Progress and performance in the primary classroom

Progress and performance in the primary classroom

edited by

Maurice Galton and Brian Simon

Routledge & Kegan Paul
London, Boston and Henley

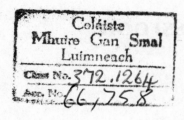
First published in 1980
by Routledge & Kegan Paul Ltd
39 Store Street, London WC1E 7DD,
9 Park Street, Boston, Mass. 02108, USA and
Broadway House, Newtown Road,
Henley-on-Thames, Oxon RG9 1EN
Set in Press Roman 10 on 12pt by
Hope Services, Abingdon, Oxon.
and printed in Great Britain by
Page Bros (Norwich) Ltd
Norwich and London

British Library Cataloguing in Publication Data

Progress and performance in the primary classroom.

1. Elementary school teaching – Great Britain
2. Academic achievement
I. Galton, Maurice
II. Simon, Brian
372.1'2'64   LB1564.G7   80-40821

ISBN 0 7100 0669 1
ISBN 0 7100 0670 5 Pbk

Contents

Contents

Contents

Figures

Tables

Introduction

This book is a sequel to a previous publication, *Inside the Primary Classroom*. In presenting a picture of classroom activity in a sample of junior and middle schools, different patterns of teacher and pupil behaviour were there identified and the relationship between them examined. In this volume the analysis is taken a stage further and the effect of these patterns on the progress of pupils over the course of a year analysed. The results, although offering little support for many contemporary criticisms of primary school practice, do cast serious doubt on the feasibility of some of the recommendations enshrined in the Plowden Report of 1967. The book should therefore be of value both to teacher educators and to those in local authorities who have responsibility for planning and administrating primary education. It should be of interest to parents whose children experience the effects of the different teaching styles described in this study.

It is hoped, however, that the book will also be widely read by primary teachers. It provides a mass of evidence and numerous examples which they may find useful in evaluating their own practice. At the same time it is hoped that the material contained in this volume will encourage teachers to take a more active part in the debate on the problems and issues identified in the course of this study. For this reason every effort has been made to eliminate technical jargon and to simplify the presentation. For the benefit of other researchers technical notes or fine details of analysis are either relegated to footnotes or placed in the Appendices.

The data have been derived from the first year's testing of the research programme, Observational Research and Classroom Learning Evaluation (ORACLE), funded by the Social Science Research Council over the period 1975 to 1980. The research team consisted of the two

1

investigators, who edit this volume, three full-time researchers, John Willcocks, Paul Croll and Anne Jasman, together with six part-time assistants who helped with the classroom observation. John Willcocks had responsibility for the day-to-day running of the programme, as well as developing and pre-testing much of the material used to measure the achievements and personality characteristics of the pupils in the study. Anne Jasman was responsible for training the observers in the use of the observation schedules and for developing the teacher-based assessment materials, some of which are reported on in this volume. Paul Croll has been responsible for the collation, processing and analysis of the vast amounts of data generated by the research. In this he has been helped by Jaya Katariya, who prepared the data for the computer with exemplary efficiency.

The format of this book differs from that of *Inside the Primary Classroom* in that two members of the research team have taken responsibility for drafting each of the individual parts. The names of those responsible are shown on the contents list. The book is, however, intended to be read as a whole. The aim of the editors has been to ensure that the argument develops logically from one part to the next.

The first chapter of Part I reviews previous research findings and provides a brief description of the tests used in the ORACLE study. In the second chapter a summary of the findings from *Inside the Primary Classroom* is presented, together with an analysis of the results of the second year's observation. These are important, since they replicate the findings of the first year of the study and show that even when a predominantly different sample of teachers were observed the same style characteristics were present. Because this is clearly an important issue it is treated at length by Paul Croll in an appendix at the end of the book.

Part II deals with the effect of teaching style on pupil progress in reading, mathematics and language use (the 'basic skills'). In Chapter 3 the levels of pupil performance at different ages are presented. Chapter 4 looks at individual differences between pupils taught by different teaching styles, and examines their degree of success with pupils of above- and below-average attainment. Chapter 5 analyses the same data using class averages rather than individual scores. This enables a very thorough investigation of the way in which a large number of related variables interact with teaching style to affect pupil progress.

Pupils' scores on basic skills were not the only measure used to assess the success of each teaching style. A number of other procedures designed to evaluate pupil performance in those skills needed for independent study have also been developed for the programme. The two chapters of Part III describe these study-skill exercises and report how pupils taught by different styles perform on them. Few previous studies have examined the influence of pupil behaviour on progress. Part IV is, however, devoted specifically to this issue. Chapter 8 contains a brief résumé of the characteristics of the various pupil types reported on in *Inside the Primary Classroom*. The relationship between these pupil types and various attitudinal characteristics, such as the degree of anxiety and motivation, is also examined. Chapter 9 deals with the effect of these variables on pupil progress.

The final part, Part V, is concerned with teacher effectiveness. In Chapter 10 the characteristics of the most successful teachers in the sample are identified and explanations of the ways in which they achieve their success proposed. In the final chapter a number of suggestions are made as to how teachers, and those responsible for in-service and initial training programmes, may make use of the results.

The research team must acknowledge the assistance of many people in bringing this part of the ORACLE programme to a successful conclusion. These include the observers, Ruth Barwood, Angela Delafield, Margaret Greig, Valerie Hallam, Janice Lea and Sarah Tann, heads and teachers in the schools and classrooms who generously allowed access to their teaching, and the officers of the three local authorities, who must remain anonymous but in whose schools these observations were carried through. We are also grateful for the financial support of the Social Science Research Council, without whose assistance none of these studies could have been undertaken.

In preparing the final draft for the press much credit must go to the project secretaries, Diana Stroud and Jaya Katariya, and also to Pat Holford who again helped with some of the drafts. Over the years of the project they have become adept at spotting inconsistencies and errors, and although final responsibility must remain with the editors they have played a vital role in coordinating the writing programme between the various members of the research team. Once again our warm thanks are due to Deanne Boydell who, as consultant to the programme, commented critically on the earlier drafts of the book.

As in *Inside the Primary Classroom*, the teacher is generally referred to as female and the pupils as males except where specific examples are quoted.

Maurice Galton
Brian Simon

University of Leicester
January 1980

3

Part 1

Research in the
primary classroom

Chapter 1

Researching the primary classroom

During the last decade primary school teachers have increasingly come under pressure from groups with a declared interest in a return to what they term 'traditional values' in education. Talk in the media of the 'wild men of the classroom' (editorial, *The Times*, 22 October 1976), together with exhortations to deter the 'half hearted progressive' and to 'curb the most extreme' (Wilkinson, 1977) offer little encouragement for teachers to engage in a rational discussion about the problems of the move away from the old selective system. In the kind of atmosphere generated by such negative criticism an open debate about the best means of preparing children for the comprehensive school becomes difficult. In addition the growth of the accountability movement, marked by the setting up of the Assessment of Performance Unit and by the rapid increase in local authority schemes for monitoring the basic skills, has added considerably to this pressure.

It is against such a background that the Social Science Research Council programme, Observational Research and Classroom Learning Evaluation (ORACLE), developed, with its emphasis on classroom observation as the main research method. It was felt that systematic observation of teacher and pupil behaviour would be of help to teachers facing these criticisms, by providing descriptions of current classroom practice against which they could evaluate aspects of their own teaching. By collecting information about pupils' performance, while at the same time engaging in these observations, it was also intended to present evidence about many of the issues which have dominated the debate between supporters of 'progressive' and 'traditional' methods.

The motivation for the research arose out of the apparently big changes taking place in primary schools from the mid to the late 1960s. In particular there developed at that time a rapid swing in primary schools towards new organizational forms within the classroom; specifically a move to abolish the classification of pupils into separate and parallel streams based on an estimate of 'intelligence' or 'ability'. This move, which began slowly in the late 1950s, gathered pace in the 1960s with official support from the Plowden Committee until, in certain areas, 'mixed ability' classes became the norm by the early 1970s (Bealing, 1972). Today all except a very small minority of primary schools adopt unstreamed methods of organization (HMI survey, 1978).

But, as outlined in an earlier book, *Inside the Primary Classroom*, the transition to non-streaming was originally accompanied by the adoption of a wide variety of organizational forms according to the predilections of individual teachers or schools. These different arrangements might range from total individualization of the teaching and learning process at one extreme to the traditional system of class teaching at the other. Alternative techniques involved the use of groupings and of group work in its various forms. In practice it seemed, as the survey carried through by the Plowden Committee discovered, that teachers moved towards a combination of individual, group and classwork in various proportions with varying emphasis. Thus complex internal classroom structures came into being, while at the same time the curriculum was also changing under the impact of the curriculum reform movement of the 1960s. Finally, a survey of primary teachers' aims highlighted the considerable diversity of purposes among primary teachers (Ashton *et al.*, 1975).

If a transformation in the nature and procedures of primary education was taking place it seemed important that these changes should be monitored, and this was one motivation for the present research. During this period it also became clear that the system of streaming or ability grouping, which was established in the inter-war period and had become part of established educational orthodoxy by the 1950s, advantaged some groups of children at the expense of others (Jackson, 1964). What then were the effects of the new systems now coming into being? What indeed were these systems? How were teachers now organizing their classrooms, and what were the major variations in organizational and teaching strategies in particular? What was the form and nature of the teacher's interactions with her pupils, and how did they relate to these organizational and curricular changes?

Progressivism: the rhetoric and the reality

Research along these lines was altogether lacking. Given a paucity of information about the processes taking place within the primary classroom, those wishing to prescribe the latest practice for new recruits to teaching, or those wishing to argue for a return to 'traditional standards', had been forced to conduct their debate in terms of the accepted rhetoric. This had closely identified class teachers with didactic presentation, while those favouring a predominantly individualized approach were, according to their 'Black Paper' critics, reluctant ever to state a fact (Cox and Dyson, 1969). At the other end of the spectrum the Plowden (1967) Committee wished to see less didactic teaching, argued strongly for an individualized approach to learning and also stressed the value of group work for promoting enquiry. The Committee, for instance, suggested that groups of pupils working together in the absence of the teacher would be 'less shy in risking a hypothesis' (Plowden, para. 758).

However, when what happens within classrooms is carefully and systematically observed, doubt arises about the validity of some of the assumptions concerning current practice which have characterized so much of the debate between those favouring progressive methods and those seeking a return to traditional teaching. A full and detailed discussion of the observational data obtained during the first year of the ORACLE study is presented in the earlier book, *Inside the Primary Classroom*, the main findings of which are summarized in Chapter 2 of this volume. One example concerns the notion of Black Paper writers that teachers who prefer an individualized approach fight shy of providing pupils with facts, preferring individuals to 'find out for themselves'. In the ORACLE study, however, it was the teachers who devoted an above-average amount of time to class teaching who more frequently engaged pupils in 'enquiry activities'. The great virtue of observational research is that, through carefully monitoring the exchanges taking place between pupils and teachers, it allows the classroom situation to be described in terms of reality rather than rhetoric.

Yet some of the rhetoric used by the media and by the writers of the Black Papers claims support from recent research, in which teachers were asked to describe their organizational arrangements, the content of the curriculum, their aims and their teaching methods, through filling in self-reporting questionnaires (Barker Lunn, 1970; Bennett, 1976). Teachers with similar practices were grouped together, and their pupils given a series of tests, mainly concerned with basic skills, at the

9

beginning and end of the school year. Differences between the pre- and post-test scores were then examined to see if pupils taught by one group of teachers, on average, achieved superior gains to those taught by another. This can be described as a 'black box' model of research into teacher effectiveness, where the actual day-to-day happenings inside the classroom are hidden away. This contrasts with the 'glass box' model used in this present study, where the classroom is open to view, and teaching behaviours are observed, quantified and used as a basis for establishing and describing differences in teaching styles.

In the most recent of these 'black box' studies, pupils taught by teachers using an 'informal' approach based for the most part on individualized teaching and learning made the least progress in basic skills of mathematics and English (Bennett, 1976). Although Bennett was cautious when attempting to interpret these results, critics of modern primary practice were not slow to assert that the relative failure of these teachers was due to their whole-hearted adoption of the Plowden approach with its emphasis on discovery teaching and learning (Bennett, 1978a). But the limited amount of observational data collected in the Lancaster study mostly concerned the amount of time pupils spent working on their set tasks. No data were presented concerning the nature of the teaching activities which could possibly justify a general condemnation of 'progressive' methods. Indeed it might be claimed, with the hindsight of the ORACLE data, that the teachers who more often taught the class as a whole succeeded for the very reason that they involved their pupils in more activities of the discovery type.

Teacher effectiveness: survey evidence in the junior school

Evidence concerning the effectiveness of progressive methods is sparse, and because of various methodological weaknesses is often difficult to interpret. In the last twenty-five years there has been a handful of British studies, which have recently been reviewed by Anthony (1979). The two earliest studies by Kemp and Warburton employed judges to rate schools on a scale which varied from 'the very *formal*, rigid, orthodox to the most *informal*, free and progressive with the curriculum organized through activities related to the needs and interests of the children' (Kemp, 1955; Warburton, 1964). Both these researchers showed that 'progressiveness' tended to correlate positively with pupil performance on tests of reading, writing and mechanical arithmetic.

More detailed was the work of Gardner, whose research into the

new 'experimental' progressive schools extended from infant to junior
level and was interrupted only for a period during the Second World
War. Although recently Gardner's later work has been dismissed by
some critics (Bennett, 1976) it is impressive for its care, knowledge and
concern about the working of new type 'progressive' schools, and for
its attempt to devise a whole range of tests reflecting the wider aims of
the informal teaching approaches they were seeking to implement.
Later studies could equally well be criticized, precisely because, by
evaluating 'pupil progress' mainly in terms of standardized tests in the
basic skills, they have propagated the notion that measurement of progress in the three Rs is the only basis for assessing the effectiveness of
different teaching methods. In devising the assessment materials for use
with the ORACLE study, much is owed to the ideas of Gardner in
developing the series of structured exercises and study-skill activities
which form part of the wide-ranging series of attainment measures used
in the present research.

In Gardner's study of junior school classrooms (Gardner, 1966) pairs
of experimental and control schools were picked out by observers. The
experimental junior schools 'devoted a considerable amount of children's
time to activities designed to make full use of their interests and purposes, devoted other time to specific teaching in English and arithmetic apart from, and in addition to, whatever arose out of the children's
spontaneous interests' and 'showed a balance between physical education, arts and sciences, creative work and skills'. Apparently schools
which allowed pupils total free choice, or those which used the 'newer
approaches' but still organized the curriculum around single-subject
teaching, were excluded. The results indicated that the experimental
schools did better on every tested attainment except mechanical arithmetic and arithmetical problems, where the control schools achieved
superior results.

Anthony (1979) criticizes Warburton's, Kemp's and Gardner's research and argues that there was an in-built bias in each of their selection
procedures which favoured the progressive schools. The observers were
told to pick out progressive schools where the children were seen to be
engaged in purposeful activities. In Gardner's research, exceptionally
'free' junior schools were rejected. Observers were directed to note
whether the children were interested in their activities, whether the
interest was lasting, and whether the pupils showed initiative and
handled materials well. Thus, according to Anthony, the schools eventually selected were not simply those with a progressive curriculum but
were schools where this curriculum could be seen to be working well in

its effects upon the children. Similar detailed considerations were not taken into account when choosing the more traditional schools, so that the progressive schools were more efficiently selected in terms of their competence than those which were to act as controls.

Anthony therefore prefers the techniques adopted by Barker Lunn (1970) and Bennett (1976). Both administered self-reporting question-naires to teachers, and their responses were subjected to cluster analysis in order to describe different teaching methods. Cluster analysis is a technique which can be used to group together people having similar characteristics, and its uses are fully described in *Inside the Primary Classroom* (p. 176). In the case of Bennett's research, teachers were grouped along a broad continuum from the 'informal' progressive pole to the 'formal' traditional one. Some teachers were then carefully selected from some of the clusters and tests of basic skills given to their classes. In Barker Lunn's study thirty-six streamed and thirty-six un-streamed junior school classes were given tests. Two groups of teachers emerged from the clustering. Type 1 teachers were very similar to Bennett's informal group, while Type 2 teachers were the opposite and were similar to Bennett's formal cluster. Anthony prefers this method of research because the samples chosen are more likely to contain both good and poor examples of each teaching type. In this sense therefore the comparison between different teaching methods was fairer than in the earlier studies.

In Barker Lunn's research, Type 2 teachers did marginally worse in English but distinctly better in arithmetic compared to Type 1 teachers. Pupils taught by Bennett's formal teachers made greatest progress at both English and mathematics. Barker Lunn also measured attitudes, and gave pupils tests of divergent thinking. Although the Type 1 tea-chers appeared more successful the differences between them and Type 2 teachers were slight. On the basis of this evidence Anthony concludes that over the period in question there has been a gradual decline in the effectiveness of progressive schooling. He argues that this is particularly so in respect of attainment in mathematics, where even Gardner's highly selected sample of progressive teachers achieved poorer results in tasks of mechanical arithmetic.

Like other writers, Anthony is forced to make the assumption that those who prefer an individualized approach to teaching and learning are more likely to make use of discovery methods. His criticism of these methods is based not on the observation of teachers working in their natural setting but on a number of carefully controlled experiments where in some cases the researcher told the teachers how to teach, although this might have been against their natural preference. Most of the studies reviewed did not involve pupils of junior school age but were carried out on American college students. The ORACLE research findings suggest that the 'Plowden type' teacher, or for that matter her 'traditional counterpart', are few and far between. The links between classroom organization, curriculum planning and what in the ORACLE study are called teaching tactics (the minute-by-minute exchanges between pupils and teachers) appear to be so complex that simple descriptions in terms of progressive and traditional labels hardly do them justice.

It is precisely the complex nature of the activity of teaching which points up the weakness of 'black box' studies based upon teacher's self-reports of their practice. Few teachers have the opportunity to see others teach or are themselves seen teaching by their fellow teachers. When asked to rate their own performance in comparison to other teachers they are forced to fall back on what they were told while training about the theory and practice of child-centred education, or to base their opinions on what they read or hear in the media about the alleged 'goings on' in progressive classrooms. Hence there is a strong possibility of circularity in statements about current teaching methods based on teachers' self-reports. The teachers make their judgments on the basis of what they read about current practice, and those who write about or criticize current teaching methods may do so as a result of these self-same reports.

It may be that this mismatch between teachers' perceptions of their teaching and their observed behaviour is unimportant in the context of the study of teacher effectiveness. Such a view would fit the model of teaching put forward by Harnischfeger and Wiley who, according to Bennett (1978b), 'dispute the underlying assumption of much research in teaching that teaching behaviour directly influences pupil achievement'. Instead they argue that 'active learning time on a particular topic is the most important determinant of a pupil's achievement' (Harnischfeger and Wiley, 1975). Thus in Bennett's Lancaster study it is argued that the superior performance of pupils taught by 'formal teachers' was due to the fact that pupils in these classes 'engaged in work related activity more frequently', while pupils in 'informal classes', of similar initial achievement, engaged in the lowest amounts of such activity, 'preferring to talk about their work or indulging in purely social interaction' (Bennett, 1976, p. 158). In Bennett's view it is the organization of the classroom and the careful structuring of the curriculum activities which is important, because within this closely controlled environment there is less scope for children to take part in time-wasting activities.

Observational studies of teaching

It should not be thought that there is no evidence in support of the alternative theory that teaching behaviour does directly influence pupil achievement. Flanders (1960) investigated whether pupils who were taught by 'indirect' teachers made more progress than those taught by 'direct' ones. 'Indirect' teachers are defined as those who accept more of the pupils' ideas, ask more questions and give more praise. 'Direct' teachers, on the other hand, offer facts and opinions, issue commands and directions and criticize students more. Bennett and other researchers have been critical of this and other early observational research on the grounds that it has often been small scale and unrepresentative. But as shown by Dunkin and Biddle (1974), when all the small-scale studies are taken together there is a clear trend in favour of indirect teaching. To use a footballing analogy, in matches between teams of pupils taught by 'indirect' and 'direct' teachers, teams who received more indirect teaching have recorded ten wins and no losses: on no occasion did those taught by more direct methods do better. The thirteen other comparative studies, where no significant relationship between teaching behaviour and pupil achievement was found, can be regarded as draws. When attitudes were examined in the same way the score sheet read eight wins, three draws and no losses, in favour of indirect teaching. Support for these trends also comes from two studies of secondary science teachers (Tisher, 1970; Eggleston *et al.*, 1976).

ORACLE research strategies

Both Bennett and Flanders claim that their findings are of practical use to teachers. Bennett suggests that his and other studies lead to a conclusion that for teaching the title of the old song should be transposed to 'it *is* what you do not the way that you do it' (Bennett, 1976, p. 160). Flanders takes the opposite view that the way teachers do it does matter (Flanders, 1976). Both sides, however, base their case on incomplete evidence. No teachers in Bennett's study, for example, were systematically observed 'doing it', while researchers using the Flanders Interaction Analysis Category System (FIAC) took little account of either classroom organization or curriculum planning, contextual variables held by Bennett to be important determinants of teacher effectiveness. Unless therefore teaching tactics, as measured by direct observation of classroom behaviour, and organizational and curriculum strategies, of the type reported in Bennett's survey, are both considered within the same study, it is not possible to determine which of these factors plays the major part in determining pupil progress.

In the ORACLE study, however, an attempt has been made to remedy some of the deficiencies of earlier research. Observational data were collected on the behaviours of both teachers and pupils. During the course of their visits to each classroom the observers also obtained information about its organization and about the curricular activities taking place. Thus it is possible to study organizational and curricular variables alongside pupil and teacher interaction; to examine, for example, whether the time the pupils spend at their tasks, as a result of more formal control in the classroom, is a better predictor of pupil performance than the use of certain teaching behaviours designed to foster enquiry activity.

In attempting to identify which of the different aspects of teaching and learning are most effective in improving pupil performance on a range of achievement measures, the present study does not aim to establish a best method over all. Rather it is concerned with drawing up a balance sheet indicating the most effective aspects of teaching for developing specific skills. In arriving at this balance sheet account must also be taken of differences between pupils, since the performance of different 'types' of pupils may also vary according to the teaching style used. Such an analysis will, it is hoped, be more detailed and informative than those achieved by earlier studies. It should thus be more relevant to the needs of practising teachers, in that it seeks to isolate important pupil and teacher behaviours relating to pupil achievement over a range of curricular activities within the context of different forms of classroom organization.

The nature of the tests used to study teaching effectiveness

A repeated criticism of previous studies has been their use of a very limited range of testing techniques to determine the effectiveness of a particular teaching approach. Since the aims of most primary teachers (Ashton *et al.*, 1975) cover a much wider range of skills than mechanical arithmetic, number problems, reading and English (the usual skills tested) there is a need to include in any study a wide range of other

15

measures. Indeed, advocates of progressive methods argue that it is precisely in those activities where creativity and imagination rather than rote learning are required that pupils taught by informal methods excel (Haddon and Lytton, 1968). Supporters of traditional teaching, however, point to the fact that it is difficult to define such terms, and even when the attempt is made assessments in many of these areas are unreliable in the technical sense. If teachers cannot define precisely what they hope to achieve and researchers are unable to develop procedures which measure these skills, then how can anyone know whether the teacher is successful? Certainly much of the thinking behind the current wave of local authority activity in monitoring for accountability purposes would seem to echo the view that it is better to stick to basics since these can be tested in a straightforward and traditional manner.

While we believe that there is a place for standardized tests in the assessment of pupil performance, their weaknesses must be acknowledged. First, such tests are 'norm-referenced'; that is, they are designed to spread people out over an approximately normal curve of distribution, with a majority of the pupils having scores close to the average for the population, and gradually decreasing proportions of the remainder having either relatively low or high scores spread out symmetrically on either side. Such tests, administered at the start of a research programme, will reflect the range of achievement among the pupils, providing the sample adequately represents the type of pupils on whom the test was standardized. When, after exposure to a particular teaching style, the pupils are again tested with the same test, the general pattern of the results will reflect these initial differences in achievement. Hence when the results of two or more groups of pupils are being compared, the scale of their progress over time cannot be attributed solely to the differences in teaching that they have received.

Norm-referenced tests mainly seek to measure the performance of each pupil relative to the others. They were primarily designed for use in selection procedures such as the 11-plus. To rely solely on such tests would therefore be unsatisfactory in terms of a hypothesis concerning the effectiveness of different teaching styles. A teacher in a classroom is not worried whether his assessment of the pupils follows a normal distribution. He is seeking to answer a more straightforward question, namely, Have my pupils learnt what I set out to teach them? Pupils are compared not with each other but against a stated criterion indicating successful learning. Thus the distribution which is of interest is a bimodal one consisting of the group who have mastered the learning task and the group who have not done so. Such a distribution, however, is not easy to achieve, and although most researchers pay lip service to the idea that in studying teacher effectiveness, mastery or 'criterion-referenced' tests of this type should be used in place of norm-referenced tests, the latter still predominate in practice (Burstall and Kay, 1978).

A second difficulty in using standardized tests concerns the reliability and validity of such assessments. A teacher makes judgments about a pupil's performance day in and day out based on the results of class work, the questions the pupil answers and asks, his behaviour in the class and so on. A test tries to make similar judgments as a result of the pupil's performance on one single occasion. In this situation there may be a whole variety of reasons why the pupil either under- or over-achieves. But a teacher's assessment is also liable to error. Many studies have shown that teachers develop certain specific expectations of pupils and that these can lead to biased judgments about a pupil's performance (Nash, 1976). This suggests that use should be made of a combination of measures which can be checked against each other, rather than relying on any one particular approach.

For these reasons three different kinds of assessment were made during the course of the ORACLE research. The first involved testing the traditional basic skills of mathematics and English. These tests were constructed from a wider range of materials known as the Richmond Tests, based on an earlier version of one of the most popular American test batteries, the IOWA Test of Basic Skills. The Richmond version attempts to move away from the norm-referenced approach of the American test. It is more like a criterion-referenced test, since each part is divided into a series of sub-tests measuring component skills or objectives. Unlike a true criterion-referenced test, however, the level necessary for mastery of each skill is not specified. For this reason tests such as the Richmond version are sometimes termed 'objective-' or 'domain-' referenced. Details of these tests are presented in Chapter 3.

The second type of test material used may be described as tests of 'study skills'. This has become a popular term, and refers to skills necessary to pursue independent study. The tests involve such activities as using reference books, map-making and map reading, interpreting and presenting data by the use of graphs, and practical activities such as model building. Some of these are included in such test batteries as the Bristol Achievement Tests and also the Richmond Tests. Often these are skills required by pupils in activities such as project and topic work. In the ORACLE study 'drawing a block graph', 'making a map of the classroom' and 'making a model of a clock-face' were chosen as three activities representing these skills. The 'clock-face' exercise was largely taken from the similar activity described by Gardner (1966).

The third type of assessment procedure used concerns what has come to be called 'teacher-based assessment'. Teachers are called on to make judgments about a pupil's progress for a variety of reasons such as determining the composition of groups, providing remedial help and making decisions about the appropriateness of the next task. During the course of a lesson a teacher may continually make such judgments, but many of these remain private and therefore go unrecorded. Researchers working in this area are attempting to help teachers make such private judgments publicly accessible by clarifying objectives and constructing checklists defining different skill levels with the aid of which assessments may be recorded. Pupils are judged to have mastered the skill if they are observed behaving consistently in a manner specified by the objective.

In the ORACLE study five skills were chosen which had been deemed important by primary teachers in the Ashton survey (1975). During the first year of fieldwork three of these skills were assessed; listening with concentration and understanding, creativity and inventiveness and acquiring information other than through reading. In order to adjust teachers' assessments for possible errors arising from the subjective element involved in completing the checklists, a series of parallel structured exercises was developed. The pupils completed these while the teachers were observing them and using the checklists to record their progress in the five skill areas. These exercises were intended to act not only as checks on the teachers' own assessments when using the checklist but also to provide guidance in the kind of behaviours that were to be assessed. Thus they served both a moderating and a training function.

The area of teacher-based assessment is an important one, particularly with the increase in emphasis on national monitoring as a result of the setting up of the Assessment of Performance Unit. Both the APU's science monitoring team and also researchers in a similar study funded by the Scottish Education Department are developing checklists to record pupil progress similar to those used by the ORACLE study (DES, 1978). This aspect of the research will therefore be treated more fully at a later stage. In examining the first-year data, only the results from the structured exercises are used, and details of these are described in Chapter 6.

Other measures used in the study

In addition to these measures of attainment and study skills, information about each pupil's liking of school, level of motivation and anxiety was also collected by means of a short questionnaire. The questionnaire was devised from a longer version entitled 'What I do in school' (WIDIS), originally used by Bennett (1976) in his study. One of the main reasons for collecting this information was that the ORACLE research programme is also concerned with the process of transfer between primary and secondary school, where previous research has shown that some pupils develop specific anxieties. The questionnaire was given on each occasion that the Richmond Tests were administered. Evidence exists which suggests that anxious children do better under certain styles of teaching (Trown and Leith, 1975). Although some doubt has been cast on the validity of such findings (Cronbach and Snow, 1977) it nevertheless seemed important to take such factors into account when attempting to assess the relative effectiveness of different teaching styles.

Table 1.1 shows the timing and the administrative details of the test programme. It can be seen that while tests of basic skills were administered at the beginning and end of the school year, both the study skills and the structured exercises were each given only on one occasion. The main reason for this was a practical one, the need not to overload the teachers, whose classes were being observed, by imposing too large a testing programme. There are obvious weaknesses in this approach, for instance the fact that some of the study-skills activities and structured exercises were administered when pupils had spent only one term with the teacher whose class was observed. Nevertheless, when the scores on the study-skill exercises are analysed in combination with the results obtained for the Richmond Tests, useful information can be obtained about the relative effectiveness of the different teaching styles. The problems and difficulties connected with such an analysis are discussed in the relevant sections of Chapter 7.

The samples

The study was carried out in fifty-eight classes in nineteen primary schools in three local authority areas. These classes were selected according to the requirements of the other project in the research programme which focused on children's transfer from primary to the

Table 1.1 Instruments used in the collection of product data
(autumn 1976 – summer 1977)

Autumn term	Modified Richmond Tests of Basic Skills in reading, language skills and mathematics + WIDIS questionnaire (October 1976).
	Block graph (November 1976)
	Structured exercises: originality and appropriateness, listening with concentration and understanding (November – December 1976)
Spring term	Map exercise (January 1977)
	Structured exercise: acquiring information other than by reading (February – March 1977)
Summer term	Clock-face (May 1977)
	Modified Richmond Tests of Basic Skills in reading, language skills and mathematics + WIDIS questionnaire (June 1977)

Data were obtained for 1,201 Pupils from 19 schools.
Testing was carried out in three local authority areas.

Local Authority A	8 classes (age 8+)	1 class (age 9+)
Local Authority B	19 classes (age 8+)	12 classes (age 9+)
	2 classes (age 8+ and 9+)	
Local Authority C	16 classes (age 10+)	

next stage in education. For this transfer study two secondary (or 'upper') schools, differing markedly in terms of their practices and procedures, were selected in each of the three local authority areas, the object of this project being to assess differences in the transfer process between the two schools in each area. For this purpose it was necessary to follow pupils through the later phase of their primary schooling before transfer. The classes studied in the process-product investigation, therefore, were those in the feeder schools to these six particular 'upper' schools. Negotiations with the heads and teachers of the primary schools concerned resulted in agreement with all such schools and classes (with the exception of one school) to participate in the process-product study now being discussed. The characteristics of the schools and teachers concerned are described in *Inside the Primary*

Classroom, but generally they seemed reasonably typical of urban and suburban schools.

In each of these classes, a total of eight pupils were chosen for systematic observation. These were selected to ensure that the sample contained a cross section of achievement levels in each class as well as equal numbers of boys and girls. All pupils were given the Richmond Tests in reading, language skills and mathematics. The scores of each pupil on these three tests were added together to give a grand total. In every class, these total scores were then divided into four quartiles. Two pupils (one boy and one girl) were randomly selected from each of the top and bottom quartiles, and four pupils (two boys and two girls) from the two middle quartiles. The pupils observed in each class therefore comprised four boys and four girls made up in the manner described.

Each class was visited for six teaching sessions (normally of one hour each) in each term of the year, a total of eighteen sessions per year. During these sessions both the sample pupils and the teachers were observed, using two observation instruments, the Pupil and the Teacher Record respectively (Boydell, 1974; 1975). In addition, data which served to place the observations in context were also collected. The observers noted systematically the teaching programme of the classes observed for the day (S1 and S2 forms) and provided descriptive accounts of the classrooms observed at the end of each visit (S3 form). During the summer term the observers collected information about grouping policies (GI form) and also details of classroom management and organization in place of this descriptive account (TQ form). More information on each of these instruments is given in Table 1.2. Fuller descriptions can be found in Chapter 1 of *Inside the Primary Classroom*.

However, before beginning the analysis of this data in relation to the progress of the ORACLE pupils, it is necessary to set the over-all scene of classroom life in the fifty-eight classrooms involved in the study. A summary of the main findings of this process data is presented in the next chapter. Particular emphasis is given to the descriptions of the different teaching styles that were identified as a result of this analysis, since the main purpose of this book is to examine their relative effectiveness. Chapter 2 is in effect a résumé of the main findings presented in *Inside the Primary Classroom*, but both new and old readers may find the summary useful. It serves to emphasize the complex nature of the modern primary classroom, and supports the argument that the differences in the performance of pupils taught by different styles must be interpreted more carefully than has commonly been done by those favouring either progressive or traditional ideologies.

Table 1.2 Instruments used in the collection of process and context data (autumn 1976–7)

Title	When completed	Focus
Pupil Record (PR)	Each target pupil was observed during each of the six observation sessions per term. Observations were made in the autumn, spring and summer terms (1976–7).	Pupils' activities and interaction with other pupils and adults.
Teacher Record (TR)	Each teacher was observed during each of the six observation sessions per term. Observations were made in the autumn, spring and summer terms (1976–7).	Teacher questions and statements, silent interaction, no interaction, the audience, its composition and curricular activity.
Session summary sheet (S1)	This was completed at the end of each observation session, therefore six were collected each term (autumn, spring and summer, 1976–7).	Physical layout of the classroom, seating of all pupils; outline of curricular contents and methods used; apparatus, resources, etc. and incidents. Order and time of observations.
Daily summary sheet (S2)	This was completed at the end of each day, therefore three were collected each term (autumn, spring and summer, 1976–7).	Class timetable, and outline of organization to include all activities whether observed or not.
Descriptive account (S3)	This was produced at the end of the six observation sessions (autumn term 1976, spring term 1977).	Prose account of the impressions of the observer as regards the teacher, classroom climate, teaching methods, etc.
Grouping instruments (GI)	This was completed for each class in the summer term 1977.	Physical layout, grouping policy and rationale.
Teachers' questionnaire (TQ)	This was completed for each class in the summer term 1977.	Classroom management/organization similar to Bennett's survey (1976).

Chapter 2

Pupils and teachers in the primary classroom

The 'informal' primary school classroom, the product of changes over the last fifteen or twenty years, is an organization of considerable complexity. This is particularly the case where the individualization of the pupils' work and of the teacher's attention is combined both with the grouping of pupils and the use of whole-class teaching in the manner prescribed in the Plowden Report (1967). The tendency to adopt this form of organization was, in fact, already under way in the schools under the impact of developments in the 1960s before the Plowden Committee reported; perhaps particularly as a result of the move towards the abolition of streaming in the primary school, concomitant with the transition to comprehensive secondary education. It is no easy task to find effective methods of describing and analysing patterns of interaction which are both reliable and valid (in the technical sense), and which discriminate effectively between classrooms of different types in terms of teaching tactics or approaches. For one thing, it was clearly important to focus on pupil behaviour, on the grounds that the activization of the pupils (if one may use the term) is held to be one of the chief characteristics of the new approaches. The search for techniques and instruments necessarily proved a lengthy affair. Preliminary systematic study of this issue commenced as far back as 1970, supported by funding from the Social Science Research Council. This was long before primary school teaching methods became a national political issue, as outlined at the start of Chapter 1.

The observational instruments

In the outcome, two observational instruments, or schedules, were developed in a series of pilot projects. They were designed to reflect the complexity of the on-going interactional 'process' within the informally organized primary school classroom, and also to differentiate effectively between patterns of interaction within these classrooms. Called the 'Pupil Record' and the 'Teacher Record', both observational instruments require the presence of a trained and skilled observer in the classroom, acting, as it is often described, as 'a fly on the wall'. The observer, positioning himself appropriately, concentrates on categorizing both pupil and teacher behaviour (as the case may be), remaining as inconspicuous as possible in order to ensure that normal relationships and behaviours are undisturbed. The object is to observe behaviours 'as they really are'.

Both instruments are fully described in the first volume of this series (*Inside the Primary Classroom*), so only a brief outline will be given here. The Pupil Record, the first to be developed, focuses on three main areas of pupil behaviour: pupil-adult interaction, pupil-pupil interaction and pupil activity. The sub-categories of the first two of these are only coded when the pupil is in fact interacting, either verbally or nonverbally, with the teacher (or other adult) or with another pupil or pupils. The third main area, pupil activity, is coded on all occasions when the pupil is being observed.

The categories of the Pupil Record are reproduced in Appendix A (Table A.1). The observer, equipped with a cassette tape recorder which feeds a signal into his earpiece every twenty-five seconds, codes the pupil's behaviour at that specific point in time. If the pupil being observed is interacting with an adult (usually the teacher), he codes each of four sub-categories which identify the relationship; whether for instance in the first case the pupil initiates the interaction, whether the pupil is being addressed by the adult, or whether he is only part of the adult's audience or simply listening to and watching the adult. The other three sub-categories are concerned with identifying the adult involved in the interaction, the nature of the adult's utterances, and with the grouping of which the pupil forms part (that is, whether the pupil is receiving individual attention, attention as member of a group or of the class as a whole). Similar relevant sub-categories enable the observer to identify specific features of pupil-pupil interaction (when that takes place), while the 'activity' category, coded on all occasions, enables a detailed analysis of pupil behaviour whether or not he is interacting with an adult or other pupils.

The method used was sampling round the class; that is, the observer focused on a given pupil making five codings at 25-second intervals, then moving to the next, and so on. Selection of the sample of pupils observed in each classroom was described in Chapter 1.

It soon became apparent in the pilot studies undertaken with the Pupil Record, that although this yielded a mass of data about pupil activity and behaviour, it picked up very little information on the teacher's activity, particularly in the informally organized primary classroom (as most were found to be). It was essential to collect information of this kind since a primary objective of the research was to identify differences in teaching approaches, or 'styles'. The Pupil Record yielded little material on this, because it was found in the pilot studies (and this was confirmed in the main study) that the system of individualization of work which is very widely used is accompanied by individualization of teacher attention. For much of the time teachers interacted privately with *individual* pupils. This meant that the Pupil Record picked up little pupil-teacher interaction, which comprised only about 15 per cent of all observations. Using the sampling technique described earlier, the teacher was often found to be interacting with pupils other than the particular one being observed at any specific moment. Therefore, while the Pupil Record did pick up data on teacher-pupil interaction, it was clear that to obtain a more complete analysis of teacher activity and behaviour it was necessary to design a second instrument focusing specifically on the teacher, to be used in conjunction with the Pupil Record. This second instrument, or schedule, is the Teacher Record; its categories are reproduced in Appendix A (Table A.2).

The Teacher Record is also described in *Inside the Primary Classroom*. It consists of a system of categories covering first, all questions and statements made by the teacher, second, different forms of 'silent interaction', and finally, what the teacher is doing when no interaction is taking place. The teacher's audience, whether an individual, a group of pupils or the class as a whole, is also coded, as is the curricular area on which the pupils are engaged at the point of interaction. Teachers' questions and statements are divided into those concerning the pupil's task, those concerning 'task supervision' and those concerning 'routine' (or management) issues. The instrument differentiates between what may be called lower- and higher-order questions and statements, and covers also such areas as praising, providing feedback on work or effort and 'critical control' (normally disciplinary). Silent marking of pupils' work, as well as reading and storytelling are also covered. Codings were made on this instrument every twenty-five seconds, as in the case of the Pupil Record (Boydell, 1974; 1975).

The main findings of the process study

One of the most striking findings of the observational study, particularly in view of the folklore about time wasting and libertarian procedures in primary schools, was the high level of pupil 'involvement' in their tasks during lesson sessions. Thus it was found that, for well over half the time (58 per cent), the 'typical' pupil was 'fully involved and co-operating on task'; that is, concentrating on the work in hand. But in addition for nearly 12 per cent of the time he was fully involved and co-operating on 'routine' activities necessary for maintaining the task, like sharpening a pencil, borrowing a rubber, getting a new sheet of paper and so on. Together these total 70 per cent of the pupils' time. However, the 'typical' pupil spends a further 4.3 per cent of his time waiting for the teacher to check over his work, ask a question and so on; usually either queueing at the teacher's desk or waiting at his table with his hand up. This may legitimately be added to the time spent co-operating on task and on routine, to give a total of very nearly 75 per cent of the 'typical' pupil's time in our study spent engaged (or involved) on his work or task. (The data are presented in this chapter in terms of the 'typical' pupil and teacher on the study. The figures presented are, therefore, derived from the averages of all observations in each case.)

On the other hand the typical pupil was 'distracted' from his work for 16 per cent of the time. During most of this time the pupil was simply distracted; that is, was temporarily not working. Active disruption and 'horseplay' were minimal, amounting to 0.1 per cent and 0.2 per cent of all observations respectively. For the remaining 9 per cent of the time the pupil's activity was indeterminate, in the sense that it was assigned to five categories which indicate partial but not full involvement on task: 'co-operating/distracted', 'interested in teacher', 'interested in pupil', 'working on another activity', 'responding to internal stimuli'.

Generally, then, the conclusion is that a 75 per cent level of work activity or 'involvement' is maintained by the 'typical' pupil in the study. Even adult workers seldom concentrate on their tasks for 100 per cent of the time since some time is needed for rest or recuperation. A 75 per cent level on average is, therefore, generally high. This evidence, objectively obtained by systematic observation, runs directly counter to much of the current folklore about the implications of modern methods in the primary school.

The analysis of pupil activity in the classroom may be taken a little further. A primary school classroom often appears, to the casual visitor, to be a buzz of activity and talk, together with a good deal of movement or mobility on the part of the pupils. But if the visitor penetrates a little more fully into what actually is going on he will find that this initial impression is partly illusory. The fact is that *some* pupils are mobile at any given time, while some others will be talking with fellow pupils in the same seated group, and yet others with the teacher. But our data bring out quite clearly that, at any given moment in a teaching session, most of the pupils are working alone, individually, on their allotted or chosen task; or at least 'engaged' on their task, for most of the time.

In practice for over half the time (58 per cent), as just described, the typical pupil is fully involved and working directly on his task. For most of this time he is working on his own, interacting with no one (40 per cent of lesson time). For some of this time he is listening to or interacting with the teacher (12 per cent of lesson time), and for a little of it he is interacting, on matters relating to his task or work, with another pupil (5 per cent of lesson time). Teacher-pupil interaction will shortly be dealt with, but the data show that pupil-pupil interaction (which mainly takes the form of talk), goes on for about one-fifth of a lesson session in the case of the typical pupil. About one-third of this interaction concerns the task in hand, but about two-thirds does not. Therefore there is conversation between pupils during lesson sessions, as any visitor to a modern primary classroom can confirm, but it is not excessive in extent, while some of it is related to the task in hand. It may be worth noting that, in this study, pupil-pupil interaction was most likely to be task related when it concerned girls only, and that the proportion of such interaction which is task related declines with age, dropping from 31 per cent of all such interaction among eight- to nine-year-olds to 22 per cent in the case of ten- to eleven-year-olds.

We may turn now to the curriculum; when the 'typical' pupil is involved in his task what, in fact, is he studying? Here the data confirm other studies, particularly the HMI survey of 1978, in that they make it very clear that the major focus of pupil activity in normal teaching sessions in the sample of primary school classrooms studied is in the areas of language and mathematics. Every coding that was made by the observers in the case of both the Pupil and the Teacher Record included a curriculum-area coding. It was, therefore, possible to reconstruct the curriculum as it was actually experienced both by pupils and teachers, and, further, using the S1 or S2 sheets compiled by observers as to the planned curriculum over the full day when observation took place, to estimate what we called 'the real curriculum'.

These three measures all differed in detail, as is bound to be the case where much of the work is individualized (as it was found to be), so that the time spent by pupils on the different areas differs to some extent from the time spent by teachers (for instance, the teachers spent substantially more time teaching reading than the typical pupil spent in learning to read, since reading in the junior school tends to be taught individually). These differences are analysed in some detail in *Inside the Primary Classroom* and will not be reiterated here. The main conclusions can however be presented quite briefly. They will be given in terms of the 'real curriculum' but bear a close relation to the results derived both from the Pupil and the Teacher Record. These indicate that about a third of the time in normal teaching sessions is devoted to number or 'mathematics' (number work, practical maths, abstract maths); another third is devoted to language (which comprises reading, writing, oral English and creative writing); while the final third is devoted both to 'general studies', which include project and topic work, and to art and crafts. It should be made clear that this breakdown refers to the normal classroom teaching sessions on which observation was focused, comprising work in the areas of mathematics, language, general studies (including science or nature study), art and crafts. It excludes physical education, TV presentations, religious instruction (when given in assembly) and games.

From this it can be concluded that the traditional curriculum, with its focus on developing skills in the fields of numeracy and literacy, persists unchanged in the schools studied. Here it is worth stressing that this information is derived from systematic observation of primary school classrooms as they actually function. These data once again call into question contemporary folklore about the supposed 'failure' of primary schools to concentrate on 'the basics'. It shows that these, in fact, form the main areas on which the schools in this study concentrate.

Some additional points may be made. For instance, it was found that the 'typical' pupil spends over 20 per cent of his time on 'writing' (practising writing and formal English exercises); on the other hand he spends only 2 per cent of his time on lessons devoted specifically to oral English, learning to express himself in an articulate manner. Topic and project work averaged at 14.8 per cent of the time for the typical pupil, but science and nature-study only 4.4 per cent.

How then does the typical teacher in our study organize this work? On the whole little class teaching takes place, but there is some. In the fifty-eight classes in our study, only four contained pupils seated in pairs, in rows, facing the teacher and the blackboard in the traditional manner of the past. The rest seated the class in groups ranging from three to eight pupils around grouped desks or tables. Usually there were five or six such groups. Organization of pupils in seated groups of this kind is the mark of the modern 'informal' primary school classroom.

But although seated in groups, we found that, overwhelmingly, the pupils are engaged in individual work; that is, the work or tasks set to pupils is largely *individualized*. The pattern of teacher interactions shows that the bulk of the teacher's time is spent on individual private exchanges with specific children in turn. Thus, in general, both the pupil's work and the teacher's attention is individualized. This, incidentally, is in accordance with the prescripts as to how the teacher should operate set out in the Plowden Report of 1967, the last authoritative pronouncement about teaching and learning in the primary school.

However, it is as a result of this practice that there arises what may be called the 'asymmetry' of teacher-pupil interaction. To focus first on the teacher is to find that she is typically extremely busy and active during lesson sessions. For 80 per cent of the time she is in fact actively interacting, in one way or another, with the pupils. For the rest of the time, 20 per cent, she is 'housekeeping', talking to another teacher or pupil from a different class, occasionally and briefly out of the room or 'resting'. Analysis of her interaction patterns in more detail indicates that for over half of the lesson time, 56 per cent, she is interacting with individual pupils; for a relatively small proportion of the time, 15 per cent, she is interacting with the whole class as a class, and for even less time, only 7 per cent, she is interacting with one or other of the groups of pupils as a group. In general, then, the picture is of the teacher actively interacting with the pupils for most of the lesson time, and mainly moving around helping or talking with individual children.

Reconstruction of the situation from the angle of the typical pupil, however, results in an entirely different picture or pattern of interaction. For the bulk of lesson time, 84 per cent, he has no interaction with the teacher whatever. For 15 to 16 per cent of the time however he does so interact, but the bulk of this interaction the pupil receives only as a member of the whole class (12 per cent of lesson time). This normally means that, as a member of the class, he is one of the teacher's audience. The typical pupil interacts with the teacher as an *individual* for only 2.3 per cent of lesson time, and as a member of a group for 1.5 per cent of lesson time. The 'asymmetry' of teacher-pupil interaction, therefore, lies precisely in this, that while the teacher spends

29

most of her time interacting with individual pupils, each specific individual child only receives individual attention from the teacher for
a very small proportion of lesson time.

No further comment will be made at this stage, except to point out
that the system of individualization inevitably means that, with classes
averaging about thirty as is the case today (and in this study), each
child typically receives very little individual attention. It appears also
from our data that on average teachers devote little attention to working
with the groups they have established. They interact primarily with
individuals within the seated (or other) groups, but clearly very little
with each group as a whole or as a single working unit. This is because
the work done when seated in groups is largely individual work.

This analysis may be taken a little further, and an examination made
of grouping practice in the primary school classrooms. The situation
here is complex and it is difficult to give a complete picture. It seems,
however, that three types of groups may be formed and may exist
simultaneously within such classes. First, what may be called 'base'
groups, that is, the seated groups found in the great majority of the
classrooms. These are not normally 'ability' ('streamed') groups. Sometimes all activities are carried on in this single type of grouping; but
sometimes only some of the activities. The second type of grouping
used may be called 'curriculum' groups. These are often established for
work in mathematics and language, and may differ in each case. Such
groups tend to have a semi-permanent membership, and are sometimes,
but by no means always, based on 'ability' (in this study under one-
fifth were so composed). These groups may have only a kind of notional
existence; that is, they do not necessarily form seated groups, but may
consist of pupils seated in different base groups whose work is individualized but structured together in terms of the level of the work-cards
or textbooks used. Thus when 'red group' works on mathematics,
pupils from different seated groups will get out the materials relevant to
the work of that particular mathematics group. The third type of
grouping is more evanescent or ephemeral. These are groups of pupils
brought together for specific, temporary activities usually as part of
topic or project work; for instance to make a collage, carry through
some measurement and so on. Once such a group has completed its
task it ceases to exist.

The internal structure of a primary school classroom is therefore
often complex and dynamic; nor is it easy for the occasional visitor to
penetrate into and grasp its complexity. The teacher on the other
hand must maintain a clear concept of this internal structure in her

mind; it is the means by which she maintains control of the complex organizational forms that individualization and group work require. However, our most striking finding concerns neither the composition nor degree of stability of these groups; it concerns their activity.

One thing that emerges quite clearly from the data is that, though pupils are typically seated in groups, for the great majority of their time they work as individuals, concentrating on their own individual tasks. Co-operative group functioning or activities – for instance, the investigation of a particular scientific problem, construction of a model, writing a play – are altogether exceptional. It is also exceptional to find a curriculum group in mathematics or language working together on a joint task. Over 90 per cent of teachers in our sample never used co-operative group work for single subjects; 70 per cent never used it for art and crafts, nor for topic or project work. Only 10 per cent of all the work observed was in fact of a co-operative group nature; some children never experienced it at all.

This may help to explain the surprisingly low level of teacher-group interaction which, it will be remembered, amounted to only 7.5 per cent of all teacher-pupil interaction (Teacher Record), as also the fact that pupils interacted with the teacher in the group situation for only 1.5 per cent of all observations (Pupil Record). The two figures, the first from the Teacher and the second from the Pupil Record tally, since if there are five groups in the class, the teacher on average will give one-fifth of all her group interactions to each group. This amounts to precisely the 1.5 per cent received by pupils in that situation.

Moving on now to the important issue of the distribution of the teacher's attention, are there any groups of pupils who get more or less than what might be called their fair share, in terms of an equitable distribution of teacher attention across the various dimensions? This question was examined in relation to three sets of pupil variables: differences in (i) achievement levels, (ii) sex and (iii) age.

As far as achievement levels are concerned, it will be remembered that the sample of pupils observed was constructed so that two pupils in each class were drawn from the top quartile, two from the bottom and four from the middle two quartiles, the pupils being allocated to these quartiles on the basis of testing at the start of the project. It was found that the teacher's attention was divided, to all intents and purposes, equally among these three groups of pupils, the high, medium and low achievers, though the latter were more likely to receive more individual attention. The same result was found for sex differences; that is, the teacher's attention was generally equally divided between the two sexes, though there was a slight (but statistically non-significant) tendency for boys to receive more attention than girls at each level (that is, individual, group and class). The sex of the teacher made no difference to the pattern of attention distribution. Again the same general result was found with age differences, which can amount to as much as twelve months in single-year classes. The older children were found to be no more likely to receive the teacher's attention than the younger children (and vice versa).

Generally speaking, then, the teacher's attention in our classrooms was distributed equally across these different groups of pupils. This seems an important finding. Further analysis, however, revealed another important and perhaps significant finding. The classes in the sample varied in size from twenty to thirty-eight, averaging 29.9. What was the effect of increasing class size on the teacher's interaction patterns? In the first place the larger the class, the less interaction with the teacher is experienced by the typical pupil, who also spends more time waiting for the teacher. But in addition it was interesting to find that, faced with larger classes, the teacher tries to compensate for this by spending a higher proportion of time actually interacting with pupils (that is, she cuts down on 'housekeeping', silently monitoring class activities and time spent out of the classroom). Nevertheless she does not adopt what might be thought to be the easiest strategy, that is, teaching (or interacting with) the class as a whole. On the contrary, she spends a smaller proportion of time in this way and a higher proportion interacting with individuals and groups. In so acting she is, perhaps unconsciously, again carrying out the Plowden prescripts, which stress the need for individualization.

A good deal of attention was devoted in our enquiry to analysing the nature and quality of teacher-pupil interaction; here the aim was to test the Plowden Committee's prescripts concerning the teacher's role in stimulating independent enquiry by pupils, as opposed to didactic teaching. For this purpose an analysis was made of all teachers' questions and statements, which account respectively for 12 per cent and 45 per cent of all teacher observations (on the Teacher Record).* It was possible to differentiate 'higher-order' and 'lower-order' questions. There were in fact two kinds of higher-order questions, namely those which were 'closed' and answered by the pupil putting forward an idea or solution where only one specific answer was acceptable (Q2 on the Teacher Record), and those which were 'open' and a variety of

* 22 per cent of teacher observations consisted of 'silent interaction', and 21 per cent of 'no-interaction'.

possible ideas and solutions were acceptable (Q3 on the Teacher Record). These higher-order questions may be contrasted with those resulting in lower-order factual answers (Q1 on the Teacher Record). Similarly it was possible to differentiate higher-order statements of ideas (S2 on the Teacher Record) from lower-order statements of fact (S1 on the Teacher Record).

Taking questioning first, it was found that higher-order closed questions formed just over 2 per cent of all observations, while higher-order open questions formed only 0.6 per cent. If these are now presented as percentages of all questioning they amount to 18 per cent and 5 per cent respectively, totalling 23 per cent. A higher proportion of all questioning consists of task supervision questions (32 per cent), while 15 per cent is on 'routine' matters. (The rest is questions of fact – 29 per cent.) Turning to teachers' statements, it was found that statements of ideas which stimulate thought and enquiry comprised 2.5 per cent of all observations (or 5.6 per cent of all statements).

Generally, then, it appears that the 'typical' teacher's questions and statements in our study are mainly concerned with containing and supervising the pupil's task activity. Only a small proportion (5.3 per cent of all teacher observations) can be classified as higher-order cognitive statements and questions. As already indicated in Chapter 1, such questions and statements paradoxically predominate (or are maximized) when the teacher is interacting with the *whole class*. They are minimized in the individual, one-to-one situation. This is a matter of some significance and interest, especially if individualization is seen, as the Plowden Committee saw it, as *the* means of promoting independent work and enquiry. The significance of these findings will become apparent later.

Some conclusions relating to 'process'

Some general conclusions can be drawn from the initial study of process within the primary school classrooms observed. First, the study has confirmed that there is a strong focus on work by the pupils; the level of involvement is generally high. Further, a high proportion of time is devoted to work in the areas of literacy and numeracy. The idea that pupils waste their time and that organization is anarchic receives no support whatever from our data, derived from systematic and detailed observation of what actually goes on in primary school classrooms.

Second, and closely related to this, little disruptive behaviour was observed, although since the typical pupil was involved in disruptive behaviour and horseplay for 0.3 per cent of observations, in a class of average size (thirty) this means that such behaviour takes place for 9 per cent of the time. On the whole the evidence, however, both from observational data and the observers' descriptive accounts, points to the conclusion that the classes are well managed and orderly. The system of grouping and individualized work, together with some class teaching, appears as an effective management system, in terms of ensuring a high level of involvement in task activity.

Third, a high proportion of the work done is individualized, although this proportion varies between teachers using different styles, as is made clear later. Nevertheless *all* teachers, however they are grouped or 'clustered', use individualization, and pupils in general mostly experience individual work. Grouping appears to be an organizational or managerial device, rather than a technique for promoting enquiry-based learning utilizing collaborative methods. There was, in fact, little co-operative group work in evidence in our sample.

Fourth and related to this, the teacher's attention is also largely individualized. Further, the teacher-pupil interaction process does not appear to have a high cognitive content; our data indicate that it is largely managerial or instructional in content, having the function of keeping things moving and assisting individual pupils with the completion of their tasks. Paradoxically, there are more questions and statements of a higher cognitive order by the teacher in the whole-class situation than in the individualized or group situation.

Thus, while our evidence confirms that, in the classes studied, there has been an important shift towards 'informal' structures relating to classroom layout, in the use of individualized teaching and learning techniques (work cards and the like) and perhaps in other ways (for instance, in relationships), there does not appear to have been any fundamental or radical transformation of the teaching/learning process in the primary schools observed. The move to individualization, which is the mark of this shift, has not been accompanied by a change in direction from didactic teaching (telling) to 'discovery' learning. In other words, 'progressivism', as presented in some detail in the Plowden Report, to which enquiry learning is fundamental, is hardly found in practice in our primary classrooms. Further, it is not at all self-evident that individualization can be the means to such a transformation. This system poses the teacher with enormous management problems. Specifically, it is our view that a solution may lie in clarifying the problems involved, and in providing more concrete assistance to teachers as regards the practice of co-operative group work in the primary class-room.

Teacher variation in the ORACLE sample

So far an outline has been presented of our findings in terms of the typical pupil and teacher. However, it was a main object of the re-search, as stated earlier, to investigate different approaches to teaching and learning within the primary school, and ultimately to identify which approaches were most effective in terms of 'outcomes'; that is, in terms of learning gains by pupils of different types. To do this in-volves differentiating teachers in terms of teaching 'styles', and, further, differentiating groups of pupils in terms of their behaviour into pupil 'types' (see Chapter 8). To carry this through involved analysis of the data derived both from the Teacher Record and from the Pupil Record. So far only averages have been presented; but these averages, of course, conceal variations. It is with these variations that we are now concerned.

Teaching styles

In *Inside the Primary Classroom* the theoretical stance of this research, so far as it concerns teaching strategies and teaching styles, was out-lined. Briefly, a teaching *strategy* is seen to consist of a teacher's attempts to translate her aims into practice, and involves decisions con-cerning such matters as classroom organization, the management of learning activities and the balance of the curriculum; her *tactics* con-cern the minute-by-minute exchanges between the teacher and pupils through which such strategies are implemented. If these teaching tactics can be shown to be consistent, this can then be defined as a *teaching style* (see Chapter 6, *Inside the Primary Classroom*). It should be noted here that this definition of teaching style depends entirely on analysis of the interaction between teachers and pupils; that is, it requires observation of teachers to describe and classify actually how they teach (the teaching process). It is not derived from self-report questionnaire data on organizational or other matters as was the case with recent re-searches into the primary classroom reviewed by Anthony (1979).

In the ORACLE study, differentiation of teaching styles was carried through by analysis of the Teacher Record data. The statistical tech-nique used was cluster analysis, a means of sorting people into groups whereby each individual in a specific group has more characteristics in common with other members of that group than with people belonging to other groups. This analysis yields four main groups of teachers operating, according to the data, similar teaching styles; for convenience, these are named respectively 'individual monitors', 'class enquirers', 'group instructors' and 'style changers'. A few words may be said about each, though a fuller description will be found in *Inside the Primary Classroom*.

A main characteristic differentiating the first three of these styles is the focus of their teaching direction, or the balance of the audience categories utilized. Individual monitors have the highest level of private, individual, one-to-one interaction; although they do use a little group and whole-class interaction, both of these are at a minimum level compared to all other styles. Class enquirers, on the other hand, maximize the use of class teaching, though even here this reaches only just under one-third of all teaching time; they combine whole-class teaching largely with individualized work, but, significantly, it is teachers using this style who maximize higher cognitive order questions and statements. Group instructors, in contradistinction to all other styles, maximize the use of grouping, so that their level of interaction with groups of pupils is very much higher than all other styles. These teachers, however, appear to concentrate on instructing the groups rather than on promoting enquiry among them.

The fourth style, the style changers, which comprises 50 per cent of the sample, appears as a mixture of the other three; as regards the balance of the audience categories, for example, these have the second highest levels of individual, group and class instruction (though some of the differences are slight).

In fact the differentiation of teachers into these groups is not dependent on the data concerning the extent of individual, group or class interaction, since when these data were excluded from the analysis the same clusters resulted from analysis of the interactional data alone. The main characteristics of each of the four teaching styles are given below.

Style 1: Individual monitors (22.4 per cent of sample)

This group has the highest level of individualized, one-to-one interaction with pupils, and, conversely, the lowest levels of interaction with pupils as members of a group or of the class as a whole; that is, they engage in very little group or class teaching, but concentrate on individuals.

In spite of this, their teaching is largely didactic, concerned with telling pupils what to do, while their questioning is mainly factual rather than probing or open-ended. With a high level of individualized work, marking (with the pupil present) accumulates rapidly, and these teachers spent a higher proportion of the time on this than any other group.

Style 2: Class enquirers (15.5 per cent of sample)

This group devotes the highest proportion of time to class teaching of any group (31 per cent); they combine this approach with individualized interaction but, although they spend a substantial proportion of time in this way (42.5 per cent), this is less than any other style. Very little time is spent interacting with pupils in groups. This group of teachers uses questioning more than any other group, especially questions relating to task work – it has the highest percentage of both open and closed questions. In addition, these teachers make more statements of ideas and problems than the other groups. The emphasis on problem solving and ideas, together with teacher control through class teaching, gives them their title.

Style 3: Group instructors (12.1 per cent of sample)

This group maximizes interaction with pupils as members of a group. Even though these teachers spend less than a fifth of lesson time in this way, this is, on average, three times as great as the rest of the sample. Their teaching appears largely didactic, though there is a high level of feedback. These teachers, through the use of grouping, appear to come closest to adopting the grouping strategy suggested by the Plowden Committee, and, though there is some evidence of problem solving, the main emphasis is placed on the informational aspects of their activity.

Style 4: Style changers (50 per cent of sample)

As already indicated, this large group of teachers has the second highest levels of individual, group and class interaction; certain features of their teaching style are also associated with one or other of the remaining groups. Examination of the data and of material from the descriptive accounts suggests that members of this group tend to change their teaching style, and to adopt the characteristics of a specific style when they change to its pattern of organization. The manner of this change however differs, and three main types of style changers were identified.

Style 4a: Infrequent changers (10.3 per cent of sample)

This group appears to have made a deliberate change in style during the observational year, though not always for the same reasons. One factor resulting in such a change was the behaviour of the pupils, which in one case, for instance, led to a switch of strategy from individualized work and responsibility to formal class teaching with all pupils engaged on the same task. In another case the motivation for change was the reverse of this — as pupils acquired the desired learning habits, the original formal structure was deliberately relaxed, with the pupils taking increased responsibility for planning their own work on an individualized basis. This sub-group reached the highest over-all level of questioning of all types, including higher cognitive order questioning and also a relatively high proportion of statements of ideas. The feedback level was also high. The group also reached the highest level of interaction of all styles (86 per cent).

Style 4b: Rotating changers (15.5 per cent of sample)

This group is identified by the organizational form of its teaching strategy. All use grouping of pupils, but in this case, while all the pupils in a given group work in one curricular area, each different group works in different curricular areas. These groups rotate from one curricular area to the next by moving bodily to the relevant table in each case. This results in the whole class shifting position at given points during the day. Among this group there is a high level of task supervision questions as also of 'critical control', which is maximized. It appears that this system may lead to disciplinary problems.

Style 4c: Habitual changers (24.2 per cent of sample)

This comparatively large group made regular changes between class and individualized instruction. Many of these appeared to be unplanned, a reaction to pupils whose behaviour was causing difficulties. This group used questioning relatively little, particularly open-ended or probing questioning or statements of ideas. The time spent in interacting with pupils in the class was the lowest of the entire sample (71.4 per cent).

38

A detailed analysis of the main style differences is given in *Inside the Primary Classroom*, including an analysis of the age and sex distribution of the teachers in each of the four main styles. Perhaps the most striking thing to emerge here is that the individual monitors were largely under thirty (and female), the group instructors had a majority in their thirties (the sexes being fairly even), while in the case of the class enquirers over half were over forty and men out-numbered women by two to one.

Further analysis was made relating specifically to the use of higher cognitive level questions and statements across all teaching styles. This is an important issue, and the reader is referred to the relevant chapter in *Inside the Primary Classroom* (Chapter 7) where this analysis is made. It was found that, although the total amount of such interaction varied across the styles, in *every case* the highest figure was recorded with a class rather than a group or individual audience. In so far as such discussion promotes a 'discovery' rather than a 'didactic' approach to teaching, it was concluded that the ORACLE teachers do not operate within the Plowden prescription, which stresses the need for individualization and group work as the most effective means to implement such an approach. Teachers' interactions with pupils as individuals or groups were shown to be overwhelmingly didactic, and this is true across all styles including, perhaps particularly, the individual monitors.

One further point should be made here. No congruence was found between the ORACLE teaching styles and those defined by Bennett (1976). These latter were arrived at through cluster analysis of questionnaire data concerning organizational features of the teacher's work, from which a reduction was made within a formal-informal continuum. Analysis based on interactional data, as in the ORACLE study, indicates that such categorization does not meet the complexities of classroom process revealed by our data. Not one of the ORACLE styles can be matched to the Bennett styles.

The replication study

The material so far presented summarizes the data and analyses derived from the project's first year of observational studies, as given in greater detail in *Inside the Primary Classroom*. Data from the second year's observational studies, carried through in 1977–8, is, however, now available and has been analysed. Replication of a study on this scale is unusual in educational research, but highly desirable as a check on initial findings. For this reason a summary of the main findings is given in Appendix B. Here it will be sufficient to refer briefly to certain issues relating both to the interactional process in primary classrooms and to the teaching-style clusters.

First, as regards process, it can in general be stated that the replication confirmed the validity of the main findings relating to interactional process of the first year's study. Data deriving from the Teacher Record indicates a close similarity in the relative frequency of use of the twenty-six categories in the two years. Here it is important to point out that the sample of second-year teachers differed largely from those studied in the first year, though they were teaching the same children in the same schools. In spite of this, the pattern of teacher behaviour was, in terms of the 'typical' teacher, very similar in both years. The main difference found was an increase in the percentage of teacher interaction with groups of pupils. This matter will be referred to again shortly.

That apart, the curriculum pattern was also shown to be very similar in the two years; as was that of the content or nature of teacher-pupil interactions, though here again there was some change in respect of teacher interactions with groups of pupils.

Pupil activity was also found to follow very similar patterns in the two years. The second year replication once again found a high level of pupil involvement in work, while the patterns of pupil-teacher and pupil-pupil interaction remained much the same as in the first year.

Of particular importance for the thesis of this book is the replication of the clustering of teachers into the various teaching styles. This is dealt with in detail in Appendix B, but here it may be said that, repeating the same procedures for the forty teachers involved in the second year, the four-cluster solution effectively differentiated these teachers both according to differences in their use of the audience categories, and in terms of their use of other categories in the Record.

The main differences between the teachers in the two years lies in the proportion of the sample grouped together under the *Group instructors* style. The proportion so clustered in the first year was 12.1 per cent; in the second year it rose to 37.5 per cent. The over-all shift in terms of teacher-group interaction referred to earlier is, in fact, explained in terms of this shift in the proportions categorized under the different styles. In addition, it was found that the second-year *Group instructors* used more higher-order questions and statements. Nevertheless it remains the case that they still predominantly used a didactic teaching approach. Thus, while the replication study does show a slight shift towards a more enquiry-based approach by *Group instructors*, the main conclusions derived from the first year study remain valid.

The fact that the replication study provided data which confirmed the validity of the four main teaching styles identified from the first year's data is, of course, of great importance for this study, which is concerned fundamentally with the relation between different teaching styles and pupil learning gains. The replication validated this analysis, by which teachers are differentiated according to objective (observed) features of their teaching styles.

This, then, completes the presentation, in summary outline, of the main findings of the process study both in the first and in the second year of observation. An analysis has been presented, so far, of the activities of the typical pupil and teacher, and of the differentiation of teachers according to teaching style. The rest of the book is concerned with the study of the relation between different teaching approaches (and forms of pupil activity) and learning on the part of the pupils. In the next three chapters the effect of teaching style on pupil progress in the basic skills is examined. This reflects not only the emphasis placed on this area in previous research, but also the concern both at national and local level with the increasing emphasis on monitoring and accountability. Next, performance in the study skills and the structured exercises described in Chapter 1 is dealt with before moving on to consider the effect on learning of differences in pupil behaviour. Finally, in Chapter 10 some of the issues relating to the concept of teaching effectiveness are discussed, and in the concluding chapter of the book, the implications of this research for teacher training are considered.

Part II

Pupil progress in basic skills

Chapter 3

Measuring pupil achievement in the basic skills

In studies concerned with the influence of teachers and schools on pupil achievement, the nature of the tests used are obviously of crucial importance. Two issues in particular need to be considered; the relevance of the measures to what teachers and schools are trying to accomplish, and the extent to which they are equally appropriate to a variety of teachers and schools, when comparisons between them are being made.

It has recently been demonstrated by Professor Rutter and his colleagues that studies which relate their measures of achievement to the aims of the schools being studied find much stronger school effects than studies using measures such as IQ and non-verbal reasoning (Rutter *et al.*, 1979). If we are concerned with the effects of schools on their pupils it is clearly important to measure the things which schools are trying to achieve. In their own study, involving twelve inner-London secondary schools, these authors argue that public examination results are the most suitable means of measuring school products, as these relate directly to the content of the school curriculum. However, the pupils in the ORACLE study were not at an age to take public examinations (at least in the local authorities in which the research was conducted), and it was necessary to find other product measures which would assess pupil achievement in those cognitive areas with which primary schools are centrally concerned.

The rest of this chapter will be concerned with describing the tests used to measure achievement in the basic skills of literacy and numeracy. It will be argued that these are among the central concerns of the primary school, and that this is true of virtually all schools and teachers. However they are not the only concerns of primary teachers, and it may be that tests in the basic skills will not do full justice to pupil achievement in some classrooms. In order to allow for this possibility

45

a number of other exercises were also devised, as mentioned in Chapter 1. These are fully described in Chapter 6.

Selection of test items

For the reasons given in Chapter 1 it was decided to base the measures of basic skills on the Richmond Tests of Basic Skills (France and Fraser, 1975). These tests are designed for children at ages from eight to thirteen, and each test is divided into six levels corresponding to the six year groups (second-year juniors to third-year secondary pupils in the conventional system of transfer at 11-plus). These levels overlap so that, for example, a second-year junior pupil attempts items one to sixty on the test of reading comprehension, and a third-year junior pupil attempts items twelve to seventy-nine. There are eleven separate tests covering different aspects of the basic skills, and they are presented together in a ninety-six-page booklet.

The full battery of Richmond Tests takes about five hours to administer, which would have been an impossible demand to make on the schools and teachers in the project. Consequently, with the consent of the publishers, abbreviated tests were constructed from selected items in the original published version. One of the advantages of the Richmond Tests is that the teachers' manual includes an extensive classification of the skills being tested by each item. Using this classification of skills three abbreviated tests were constructed in the range of difficulty of the first four levels of the Richmond Tests, labelled 'Reading', 'Mathematics' and 'Language skills'. Each of the three tests consisted of thirty multiple-choice items. As the hardest items in the abbreviated tests were designed for children of twelve, it was felt that it would be unduly discouraging to present the youngest children in the study with the full tests, and a shortened version of each, with the hardest items removed, was prepared for administration to the second-year juniors in the initial round of testing. The item numbers from the published Richmond Tests included in the abbreviated tests are given in Appendix A (Table A.3).

(i) *Reading*

It is well established that the development of reading ability is one of the principal aims of the primary school. In the Schools Council study *The Aims of Primary Education* (Ashton *et al.*, 1975) the aim that children should 'read with understanding' was ranked second only to the aim of being 'happy, cheerful and well balanced' in teachers' rankings of seventy-two aims of primary education. Being able to 'read fluently and accurately' was ranked fourth and having a 'wide vocabulary' fifteenth in this list. No other cognitive area was ranked higher than were abilities related to reading. As was seen in Chapter 2 relatively little time is explicitly devoted to developing reading ability. By the time children reach the age of the youngest pupils in this study not many of them need to be taught to read, but reading is a continual aspect of many other classroom activities.

The items in the reading test are taken from the Richmond Tests of vocabulary and reading comprehension. The first half of the test consists of thirteen vocabulary items in which the pupil has to identify the synonym for a word from a list of four other words. The remainder of the test consists of short passages followed by questions testing comprehension, and the pupils have to identify the correct answer. These are designed to test various aspects of comprehension, but the majority of items used in the abbreviated test come from the skills classification, 'recognize and understand stated or implied factual details and relationships'.

(ii) *Mathematics*

Mathematics, like reading, was one of the areas ranked most highly in the *Aims of Primary Education* project. The ability to use mathematics in everyday life ('The child should know how to use mathematical techniques in his everyday life; for instance, estimating distances, classifying objects, using money') was ranked joint fifteenth equal to 'The child should have a wide vocabulary.' Knowledge of the four rules of arithmetic was ranked twentieth. Both of these fell into the category 'of major importance'. The attention given to mathematics in the primary schools in this study amply confirmed these rankings. As was shown in Chapter 2, a third of lesson time was devoted to mathematics.

The thirty-item mathematics test is derived from the two Richmond Tests concerned with mathematics, mathematics concepts and mathematics problem solving.

(iii) *Language skills*

The test of language skills was derived by taking items from four Richmond Tests; spelling, punctuation, use of capitals and usage. These are rather more formal skills of literacy than comprehension and vocabulary, and they were less highly ranked by teachers in the *Aims of Primary Education* project than the other skills measured by the tests. 'Correct spelling' was included in the category of major importance, but was ranked relatively low within it. 'Basic grammar' was categorized only as important rather than of major importance. Nevertheless, as was shown in Chapter 2, plenty of attention was given to these matters in the primary schools where the ORACLE research took place. In nearly three-quarters of the classrooms studied there were weekly tests of spelling.

Reliability and validity

Items were selected from the Richmond Tests for inclusion in the three tests described above on the basis of their immediate or 'face' validity. It was then necessary to establish empirically that they were a representative subset of items concerned with the skills they were intended to measure. This was done by administering the full version of those Richmond Tests from which items were selected to groups of children of appropriate ages. The results of the complete tests were then compared with results taken only from the selected items in the shortened versions. The comparison of the group mean scores on the complete test with the group mean scores on the selected items indicates the extent to which the selected items were representative of the level of difficulty of the full test. The correlation between individuals' scores on the full and partial tests was used to indicate the extent to which the selected items measure the same abilities as the full test (Pearson product-moment coefficient).

These calculations were made separately for the three tests (mathematics, language and reading). The results, presented in Table 3.1, indicate that the full and abbreviated forms of the test have very similar levels of difficulty as well as high inter-correlations. This establishes empirically that the abbreviated form of the test contained a representative selection of items and that the selected items measured the same abilities as the full test.

This pilot exercise was also used to provide preliminary reliability figures for the new tests. However, reliabilities were later calculated after the first full administration of the tests to 1,404 pupils in the three local authority areas. Taking the three tests together a reliability coefficient of 0.91 was obtained for both the full and shortened versions

Table 3.1 A comparison of the full and abbreviated forms of the Richmond Tests

	Number of children	Scores on full test	Scores on abbreviated test	Correlation coefficient
Mathematics	90	27	26	0.86
Language	62	47	47	0.89
Reading	62	46	51	0.89

The same children took the language and reading tests. A different group took the mathematics test. Scores are expressed as the average percentage of questions answered correctly.

(Spearman-Brown split half). Separate reliabilities were also obtained for the individual tests. Only one fell below 0.8, and this was a value of 0.79 for the shortened mathematics test. Reliability measures are given in full in Table 3.2.

Table 3.2 Test reliability of ORACLE tests

	Full version (N = 734)	Shortened version (N = 670)
Total score	0.91	0.91
Maths	0.81	0.79
Language	0.86	0.95
Reading	0.80	0.84

Initial pupil achievement in the basic skills

The tests were administered to 1,404 children in sixty classrooms at the beginning of the research in September 1976. The results from this initial round of testing were used to stratify the children by achievement levels in each class, prior to selecting a sample of children for detailed observation, and later as a base line from which to assess pupil achievement when the children were re-tested at the end of the year. Full results for the three tests are given in Table 3.3. These figures are given as the average percentage of questions in each area of the tests answered correctly by children of each age group, and by boys and girls. Although test scores were originally obtained from 1,404 children, during the first year of the study two classrooms were dropped because the secondary school to which the pupils would transfer was changed, and some children who had taken the test at the beginning of the year were not re-tested, mainly because they had left the school. The figures given in Table 3.3 are based on the 1,201 children in fifty-eight classrooms who remained in the study throughout the year.

Table 3.3 Initial test results of the pupils remaining in the study throughout the first year

	Age			Sex		All
	8	9	10	Boys	Girls	pupils
Maths concepts	28*	41	51	38	36	37
Maths problems	30	46	53	41	39	40
Total maths	29	43	52	40	38	39
Spelling	26	43	48	35	37	36
Use of capitals	12	25	32	19	23	21
Punctuation	18	26	25	22	22	22
Usage	27	38	40	33	33	33
Total language skills	21	33	37	27	29	28
Vocabulary	33	47	51	41	41	41
Comprehension	35	52	62	46	46	46
Total reading	34	50	58	44	44	44
N =	580	306	315	586	615	1201

*All figures are the average percentage of questions answered correctly by children in each category.

The results show that, as would be expected, older children performed more successfully on the test than the younger children, and that this was true for all three tests. Boys and girls had virtually identical over-all test scores. However there were slight variations between the different tests. Boys did slightly better on the test of mathematics and girls slightly better on the test of language skills. Scores for reading were identical for boys and girls.

The reading test was the test on which children scored highest at all age levels, and within this test the comprehension items were answered most successfully. These consisted of questions designed to measure comprehension of short passages. Slightly lower scores were achieved on the vocabulary items where children had to identify synonyms for words. The easiest words were 'even' (synonym 'smooth') and 'healed' ('got well'). In the first round of testing over four-fifths of the ten-year-olds (the oldest age group in the sample) gave the correct answer for each of these. Among the eight-year-olds (the youngest age group) 'even' was correctly identified by 73 per cent and 'healed' by 63 per cent. Much harder were 'suburb of a city' (correct answer, 'outlying part') and 'leisure' ('free time'). Fewer than one in four of the ten-year-olds gave the correct answers for these items.

Average scores for the maths test were rather lower than scores for reading. However, scores varied considerably between different computational procedures in the test. Questions involving simple addition and subtraction were answered correctly by the great majority of children. Questions applying these operations and multiplication to problems with money were also answered correctly by a high proportion of the sample. The children were, in general, able to cope with practical problems of this kind. However, problems involving divisions, fractions and decimals were only answered correctly by a much smaller proportion of children. A recent report on mathematics in primary schools found that children performed badly on fractions and decimals and also on notation and place value (Ward, 1979, pp. 39–40). These results were confirmed in the present study.

As was noted earlier, the areas assessed in the language skills test did not receive such high ranks in the Schools Council study, *The Aims of Primary Education,* as the mathematics and reading skills tested. The results discussed below suggest that less importance is attached to them, especially punctuation and the use of capitals, in many of the classrooms in which children were tested.

The language-skills test consisted of nine items to test spelling, six to test the use of capitals, eight to test punctuation and six to test usage. The format of all the items was the same. Three or four words or sentences were presented and the child was asked to underline the one containing an error, or else to underline 'no mistakes'. The examples of mis-spelling included 'radeo', correctly identified by 59 per cent of eight-year-olds and 86 per cent of ten-year-olds, 'feild' (28 per cent of eight-year-olds and 57 per cent of ten-year-olds) and 'gloomey', which was correctly answered by only 18 per cent of the older children. Spelling was the area of language skills in which children performed best. The results for the use of capital letters were rather poorer. Two-thirds of the ten-year-olds and 29 per cent of the eight-year-olds knew that 'sunday' should have a capital, but this dropped to 49 per cent and 23 per cent who knew that 'african' has a capital. Perhaps rather surprisingly the figures were even poorer for 'doctor Lewis'. Only 25 per cent of the oldest and 12 per cent of the youngest children realized that this was an error. Hardly any of the children could sort out the use of capitals in an item involving reported speech, and dealing with reported speech generally seemed to pose very considerable difficulties for the ORACLE sample of children.

This problem with reported speech occurred again in the items testing punctuation, where items of this kind had a very low proportion of correct answers. More surprisingly only 31 per cent of ten-year-olds and 16 per cent of eight-year-olds realized that a question mark was missing at the end of the sentence, 'Do you know why the River Thames is called Old Father Thames.'

The results for usage were rather better than those for the preceding two areas of language skills. An error such as 'Me and him . . .' was correctly identified by 67 per cent of ten-year-olds and 58 per cent of eight-year-olds, but only 40 per cent and 27 per cent of pupils realized that 'Us boys . . .' was wrong. Just under a quarter of the older children correctly identified 'delightfulest' as a mistake.

It is worth noting that the degree of success with which children tackled various areas of the tests follows exactly the order in which these areas were ranked as important in *The Aims of Primary Education*. Reading was the highest ranked of all cognitive areas by teachers and, as Table 3.3 shows, children did better on reading comprehension than on any other area of the tests. A 'wide vocabulary' and 'everyday mathematics' were ranked next highest of the skills measured here, and these are the skills on which children achieved the next highest scores. Of the more formal language skills, spelling was the only one to be rated as of major importance in teachers' aims, and it was rated very much lower than reading and mathematics. Scores for spelling were poorer than for reading and mathematics but better than the scores for other language skills. Capitals and punctuation, which were the skills children performed least well at in the tests, did not receive a specific mention in teachers' aims but were presumably included in 'basic grammar' which was relatively lowly rated. This clear relationship between the test scores and primary teachers' stated aims suggests that the variation in scores reflects the emphasis given to various areas of the curriculum, and is not just an artefact of the items chosen.

However, the description of levels of attainment in different skills was not the main aim of the testing programme. The chief purpose of the tests was to compare pupils and teaching methods by analysing the change in scores over the year. This forms the subject matter of the next two chapters.

Chapter 4

Teaching styles and progress in basic skills

Whenever the question of primary school practice is raised pupil progress, particularly in basic skills, is always a central issue. For this reason the main focus of the ORACLE research programme involved the analysis of what is termed process-product data. Process variables have to do with the daily drama which is played out in the classroom, consisting of the observable behaviours of both teachers and their pupils. Products have to do with the outcomes of pupil learning. Research of this type usually concerns itself only with short-term products such as pupil performance on various achievement tests, or measures of pupil attitude. Teachers however are also concerned with long-term outcomes, and must hope, for example, that the skills and habits of behaviour acquired by their pupils play a part in helping children to succeed after transfer to the secondary stage. These longer-term effects will be the subject of a later book, but here in this chapter attention is given to the progress that pupils made, during the course of one year, in reading, mathematics and language skills.

Process-product studies attempt to establish relationships between pupil achievement and teacher and pupil behaviour. The aim is to identify aspects of successful practice in certain teachers for the benefit of others. In any study there will be a large number of process variables which must be taken into account, but fortunately a rather complicated analysis can be simplified, because certain teachers tend to share common characteristics. In the present study, for example, a group of teachers who favoured an individualized approach tended to give feedback through silent marking rather than by spoken comments, and also asked relatively fewer questions than other groups of teachers. The particular unique observable characteristics of any group constitute their 'teaching style'. The issues involved in identifying such teaching styles were fully discussed in *Inside the Primary Classroom* where six distinct styles were identified. Summaries of the main characteristics of each style are presented in Chapter 2 of this book.

There is always a danger with an analysis of this kind that the teaching styles identified have no validity outside the sample of teachers from whom they were derived. If different teachers were observed then different patterns of behaviour would emerge. A most important finding therefore is that the teaching styles obtained from the analysis of observation of fifty-eight teachers, whose pupils' progress is considered in this chapter, have been replicated on a further sample of teachers during the following year of the study. This second-year sample contained less than 25 per cent of the original fifty-eight teachers. The fact that the characteristics of these teaching styles remain stable from one year to the next increases confidence that they are indeed valid measures of classroom behaviour and are not just an artefact of the sampling.

Pupil progress was measured using the modified version of the Richmond Tests described in the previous chapter. Pupils took these tests at the beginning of the school year. The same set of tests was again given to the pupils towards the end of the year. In between the two test administrations most of the children were in contact with one particular teaching style. By examining these two sets of scores the analysis aims to discover whether groups of pupils taught by a particular style made greater progress in terms of their gains on the Richmond Tests than did pupils who were taught by other styles.

Research issues in process-product studies

There are however a number of problems in carrying out such an analysis, and considerable discussion has taken place among researchers about the correct procedure to adopt. The arguments centre on four main issues.

1 How should changes in scores between the two test administrations be measured, in order to make an appropriate comparison between groups of teachers?
2 What is the appropriate unit of analysis for measuring these changes?
3 What criteria should be used when deciding whether differences between the groups of teachers are to be judged significant?
4 Are the comparisons fair, in that the tests used are equally appropriate to all the groups of teachers involved?

At the moment there appears to be no consensus among educational researchers as to a best over-all procedure in such cases. It is therefore necessary to evaluate carefully the methods used in this present analysis. Although much of the discussion relates to technical issues which are beyond the scope of this book, there is one matter that is central to an understanding and interpretation of the data presented in the following chapters: the use of gain scores to represent pupil progress. This issue is therefore discussed in some detail, before considering the results derived from the Richmond Tests of basic skills.

Measuring change

A critical issue in all process-product studies is the measurement of change. How can differences in the performance of groups of pupils at the beginning and end of their exposure to a particular style of teaching best be assessed so that comparisons between the various groups of teachers can be made?

Obviously it would be ideal if the levels of achievement of each group of pupils taught by different styles were equal at the start of the study. Differences in the post-test scores could then be directly related to the effect of different styles. If, however, the researcher sets out to match the groups exactly in respect of their initial attainment, then this may result in their being unequal with regard to other important variables. In practice, therefore, the desired condition can only be approximately realized by allocating pupils randomly to each teaching style. With such an arrangement every pupil would have an equal chance of being taught by a particular teaching style, so that over-all the groups would tend to be balanced not only in respect of their initial attainment but also on those other factors which might affect the post-test scores. In such a carefully designed experiment any differences between the groups on the post-test could be directly attributed to the treatment.

Such studies are open to criticism, in that they do not accurately reflect the real-life situation in the classroom, where levels of attainment for classes of equal age may vary from school to school according to such factors as the socio-economic characteristics of the catchment area, or the type of grouping policy adopted by the staff. Any differences attributable to these factors ought to be investigated rather than controlled for in the research design, if the results are to be directly relevant to a teacher with, for example, a mixed-ability class consisting of pupils whose parents mainly belong to groups four and five of the socio-economic status scale. Added to this, in large-scale studies the disruption that would result in attempting to allocate pupils randomly within a school is such that it is not surprising that there are few cases where a researcher has been bold enough to suggest the possibility to the head teacher.

A further problem is that once pupils have been allocated to a particular treatment it is not possible for them to be moved to another class if the results of the experiments are to be meaningful. This can raise serious issues, particularly if the teachers believe that a particular treatment is doing certain pupils harm by retarding their progress. According to Parlett and Hamilton (1976) this happened in the experiment designed to assess the effectiveness of the i.t.a. approach to the teaching of reading (Downing, 1967).

Most research is therefore conducted in 'natural' settings, where each school is left to carry out its own procedure for assigning a teacher and her pupils to a particular class. Differences in the level of attainment are therefore likely to exist from class to class across schools. Since the groups of pupils start off unequal it is not possible to use the post-test scores by themselves to measure progress during the course of the year. In this situation a correction must be made for the effects of these initial differences. It is the nature of this correction which has given rise to disagreement among researchers (Harris, 1963; Cronbach and Furby, 1970).

The use of raw-score gains to measure pupil progress

The simplest approach is to calculate *difference scores* by subtracting the pre-test from the post-test score. This procedure has the advantage that it is easy to do and simple to interpret. Difficulties arise, however, because an individual's score is at best only an approximate estimate of his true level of achievement. Some individuals' scores will over-estimate this level, while some will underestimate it. The reliability of a test indicates the degree of error involved in using the observed scores as estimates of the true achievement level of the candidates taking the test. The theory of test reliability predicts that when a pre-test score is subtracted from a post-test one, the reliability of the simple difference score will be less than that for either the pre-test or the post-test.[1] In process-product studies this low reliability may mask real differences between teaching styles.

A further difficulty arises in that, because of this unreliability, the pre-test scores tend to correlate negatively with the simple gain scores. Pupils with low scores on the pre-test will therefore tend to make greater gains than pupils with high scores. This has unfortunate consequences when analysing process-product studies such as ORACLE. Teachers usually wish to know whether a particular teaching style is equally effective across the whole ability range. This issue can be investigated by using the pre-test scores to sub-divide pupils into above- and below-average categories. When the simple difference scores are used, their negative correlation with the pre-test introduces a potential bias into results. The above-average pupils appear to make less progress while the below-average ones make more.

The use of residual-change scores to measure pupil progress

Mainly for this reason, another method of correcting for initial differences on the pre-test has increasingly come to be used. This involves the calculation of what is known as the *residual-change* score. Figure 4.1 illustrates the procedure. When two variables are correlated together a simple way of examining the relationship is by means of a scatter plot, where the scores on one variable, in this case the post-test, are plotted against the other, the pre-test. Thus the point A on the diagram represents the pupil whose score on the pre-test was x and whose score on the post-test was y. The straight line drawn through the scatter of points is called the *regression line*. The line can be used to predict the post-test score from a knowledge of the pre-test one. The higher the correlation the better the prediction. When the value of the correlation coefficient is positive and equals one, its maximum value, then the predicted post-test score and the actual post-test score are the same. The *residual-change* score is the difference between the observed and the predicted post-test score. In the diagram the predicted post-test score for pupil A is z. Thus this pupil's residual-change score would be (y – z). The magnitude of this difference represents the extent to which pupil A has progressed more than expected, if judged on his level of achievement at the beginning of the school year. Unlike simple difference scores, residual-change scores are uncorrelated with the pre-test and also tend to have higher reliability. However, there are a number of problems attached to their use and interpretation.

To begin with, the residual-change score is not a 'true' gain score in which the influence of initial achievement has been removed. It is

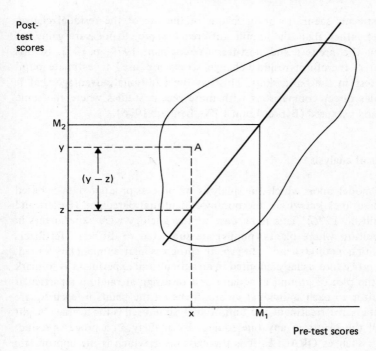

Figure 4.1 Calculating residual-change scores

simply the difference between the post-test score and that which would have been predicted from the pupil's initial achievement. It is based solely on the performance of other children taking the tests, where some individuals do well or badly in comparison with others. In Figure 4.1, if all the residual-change scores of the pupils who did better than predicted were added together, their total would be balanced by the sum of the scores of the pupils whose performance fell below the expected value. The inclusion of another group of children could therefore change an individual's predicted post-test score. In studies such as ORACLE, where the relationship between teaching style and pupil performance is studied, scores on the pre-test should also be influenced by teaching received in the previous years of schooling. Thus the predicted score is difficult to interpret, based as it is partly on the pupil's earlier achievement and partly on the kind of teaching previously received. This in turn means that the interpretation of pupil progress in terms of residual change scores becomes more difficult.

Despite such problems, however, the recommendation of most

statisticians seems to be in favour of the use of the residual change score, rather than the simple difference score, to measure gains between the pre-test and post-test (Youngman, 1979, p. 191). In this chapter, therefore, residual-change scores are used to estimate pupil progress in the basic skills. This has the additional advantage that it enables direct comparisons with more recent studies where the same method was used (Barker Lunn 1970, Bennett 1976).

Units of analysis

The model upon which the analysis of process-product data is based is sometimes known as 'the botany-agricultural paradigm' (Parlett and Hamilton, 1976). This is because of the analogy with experiments in agriculture where plants (pupils) are subjected to different fertilizers (teaching methods) and their growth (progress in attainment) measured. The procedure usually adopted in an agricultural experiment is to mark out the plot of ground in squares and to assign at random a particular fertilizer to each individual square. Since all the plants in each square get the same treatment the unit of analysis chosen is the average height of all the plants in any one square. By analogy, in a process-product study such as ORACLE, it is the class mean which is the appropriate unit of analysis, since all the pupils in a class are taught by the same teacher.

When class means are used as the unit of analysis the size of the sample is reduced considerably. For example, in the ORACLE study 1,200 pupils completed the Richmond Test, but these came from only fifty-eight classes. In addition, when the class average is used, possible relationships between a particular teaching style and the characteristics of certain types of pupil cannot be investigated. For example, it is no longer possible to obtain information about the effects of different teaching styles on the progress of different types of pupils with above- and below-average attainment. The effects of different teaching styles on the progress of such pupils within a class is clearly of interest to teachers.

Recent studies, such as Barker Lunn (1970) and Bennett (1976), have tended to use the individual pupil rather than the class as the unit of analysis. In the absence of any clear consensus about which unit of analysis to adopt it seemed sensible to take a pragmatic approach and to use both. The results presented in this chapter will be based on the scores of individual pupils and not on class averages. The analysis for class averages will, however, be presented in the following chapter, and any discrepancies between the two sets of results commented upon.

There are thus three different units of analysis in the ORACLE study.

Unit A: The total sample   All the pupils in the fifty-eight classes who took the tests during the first year of the study.

Unit B: The observed sample   The stratified random sample of eight pupils in each of fifty-eight classes who were observed using the Pupil Record.

Unit C: The class sample   The fifty-eight classes involved in the study.

In collating data for individual pupils, sample B rather than the full sample A was used. This makes possible direct comparison between teaching style, pupil types and pupil progress in the final chapters of the book, since it is from this sample that pupil types have been identified.

Significance of results

Significance tests are properly used to make inferences from a randomly selected sample to a known population, and to test for non-random effects in experiments of the botany-agricultural kind described previously. Many studies where random sampling is not possible still report significance levels of their results (Barker Lunn, 1970; Bennett, 1976; Rutter *et al.*, 1979). Here the tests of significance are used to give an indication of the order of magnitude of the results obtained. Reporting significance levels enables such researchers to interpret their results in a consistent manner throughout, and also provides a convenient way to compare the results with other studies. It is in this sense that they are used in the ORACLE study where significance levels of 5 per cent and 1 per cent are reported.[2]

Are the comparisons fair?

When examining the scores of pupils who have been subjected to different teaching approaches, the question arises as to whether the test items on which the pupils are compared are appropriate in all cases. This issue has already been commented upon in the previous chapter, where Rutter's findings were cited to support the argument that the measures used as products should reflect both the aims and the classroom practice of the teachers (Rutter *et al.*, 1979).

The pupils taking part in the ORACLE study do not take public examinations but, as was shown in Chapter 3, the basic skills of reading, mathematics and English as measured by the Richmond Tests do reflect aspects of learning with which teachers in the primary schools are centrally concerned. The observation data presented in *Inside the Primary Classroom* confirm that this was also the case for teachers in this study. Furthermore, many of the comments of the observers in their descriptive accounts of lessons concerned work-sheets and activities which were closely related to the skills which the Richmond Tests measured. Recent surveys, for example, that of HMI, reinforce the ORACLE findings that a large proportion of time is given to the study of these curricular areas (HMI, 1978).

It may be, however, that more emphasis is given to these basic skills in some classes than in others. Evaluation of the different teaching styles solely in terms of the range of basic skills could therefore be misleading in some cases. For this reason measures in the other areas outlined earlier in Chapter 1 are included in the final appraisal of the ORACLE pupils' progress and performance. Analysis of the results relating to these latter areas are presented in Chapters 6 and 7. In the rest of this chapter and in the one that follows, the focus is on the assessment of basic skills.

Progress in mathematics

Table 4.1 sets out the results for progress in mathematics for the six identified teaching styles. Row 1 gives the raw score pre-test means which were obtained from the scores of the eight target pupils in every class taught by a particular teaching style. The post-test means obtained in the same way are given in row 2. The raw score gain (simple difference score) for each style is then the difference between these pairs of pre-test and post-test means (row 3). They are included by way of comparison with the residual-change scores in row 4.

It is these residual change scores which are used here to evaluate pupil progress in mathematics. The positive value indicates that the pupil's post-test score was better than predicted by his pre-test result. The mean residual-change scores, reported in row 4, therefore indicate whether the pupils taught by a particular style did better or worse than expected.

Perhaps the most striking feature from the pre-test data was the level of achievement of the group taught by the *individual monitors* (row 1).

Table 4.1 Teaching style and progress in mathematics

	Individual monitors	Class enquirers	Group instructors	Infrequent changers	Rotating changers	Habitual changers	All pupils
1 Pre-test means	15.2	10.4	9.3	11.9	10.8	11.6	11.7
2 Post-test means	18.6	17.7	15.8	16.6	15.8	16.3	16.8
3 Raw-score gains	+3.4	+7.3	+6.5	+4.7	+5.0	+4.7	+5.1
4 Residual-change score allowing for pre-test differences	−0.5	+1.8	+0.2	+0.4	−0.5	−0.7	0
5 Residual-change score allowing for pre-test and time on task differences	−0.5	+1.7	+0.2	+0.4	−0.5	−0.6	0
Number of pupils (sample B)	97	67	49	43	64	89	409

Their pre-test mean was considerably higher than that of any other group, partly because the schools in local authority area C contributed the majority of teachers to this style, and the group therefore contained a high proportion of older children. The data in the third row, which gives the difference between the pre-test and post-test means, indicate that all groups improved during the course of the year, particularly those taught by the *class enquirers* and *group instructors* who had the lowest pre-test means. When differences in initial achievement were taken into account the *class enquirers* still made the most progress in terms of the residual-change scores (row 4) but the *infrequent changers* did better than the *group instructors*. In the light of the earlier discussion it should be observed from Table 4.1 that, when the whole sample of pupils is considered, the sum of all their residual-change scores is zero. This is because the adjustment of each score within a style is a function of the sample, and an improvement in the average score for one group of pupils must be balanced by a downward adjustment elsewhere among the remaining styles. The result is significant at the 1 per cent level, so that differences between the residual-change scores of this magnitude would have been likely to occur, as a result of sampling fluctuations, only one time in a hundred. This result, however, only informs us about the gap between the style with the highest positive score, the *class enquirers*, and the group who were the least successful, the *habitual changers*. A further test of significance was carried out to examine the differences between the *class enquirers* and the remaining teaching styles. In comparison with the most successful style, the residual-change scores of the *individual monitors* and the *rotating changers* both differed at the 1 per cent level. The difference between the *class enquirers* and the *group instructors* was at the 5 per cent level, while that with the *infrequent changers* just failed to reach this value. The procedures used were taken from Winer (1970), Chapter 3.

In the fifth row of Table 4.1 the residual-change scores for each teaching style are presented when a second variable, the time pupils spend on their tasks, is introduced as an additional covariate. Harnischfeger and Wiley (1975) have argued that the *major* influence on a pupil's progress is the 'active learning time' rather than the quality and nature of the teaching received, in so far as this is concerned to promote objectives other than keeping children working on their task. Bennett has chosen to interpret the Lancaster findings (Bennett, 1976), that formal teachers are more successful than informal ones, in terms of this theory. In his informal classrooms, with the emphasis on individualized instruction, there was more time wasting, and longer periods of transition from one activity to another, than there was in the formal classes. Thus pupils in formal classes, where there was a higher percentage of class teaching, spent more time working at their tasks, and it is to this factor that Bennett attributes most of their success (Bennett, 1978b).

The analysis of covariance procedure, used to adjust the post-test scores for initial differences between the groups on the pre-test, can again be used to examine this theory of Harnischfeger and Wiley. Here, by including the amount of time which the pupils spend working at their task in the covariate, a new predicted post-test score can be obtained, and a new residual-change score calculated for each pupil. The new residual-change scores take into account the fact that pupils taught by different styles spend different amounts of time working at their mathematics tasks. If Harnischfeger and Wiley's theory is correct, then these differences in the time spent on the task should predict most of the pupils' observed post-test scores. The differences between the residual scores of the groups taught by the varying styles should therefore disappear, since it is the difference in the time pupils spent working which is held to be responsible for a major part of the variation in the levels of attainment across the groups.

The scores in Table 4.1 are for the target pupils who, for part of the time during which they were observed, were engaged on mathematical activities such as number work and problem solving, or practical activities including measuring and using money. As part of the observation procedure, pupils were coded COOP TK whenever they were co-operating on a set task, and a note was also made of the nature of the activity. Thus, for each of these pupils, the proportion of total observation time during mathematics when they were working on their tasks could be obtained and then correlated against their raw post-test score. The residual change between the actual post-test score and that predicted from this regression line was calculated for each style in the manner described previously.

It can be seen from the fifth row of the table that this second adjustment had a negligible effect. The analysis of covariance in Appendix C1 confirms that this was so. When 'time on task' is introduced as an additional term, only 1 per cent of the total variation can be attributed to the 'time on task' variable. Thus with the ORACLE sample of pupils and these particular tests of mathematical achievement, the theory of teacher effectiveness suggested by Harnischfeger and Wiley did not hold.

Table 4.2 Teaching style and progress in language skills

	Individual monitors	Class enquirers	Group instructors	Infrequent changers	Rotating changers	Habitual changers	All pupils
1 Pre-test means	10.4	7.3	6.9	9.3	8.0	9.8	8.8
2 Post-test means	13.6	13.6	12.9	13.6	10.8	13.8	13.0
3 Raw-score gains	+3.2	+6.3	+6.0	+4.3	+2.8	+4.0	+4.2
4 Residual-change score allowing for pre-test differences	−0.5	+1.5	+1.1	+0.5	−1.8	−0.2	0
5 Residual-change score allowing for pre-test and time on task differences	−0.4	+1.5	+1.2	+0.5	−1.9	−0.2	0
Number of pupils (Sample B)	97	67	49	43	62	92	410

Progress in language skills

The skills assessed in this part of the Richmond Test concern the pupils' ability to spell correctly and recognize errors in punctuation and grammar in written English. The method of analysis was similar to that for the mathematics test, and the data presented in Table 4.2 show both the raw-score gains and the average residual-change scores for each of the six teaching styles. Again the *individual monitors* had the highest pre-test mean, but the differences between them and the remaining groups was not so large as for mathematics (row 1). Also, as before, the groups of pupils taught by each style improved by the time the post-test was administered, with the *class enquirers* and *group instructors* making greatest progress (row 3). When allowance was made for in-equalities between the group means on the pre-test then the residual-change scores (row 4) followed the same rank order as the raw-score differences, and over-all, were significant at the 1 per cent level (Appendix C1).

Examining group differences, pupils taught by the *class enquirers* have the highest residual score (row 4). Unlike the results for mathematics, however, there were fewer statistically significant differences between their score and those of the remaining teaching styles. Only the change scores of the *individual monitors, rotating changers* and *habitual changers* differed significantly from that of the *class enquirers*. The difference for the *habitual changers* was at the 5 per cent level of significance, while that for the other two styles was at the 1 per cent level.

Looking at the residuals in the fifth row of Table 4.2, it can be seen that when time on task, defined as the time spent by the pupils on writing activities, was included with the pre-test in obtaining the regression line none of the values for the mean scores of pupils taught by each teaching style changed by more than one unit in the first place of decimals. The failure of the time-on-task variable to account for a significant proportion of differences in post-test means can be seen from Appendix C, Table C.1, where a summary of the analysis of covariance is presented. Adding the second variable to the covariate reduces the unexplained variation by less than 0.1 per cent. As with the mathematics, this result offers little support for Harnischfeger and Wiley's explanation of pupil progress.

Progress in reading, word recognition and comprehension

The data are presented in Table 4.3 in a similar manner to that for the

Table 4.3 Teaching style and progress in reading

	Individual monitors	Class enquirers	Group instructors	Infrequent changers	Rotating changers	Habitual changers	All pupils
1 Pre-test means	14.6	12.0	11.0	12.2	11.5	13.4	12.7
2 Post-test means	20.6	18.4	17.9	20.9	17.2	18.5	18.8
3 Raw-score gains	+6.0	+6.4	+6.9	+8.7	+5.7	+5.1	+6.1
4 Residual-change score allowing for pre-test differences	+0.5	0	−0.1	+2.7	−1.0	−1.0	0
5 Residual-change score allowing for pre-test and time on task differences	+0.5	0	−0.2	+2.8	−1.0	−1.0	0
Number of pupils (sample B)	97	67	49	43	61	93	410

two other areas of basic skills. *Individual monitors* again have the highest pre-test mean. Comparing the raw-score pre-test and post-test means, however, it can be seen from row 3 that it was the *infrequent changers* and not *class enquirers* who made the largest gains. When allowance was made for the inequalities of the styles on the pre-test then this result remained unchanged and the *infrequent changers* appeared to have made greatest progress over the school year (row 4). *Individual monitors* were the next most successful group. The difference between the residual-change score of the *infrequent changers* and the *individual monitors* was however significant at the 5 per cent level, as was that for both *group instructors* and *class enquirers*. The difference between the *infrequent changers* and the remaining two styles were both significant at the 1 per cent level.

The fifth row shows the residual-change scores when both the pre-test and time on task are used as covariates. It can be seen that, once more, the addition of the time-on-task variable makes a negligible difference to the mean residual-change scores. The data from the analysis of covariance in Appendix C (Table C.1) show that time on task accounts for none of the variation. One possible explanation for this particular result is that the time-on-task variable in this case was determined by the time the pupils spent on activities such as reading aloud in class or reading individually to the teacher. In junior school classrooms little time is allocated to such formal reading activities, and the observation schedule did not permit the recording under a separate category of the time spent when pupils were reading from books or work-sheets in connection with other activities. There may be too little data to show up differences between the styles on the amount of time given to these formal reading activities, and if so, it would not be possible to establish a relationship between this variable and the pupils' reading progress. Even if the assumption is made that the total amount of time which pupils spend on all their tasks is proportional to the time spent on informal reading activities (using books, work-sheets and so on), and this variable is introduced into the analysis, there is little change in the result. Total time spent on all tasks accounted for only 3 per cent of the variation in reading post-test scores. Thus in both cases there is little support for the theory that the time on task variable is 'the most important determinant of pupils' progress' in reading.

Table 4.4 Summary of results for teaching style and achievement in basic skills

1	2	3	4	5
Test area	Most successful style	Not significantly different from most successful style	Significant at 5 per cent from most successful style	Significant at 1 per cent from most successful style
Mathematics	Class enquirers	Infrequent changers	Group instructors	Rotating changers Individual monitors Habitual changers
Language skills	Class enquirers	Group instructors Infrequent changers	Habitual changers	Individual monitors Rotating changers
Reading	Infrequent changers		Individual monitors Class enquirers Group instructors	Habitual changers Rotating changers

Pupil progress: summarizing the results

Table 4.4 presents a summary of all the major findings with respect to the basic skills. In comparison with the research discussed in the first chapter of the book, two features of this table are particularly striking. First, unlike previous studies, based largely on self-reporting questionnaires, *no over-all best style emerges for all three tests*. While the *class enquirers* were most successful in mathematics and language skills, it is the pupils of the *infrequent changers* who make the greatest gains in reading. However, in language skills the *class enquirers* enjoyed no over-all superiority from either the *group instructors* or the *infrequent changers*. In mathematics the progress of pupils taught by *infrequent changers* did not differ significantly from that achieved by the group taught by the *class enquirers*.

The finding that, as far as the basic skills were concerned, there was no 'best buy' would seem important in the continuing debate about teacher effectiveness. Past research has usually been concerned to establish the over-all superiority of one particular teaching method over the remainder, but here there appear to be three different styles, allied to different proportions of class, individual and group work, which are available to teachers interested in improving pupil performance in the basic skills.

The least successful style would seem to be that of the *rotating changers*, who have considerable problems in improving the level of their pupils' achievement in basic skills. In each of the cells in column five of Table 4.4 the styles are written in rank order of their residual-change score. The most successful style is placed at the top and the least successful at the bottom. The difference between the change score of the most successful style and that of pupils taught by the *rotating changers* was, in every case, significant at the 1 per cent level and was, in absolute terms, the largest difference for language skills. In the previous book, *Inside the Primary Classroom*, the manner in which these changes from one curricular area to another tended to break down a pupil's concentration, and lower his interest in the set task, was described. In both this group of pupils and those of the *habitual changers* and the *individual monitors*, who were also less successful than either the *class enquirers, infrequent changers* or *group instructors*, the number of pupils who were involved in high levels of distraction was appreciably greater than would be expected from the over-all proportion in the sample. For the *rotating changers*, in particular, there were also fewer pupils who maintained a high level of work activity. It would seem, therefore, that both in terms of test results and also in terms of pupil behaviour there are particular problems associated with this style of teaching. A more detailed discussion of these differences will be found in the section on pupil behaviour (Chapters 8 and 9).

The second point of interest concerns the pattern of success between the different styles in respect to the three test areas. In Chapter 1 mention was made of Anthony's (1979) review of previous research concerning effective mathematics teaching. He concluded that even in earlier studies tending to favour progressive methods, there was a consistent trend which showed that pupils of teachers using a class rather than an individualized organizational strategy performed better on tests of numerical computation and intellectual problem solving. The result, presented here, confirms this conclusion, in that the *class enquirers*, the teachers who spent up to a third of their time on class-based instruction, achieved a statistically significant superiority, in terms of the pupil gains over the year, when compared to all other styles with the exception of the *infrequent changers*. This style, however, made the second highest use of class instruction.

In the face of evidence from this result and from the studies listed by Anthony, all using different methodologies, and covering a period of nearly twenty years, it must be concluded that there is something about an approach based on class teaching which is helpful in getting pupils to solve mathematical problems of the type represented by traditional standardized tests. This is an important finding, even if there still remains the controversy about the exact nature of what that 'something' is, since both these successful styles also engaged in the greatest number of 'higher-order cognitive interactions' (open questions, statements of ideas and so on). Further discussion of this issue will be found in Chapter 10.

However, Anthony's other conclusion, that the evidence of more recent studies suggests that an approach based on individualized instruction has been less successful for teaching basic skills of English, was not supported. Although the *class enquirers* were the most successful in developing language skills, the difference between their change score and that of either the *group instructors* or the *infrequent changers* was not statistically significant. In reading and comprehension it was the *infrequent changers* who did best, thereby contributing to their being the most successful style over all.

The findings presented here are much closer to the results obtained by Gardner (1966), and make sense in terms of the data collected from the Teacher and Pupil Records. The *infrequent changers* interacted more frequently with their pupils than did teachers using the other styles. A higher proportion of their pupils either sought or were selected for attention, either privately or as the focus of the group or class. It would seem logical to expect that the pupils who were heard reading individually, or who talked to the teacher about the meaning of what they had read, would reap the benefits, and this result appears to support this view.

Pupil progress and initial achievement

It is also of interest to analyse the results in more detail by breaking down each class of pupils into different levels of achievement, based on their initial pre-test scores. High achievers were in the top quartile of the class, low achievers in the bottom quartile, while the medium achievers consisted of pupils in the two middle quartiles. Much has been heard recently of the criticism that modern teaching methods hold back the 'bright child' because the level of teaching tends towards the 'lowest common denominator'. In *Inside the Primary Classroom* it was shown that, in terms of distribution of a teacher's attention, neither high nor low achievers were particularly favoured. Many teachers, however, intuitively feel that different teaching approaches are more suitable for pupils with different levels of achievement. By comparing pupil progress in the basic skills at three initial levels of attainment it becomes possible to explore this issue within the ORACLE sample.

Table 4.5 shows the rank order of the residual-change scores for each style for the high, medium and low achievers respectively. For the purpose of this discussion it was found simpler to present the over-all trends rather than lengthy and detailed tables of the actual scores. These can be found in Appendix C (Table C.2). Table 4.5 shows that, although there were some statistically significant differences between the styles when the initial achievement of pupils was taken into account in this way, the trend in favour of the more successful styles tended to operate right across all levels of achievement within the sample. For the high achievers the *class enquirers* seemed to have the most effective approach. Classes of pupils taught by this style were most successful in mathematics and language skills and came out second in reading. Perhaps surprising, however, is that the second most successful style with high achieving pupils was that of the *individual monitors*, who in Table 4.4 appeared to be, over-all, one of the least successful styles. Only in language skills were they among the bottom three styles in terms of effectiveness for the high achieving pupils.

Table 4.5 Teaching styles and basic skills: summary of rank orders of adjusted scores for different levels of initial achievement

Test area	Teaching styles					
	1 Individual monitors	2 Class enquirers	3 Group instructors	4 Infrequent changers	5 Rotating changers	6 Habitual changers
Mathematics						
All pupils	4	1	3	2	4	6**
High achievers	2	1	6	3	5	3+
Medium achievers	4	1	3	2	6	5+
Low achievers	4	1	5	2	3	6
Language skills						
All pupils	5	1	2	3	6	4**
High achievers	4	1	2	3	6	5*
Medium achievers	5	1	2	4	6	3+
Low achievers	3	3	2	1	6	5
Reading						
All pupils	2	3	4	1	5	5**
High achievers	1	2	4	2	6	5*
Medium achievers	2	3	3	1	5	6*
Low achievers	2	5	5	1	4	3

* significant at the 5 per cent level

** significant at or beyond the 1 per cent level

+ significant between the 5 per cent and 10 per cent level

Lowest rank is the most successful style in each case.

Differences do not reach statistical significance for low achievers (F ratio less than one).

For medium achievers the *class enquirers* were the most successful in both mathematics and language skills, but not for reading, where the *infrequent changers* had the highest positive residual-change score. For low achievers none of the results reached statistical significance but the trend was strongly in favour of the *infrequent changers*, particularly for language skills and for reading. The data suggest that the groups who are less successful across all achievement levels are the *rotating changers* and *habitual changers*.

Both the *individual monitors* and *infrequent changers* had the highest proportions of pupils either seeking or receiving individual attention. It would seem, from Table 4.5, that for pupils of all levels of achievement individual instruction is important for success in reading with understanding. In contrast to the findings of the Lancaster study (Bennett, 1976) the data on reading from the ORACLE research support the view of the Bullock Committee that 'independent work by individuals and groups provides the best sustained context for effective instruction by a teacher and should therefore be the principal form of classroom activity' (Bullock, 1975, para. 13. 15).

While the *group instructors* in this study were not so successful in promoting progress in reading, the evidence from *Inside the Primary Classroom* showed that the groups did not function as collaborative learning units. For much of the time pupils worked in relative isolation with little contact with the teacher.

The value of some degree of class instruction as an aid to successful learning in mathematics receives further support from the more detailed results presented here. The *class enquirers* achieved greater gains across all three achievement levels. The same was true with the exception of low achievers for language skills.

These results suggest that teachers need to think carefully about both the forms of organization and the kinds of interactions which they employ when teaching the different curriculum areas assessed by these tests. Teachers with the highest level of class involvement did best in fostering mathematics and language skills irrespective of whether the pupils were high, medium or low achievers. Those using the highest amount of individualized teaching were the more successful in the reading comprehension tests.

In this study, however, much emphasis has been placed on the kind of interactions which take place between the teacher and the pupils within these organizational settings. Each teaching style was defined in terms of a distinct pattern of such interactions. Both the *class enquirers* and the *infrequent changers*, who appeared to be the most successful styles over-all, have high levels of interaction with pupils in both class and individualized settings. Both styles also make the greatest use of what might be identified as higher-order interactions involving the presentation of ideas and encouraging more open-ended discussion (see Chapter 2, p. 39).

These links between form of organization (reflecting the teacher's strategy), the kinds of interactions engaged in by the teacher within these different forms (the teacher's tactics) and their pupils' progress will be explored further in the final chapters. This examination of pupil progress has used the scores of individual pupils as the basic unit of analysis. This, as we have seen, has many advantages when seeking to interpret the results, but the procedure is open to criticism from statistical considerations. Some researchers argue that the use of the class mean as the unit of analysis is more appropriate. It seems proper, therefore, to repeat the analysis using class averages rather than individual scores and to compare the two sets of results, before going on to examine other alternative forms of assessment in later chapters.

Notes

1 Tests theory assumes that any particular test score is made up of two components; an element due to the individual's true score on the attribute being measured and an element of random error. A reliability coefficient of 0.9 (the approximate reliabilities of the achievement tests used in the ORACLE project) is interpreted as an estimate of the proportion of variance in the test that is true variance, that is, not due to error. When an individual takes two tests, or takes a single test on two occasions in time, the error component of his score is uncorrelated between the two tests, as it is a random component. However, if the tests themselves are correlated (as two achievement tests or a pre-test and post-test almost always will be) the presence of random error introduces complications when scores on the two tests are being compared.

A gain score made up of the simple difference between two correlated scores will tend to have a low reliability. How this arises can be illustrated by imagining the situation when the two tests are perfectly correlated. In this case, if an individual's scores on the two tests are expressed as standard scores, then the difference between the two will be entirely due to error and the difference score will have a reliability of zero. In the case of two tests having reliabilities of 0.90 and intercorrelations of 0.75, the reliability of the difference score is 0.60 (see O'Connor, 1972).

Although the error components in the pre- and post-test scores are uncorrelated, the same is not true of comparisons involving difference scores. In particular, there is a negative correlation between the error components in the pre-test and those in the difference scores. People who score below their true level of attainment on the pre-test will appear to have made larger gains than they really have, while the opposite will be true of people scoring above their true level. This results in an inbuilt tendency for the pre-test and the measure of change to correlate negatively.

Comparing pre- and post-tests on the basis of residual scores through an analysis of covariance, increases the reliability of the measure of change and eliminates the inbuilt negative correlations with pre-test.

2 Statistical significance is properly used to assess the likelihood that an observed result is due to chance sampling fluctuations rather than real differences in the population from which the samples were drawn.

Researchers testing for statistical significance begin with the assumption that in the population as a whole there is no relationship between the variables being studied. This assumption is known as the null hypothesis. In the present study the null hypothesis is the idea that using different teaching styles on the population of children which our samples represent has no effect on their progress. Any observed differences in the progress of pupils taught by different styles are assumed to be the result of chance fluctuation in the selection of the sample.

A 5 per cent significance level indicates the magnitude of these observed differences which would be expected five times in every hundred cases if the null hypothesis holds true. It is not to be taken to mean that there is a 95 per cent chance of any result being correct, as some researchers appear to suggest. The significance level only assesses the probability of a specific result being due to chance when the null hypothesis is true.

Chapter 5

Teaching styles and class progress in basic skills

The preceding chapter was concerned with progress in mathematics, language skills and reading, based on the analysis of the scores of individual pupils. This analysis showed that teaching style did have an effect on pupil progress in these basic skills, that children taught in classrooms where the teachers belonged to the teaching styles described either as *class enquirers* or *infrequent changers* performed better at the end of the year than had been expected from their scores at the beginning of the year, while children from the classrooms of either *rotating* or *habitual changers* tended to perform below expectations.

In this chapter these results will be investigated further in two ways. First, the relationship between teaching style and pupil progress will be re-examined using class averages rather than individual pupil scores as the units of analysis. Second, possible explanations for these results, other than teaching style, will be considered.

Analysis of progress using class averages

In Chapter 4 the difficulties involved in selecting appropriate units of analysis in classroom-based research were discussed. There the analysis involved pre- and post-test scores of eight target pupils from each class. The basis for calculating the statistical significance of the results, however, depended upon the assumption that each unit of analysis had been independently sampled. This is clearly not so when individual scores are used to determine the effects of teaching style. Certain pupils have in common the same class and the same teacher. The correct unit is therefore the average score for the class.

With only one score per class, however, it is no longer possible to investigate how different types of pupil respond to a particular teaching method. Using the class average assumes that the effect of the style employed by a particular teacher is constant for all her pupils. This assumption would seem questionable, particularly in primary classrooms where the emphasis is on an individualized approach. However, since both units of analysis have their advantages it is desirable to analyse the data from the Richmond Tests using the mean scores of the fifty-eight classrooms in the study to complement the earlier treatment based on individual scores.

The statistical method used is the same as before, namely analysis of covariance fully described in the previous chapter. The method adjusts class average post-test scores so that they can be expressed as residual-change scores. These estimate the extent to which classes did better or worse at the end of the year than was predicted from their scores at the beginning of the year. The teaching styles being compared are exactly the same as in the previous analysis. The main difference from the analysis of individual pupil scores is the sample size. This has been reduced from 410 to fifty-eight. Other things being equal, the results are now not so likely to reach statistical significance, because the effect of chance sampling factors are less likely to even out in small samples than in big ones. However, using class averages does remove one source of error (in the statistical sense). Variations between individual pupils in the class which are not accounted for by teaching style do not occur when the unit is the class average.

Analyses of covariance were carried out in turn for language skills, reading and mathematics. The individual analysis in the previous chapter was based on the eight target children in each class, but here the class averages were based on all the children in the class. In Table 5.1 the residual-change scores for the six teaching styles are given, together with levels of significance, when initial differences on the pre-tests are taken into account. With the exception of mathematics the results confirm the findings of the previous analysis based on the scores of the eight target pupils. The first row of Table 5.1 presents the results for language skills. As in the original analysis, the *class enquirers* had the highest residual-change score. *Infrequent changers* and *group instructors* were second and third highest, and although this is the reverse of their order in the individual analysis these differences were not significant. The other three styles all had negative residual-change scores as before. The differences between the average scores of these styles and that of the *class enquirers*, the most successful style, were significant at the 5 per cent level.

Table 5.1 The variation of class progress in basic skills across teaching styles (using residual-change scores with pre-test as the controlling variable)

| | Teaching styles | | | | | | |
Skill area	Individual monitors	Class enquirers	Group instructors	Infrequent changers	Rotating changers	Habitual changers	Significance level
Language	−0.8	1.7	0.5	1.1	−1.4	−0.3	*
Reading	0.8	0.8	0.3	1.3	−1.1	−1.1	*
Mathematics	−0.5	1.4	0	0.6	−0.6	−0.3	†
Number of classes	13	9	7	6	9	14	58

* significant at the 5 per cent level
† significant at the 10 per cent level

The results for the reading test are given in the second row of Table 5.1. As with the results for language skills, the ordering of the residual scores showed some differences from that in the individual analysis but the over-all picture was very similar. *Infrequent changers* had the highest residual score, as they had in the individual analysis. The *individual monitors* were equal second with the *class enquirers*, whereas previously they had been above them. *Group instructors* now had a small positive rather than a small negative residual-change score, while the remaining two styles had the lowest residuals, as before. Like the results for language skills, the over-all difference in the average score for the *infrequent changers*, the most successful style, and the two styles having the lowest residuals was significant at the 5 per cent level.

The results for mathematics given in the third row of Table 5.1 differed from the preceding results in that they did not meet statistical significance at the 5 per cent level, although they would be significant if a 10 per cent ($p < 0.1$) level were adopted. The residual-change scores, however, followed the same pattern as in the analysis of individual pupils. *Class enquirers* had the highest average residual-change score, followed by *infrequent changers* and *group instructors*, while the other three styles performed less well.

In general the analysis of class means confirmed the results reported in the previous chapter. The rank order of the residual-change scores for the various teaching styles was very similar in the two analyses, and only the mathematics results did not reach statistical significance at the 5 per cent level. The procedure adopted here of aggregating a very large number of scores on individual pupils into a much smaller number of class average scores is, however, a very conservative one. Using class averages as the unit of analysis rather than individual scores is therefore a much harder test of the hypothesis that the progress pupils make in the basic skills differs with teaching style. Given the conservative nature of the procedure, it is most reassuring that the results of the second analysis show that the relative differences between the most successful and least successful styles follow a similar pattern to that obtained when individual pupil scores were used as the unit of analysis.

Alternative explanations of pupil progress

The results discussed here reinforce the view that pupils taught by certain teaching styles are more successful than others in achieving progress in the basic skills. Teachers belonging to the groups of *class enquirers* or *infrequent changers* do considerably better over-all, although the *group instructors* also have above-average gains. The remaining three styles generally scored below average, with the one exception of the *individual monitors* who were among the most successful styles for reading.

The two questions which immediately come to mind following such results concern causality. Did the differences in style 'cause' the differences in progress, and if so what was it about the styles which caused these changes? The problem with such questions is that causality cannot be inferred from the results of non-experimental research. This is because the observed relationship between two variables (e.g., teaching styles and achievement) may come about not because one has a causal influence on the other but because they are both dependent for their effect on some third variable.

In principle it is not difficult to investigate specific effects of this kind by controlling for the effect of a third variable on the other two, and seeing if the original relationship remains. The issue is, therefore, not whether other factors may be causally related to the two variables of interest, but the uncertainty that all possible third variables have been taken into account. No matter how many variables are controlled for in non-experimental research, there will always be the possibility that a factor which has not been considered is really responsible for an observed relationship.

This problem should not be allowed to dominate the analysis of researches where it is not possible to have experimental control. In principle anything can be explained by factors that no one has thought of yet, and while this should make us cautious in interpreting any results it should not deter us from examining the influence of those factors of which we are aware, and which are related to the variables in an observed relationship.

A number of variables will therefore be introduced in the analysis in an attempt to explain the findings. However, they will not all influence teaching style in the same way, and therefore the extent to which it is appropriate to control for them will differ. For the purpose of discussion they will be considered under three headings:

1 *Variables external to teaching style*
These include socio-economic status of pupils, class size and such outside constraints as the 11-plus. If the observed relationship between teaching style and progress disappears when such factors are introduced into the analysis, then the effects of style may be said to have been explained away.

2   *Variables directly associated with teaching style*
These factors are themselves part of the teaching process, and include
the time pupils spend working and the proportion of the time which
the teacher devotes to class or group work. These factors are of
interest because they offer possible explanations as to how teaching
styles achieve their effects.
3   *Variables where the relationship with teaching style is problematic*
It is not clear how or why factors in this category achieve their effects.
Under this heading are such variables as the age of the teacher, the time
devoted to certain subject areas, the type of classroom and the age
composition of the class. Because the nature of the relationship
between teaching style and these variables is unclear it is also difficult
to decide whether it is appropriate to control for them.

In order to demonstrate that such variables account for the observed
effects of teaching style on pupil progress, certain conditions must be
met. First, they must discriminate between successful and unsuccessful
teaching styles. Next, their relationship with pupil progress must be
consistent with the pattern of differences between the teaching styles.
For example, if middle-class pupils make greater progress than working-
class pupils, then a higher proportion of the latter should be taught by
the unsuccessful styles. Finally, if both the above conditions are met,
then the inclusion of the variable as an additional controlling factor in
the analysis of covariance should cause the observed relationship between teaching style and pupil progress to disappear.

The procedure for data analysis is as follows. First, for each teaching
style, the scores on the various factors are calculated and expressed
either as percentages or averages, as appropriate. Teaching styles are
then divided into two groups; those with above-average residual-change
scores (*class enquirers, infrequent changers* and *group instructors*) and
those with below-average residuals (*individual monitors, rotating
changers* and *habitual changers*). Examining the variation in scores for
each of the variables in this way determines the extent to which they
discriminate between teaching styles. Where they do, the correlations
between these variables and pupil progress are considered. Values are
given first for all classrooms, and then separately for classes taught by
above-average and below-average styles. Finally, when such factors are
shown to influence both style and progress in a consistent manner,
their effects on the residual-change scores are examined.

Variables external to teaching style

One class of variables consists of those which have no necessary connection with teaching style, but which may have a causal relationship with pupil progress. Two such possible factors are the socio-economic status of the pupils and the existence of an external constraint such as the 11-plus. It has been suggested that one or both of these may have had a confounding effect on the Lancaster study of pupil progress (Gray and Satterly, 1976). One argument is that pupils from more prosperous social backgrounds are known to have an advantage at school, and that if a particular teaching style had a disproportionate number of such children, either by chance or because parental pressures influence the choice of teaching methods, the observed relationship between progress and teaching styles would be explained. A similar argument applies to the 11-plus. In 11-plus areas children may be motivated to do well at achievement tests and certain teaching styles may predominate, but there need be no necessary connection between them. These are examples of what are termed in statistics spurious relationships.[1] If they were found to exist in the present case, the relationship between teaching styles and progress would be not so much explained, as explained away.

A variable similar to these is the number of children in the class. This is not an external factor but a feature of the classroom. Nevertheless, if class size affected both pupil performance and teaching style, and if the differences in performance associated with teaching style disappeared when differences in class size were controlled, it would be reasonable to describe the association between teaching style and performance as spurious, and to reject it as an explanation for pupil progress.

Of these external variables, the question of possible effects of the 11-plus is most easily dealt with, since none of the local authority areas in which the research was conducted made use of external examinations for selection purposes. In Table 5.2, therefore, only data for class size and socio-economic status is given. The figures for class size represent the average number of pupils in classes taught by different styles, while variation in socio-economic status is presented as the percentage of the different occupational categories within each style.

The socio-economic status of parents was derived from the occupation of the fathers of pupils in the class. Such data is, however, notoriously difficult to classify. In some schools, where this information was either not available or thought to be unreliable, it was supplemented

Table 5.2 Differences in 'external', 'associated' and 'problematic' variables across teaching styles

Type of variable	Measure used	Teaching style						Above-average styles	Below-average styles
		1	2	3	4a	4b	4c		
External	Average class size	29.0	28.9	30.9	32.2	31.4	29.1	30.4	29.6
Socio-economic status of parents (per cent)	Professional and managerial	14.5	8.2	13.1	4.8	8.0	5.7	9.0	9.5
	Other non-manual	19.1	24.3	20.5	18.6	25.4	37.3	21.5	27.7
	Skilled manual	46.0	39.1	29.2	43.7	38.1	31.4	38.3	38.3
	Other manual	20.4	28.4	37.2	32.9	28.5	25.6	31.2	24.5
	Total percentage	100.0	100.0	100.0	100.0	100.0	100.0	100.0	100.0
Associated	Average percentage of time spent working	56.4	64.9	56.0	56.8	56.0	58.3	59.9	57.0
	Average percentage of time spent on class and group work	12.5	37.3	29.1	23.0	20.9	20.2	30.8	17.6
Problematic	Average percentage of time spent on basic skills (maths, language, reading)	63.0	63.3	65.6	64.6	65.2	51.4	64.4	59.1
	Average age of teacher	30.8	41.1	40.0	35.8	39.2	30.0	39.3	32.6
	Percentage of open-plan classes	39	0	0	17	44	35	5	38
	Percentage of vertically grouped classes	8	11	14	33	55	35	18	30

KEY: 1 = Individual monitors   2 = Class enquirers   3 = Group instructors   4a = Infrequent changers   4b = Rotating changers
4c = Habitual changers

by the 1971 census data for the school catchment areas. In such cases all the classes within a particular school were assumed to have the same socio-economic composition.

Table 5.2 shows that the average class size of about thirty children to a class was fairly uniform across all six teaching styles and virtually identical between the above- and below-average styles. Socio-economic status also did not seem to vary in any systematic fashion between teaching styles. Although the percentage of children from families in different occupational categories differed somewhat between styles, these differences did not form a pattern which could account for the differences in progress. Over-all, the above-average teaching styles had a slightly higher proportion of children whose parents were in manual occupations compared with children in the below-average styles. None of these three variables differed between styles in a way that could account for the differences in progress across teaching style. Further investigation is therefore unnecessary.

Variables directly associated with teaching style

Another different class of variables includes such measures as the proportion of lesson time that children spend working, and the amount of time a teacher devotes to class or group work. These variables are themselves part of the classroom process. If, therefore, the effect of teaching style on pupil progress disappears when such variables are introduced into the analysis of covariance, then this result would not have explained away the differences between styles but instead explained how they came about. Such an analysis would underline the value of basing the typology of teaching styles on direct observation; it becomes possible not only to describe the effects of teaching styles but to give an indication of how they achieve their effects.

The amounts of class and group work were variables in the cluster analysis from which teaching styles were derived. However, it was shown in *Inside the Primary Classroom* that the clusters were determined by the pattern of teacher-pupil interaction, rather than by these organizational variables. The amount of time which children spend working is also likely to be affected by the teacher's behaviour in the classroom. Both these variables would therefore be expected to differ across teaching styles, and Table 5.2 shows that this is so. Not surprisingly the *class enquirers* and *group instructors* have very much higher than average amounts of class or group teaching, and the *class*

Table 5.3 Correlation of residual-change scores with other factors associated with progress in the basic skills

Type of variable	Factor correlated with residual-change scores	All classrooms				Classes with above-average styles				Classes with below-average styles			
		Skill area			Total scores	Skill area			Total scores	Skill area			Total scores
		1	2	3		1	2	3		1	2	3	
Associated	Percentage of time spent working	04*	24	26	20	11	23	0	12	−13	10	28	14
	Percentage of time spent on class and group work	24	25	20	29	33	22	19	28	−11	−25	−23	−23
Problematic	Percentage of time on subject	17	−16	04	−10	−12	−14	−45	−24	28	−35	−06	−18
	Teacher age	16	24	17	25	14	18	11	15	−10	0	02	−01
	Number of classes				58				22				36

* decimal points omitted for convenience

KEY: 1 = Maths scores   2 = Language scores   3 = Reading scores *enquirers* have a greater proportion of time spent working than the other styles. However, the pattern of the relationships makes it unlikely that these variables will totally explain the effects of teaching style. Pupils of the *infrequent changers*, over-all the most successful style, spent approximately the same amount of time on work as the children taught by *rotating changers*, the least successful. Although the average time spent on class or group work does discriminate between successful and unsuccessful styles, the *infrequent changers* make less use of these strategies than the *group instructors*, who were considerably less effective.

Table 5.3 shows the complicated nature of the relationship of these two variables with pupil progress. For each classroom, the correlations between the average percentage of time pupils spent working per class and the average amount of time devoted to group and class work were correlated in turn with the mean class residual gain. This was done separately for mathematics, language skills and reading, and also for the combined total scores. The analysis was then repeated, first for classes taught by the above-average styles and then for classes taught by the below-average ones.

For all teachers together there were moderate correlations between the variables and the average class residual-change scores (for the combined scores $r = 0.20$ for the proportion of time working; $r = 0.29$ for class and group teaching). However, when these correlations were calculated separately for the more successful and less successful styles the form of the relationship changed. The correlations of the residuals with the proportion of time spent working were in each case reduced, while the correlations with the amount of time spent on class and group work became negative in the case of the less successful styles. These results therefore tend to confirm an effect of teaching styles independent of these variables. When teaching styles were controlled the relationship was reduced or reversed. In particular, among the least successful styles which made little use of class or group teaching, such approaches were negatively related to pupil progress.

As would be expected from these results, using these variables as extra covariates in the analysis of covariance does not make much difference to the adjusted post-test scores, although it does reduce the level of statistical significance. In Table 5.4 the average residual-change scores for the six styles, with both variables as extra covariates, are presented. In all cases the order of differences between styles remained virtually the same, although the differences were not now significant at the 5 per cent level. These variables, particularly the time

Table 5.4 Class average residual-change scores for factors associated with teaching style

Controlling variables	Skill area	Teaching style							Significance level
		Individual monitors	Class enquirers	Group instructors	Infrequent changers	Rotating changers	Habitual changers	
Pre-test, class plus group work and percentage of time working	Language	-1.0	1.8	0.8	1.2	-1.2	-0.4	NS
	Reading	0.4	0.4	0.1	1.3	-0.3	-1.0	NS
	Mathematics	-0.4	1.3	-0.3	0.5	-0.6	-0.2	NS
Number of classes		13	9	7	6	9	14	

allocated to class and group work, do go some way towards explaining how some of the styles achieved their success. The data, however, do not suggest that increasing the amount of such activity will in itself guarantee an improvement in pupils' progress. With the less successful styles, increasing either group or class work tended to be counter-productive. It was shown in *Inside the Primary Classroom* that the use of class work, in particular, was closely associated with the use of higher-order interactions. This suggests that it may be the nature of the interactions which are shared by the whole class that differentiate between the successful and unsuccessful teachers. This point will be developed in Chapter 10, when the characteristics of effective teaching are examined in greater detail.

Variables where the relationship with teaching style is problematic

A third class of variables presents more of a problem, as it is not immediately clear if it is appropriate to control for them, nor how the results should be interpreted if they are controlled. These are variables associated with the teacher, but not themselves part of the teaching style. In this study, two such variables are the age of the teacher and the amount of time spent on different parts of the curriculum. In *Inside the Primary Classroom* it was shown that certain styles of teaching were more likely to be used in either open-plan areas or vertically grouped classes. Both these factors must therefore be included in the analysis, although in either case it is again not immediately obvious how to explain their effect.

Other studies concerned with the effects of teaching on pupil progress have been criticized for not controlling for such variables, in particular for not controlling for the teacher's age or experience. Gray and Satterly, for example, criticize the Lancaster study of pupil progress for this among other reasons (Gray and Satterly, 1976).

However, it has also been argued recently that it is not appropriate to control for such variables, as their influence is part of the teacher effects being investigated (Youngman, 1979, pp. 193-4). Here we come back to the main concern of this chapter, that of explaining (or perhaps explaining away) the observed relationships. If it turns out that the time spent working on a part of the curriculum is the major determinant of pupil progress, and that the effects of teaching style disappear when it is controlled, then this could be regarded as an explanation of how the successful styles achieve their effects. On the other hand, it could be argued that time spent on different parts of the curriculum is in no sense a necessary part of a teaching style, at least as style is defined in the present study, and that all teachers could increase or decrease the amount of time they devote to different subjects, if they thought it appropriate, without altering their approach to teaching. Looked at this way, the time spent on various subjects is a different kind of variable from the proportion of their time children spend working, and the time spent in class or group work.

Similar problems arise with the age or experience of the teacher. Any effect associated with teacher age is clearly a teacher effect. But if the effects of teaching style disappear when teacher age is controlled then it may be misleading to attribute these effects to teaching style. Nevertheless, to attribute teacher effects to age or experience only raises further questions. It seems unlikely that it is age or experience in themselves which produce effects; it must be something that older or more experienced teachers *do*. As teachers have been extensively observed in the present study, it may be that the effects of age or experience are contained in the observations of teaching style.

This raises the possibility that teachers of different ages get different results because they teach differently. If the evidence supports this view, then it provides a rather different answer to the question of whether factors associated with the teacher but not themselves part of teaching style should be controlled in the analysis. If the concern is with explaining teaching effects rather than simply establishing them, then some account must be taken of the variables such as age. The interpretation of any results, however, may well depend on other kinds of relationships present in the data. It may be, for example, that if children in open-plan classrooms also make less progress, then the relationship with teacher experience is partially explained by the fact that the older teachers are less likely to teach in such schools.

The issues raised by the above discussion also apply to other variables, such as pupil motivation, which are dealt with in Chapters 8 and 9. The pupil variables examined so far have been the socio-economic status of the children's background and, implicitly, the pupils' prior achievement, which has been used throughout as the covariate in the analysis of teaching style and progress. Both these factors have been controlled as external variables, and have failed to explain away the effect of style.

Unlike socio-economic status or initial achievement, it is not immediately obvious how a variable such as pupil motivation should be introduced into the analysis. Teaching styles may be influenced by levels of pupil motivation, but they may also influence them. In this case pupil motivation could be a way in which a teaching style produces its effects. As with factors such as the time given to teaching basics and the age of the teacher, the appropriate form of analysis will depend upon the nature of the relationships.

The amount of time spent on the basic skills is very much in the teacher's (or the school's) hands, but is not part of teaching style as it has been defined in this research. In fact, with one exception the styles were remarkably uniform with regard to the total amount of time spent on mathematics, language skills and reading. As Table 5.2 (p. 85) shows, just under two-thirds of lesson time was devoted to these areas, the remainder being spent on topic or project work, art and craft (for the purpose of the research 'lesson time' excludes PE, music, drama and so on). Only the *habitual changers* were below this figure, spending no more than half the lesson time on these areas.

Returning to Table 5.3 (p. 87), where correlations of the time spent on basics and class residual-change scores are tabulated, it can be seen that no consistent trend emerges. For all classrooms the correlation with the combined residual score was small and negative. When classes were divided into those taught by successful and unsuccessful styles, then the negative relationship was strengthened both for individual subject areas and for the combined score. The one positive correlation ($r = + 0.28$) was obtained in mathematics for classes taught by the less successful styles. This negative result does not mean that the less time a teacher spends on basic skills the more progress her pupils will make. In *Inside the Primary Classroom* it was shown that, on average, teachers in the sample spent about two-thirds of their time on mathematics, language and reading. This result demonstrates that, above the threshold value, a greater emphasis on these aspects of the curriculum does not result in greater pupil success.

However, when interpreting this finding, it should be borne in mind that the time spent on basics is expressed as a proportion of the total lesson time in Table 5.3. It is therefore possible that two teachers could have the same percentage figure but that one could devote more time to basic skills, by virtue of spending more time teaching in the classroom. This could come about if the other teacher had devoted more of the lesson time to activities such as PE and cookery, which took place outside the classroom area and were therefore not observed. Although, therefore, the figures may not estimate the absolute amount of time spent on basics, they do serve to represent the emphasis given to these subjects as opposed to other curriculum areas.

Table 5.5 Class average residual-change scores for each teaching style with age and time on subject as additional controlling variables

Controlling variables	Subject area	Teaching style						Significance level
		Individual monitors	Class enquirers	Group instructors	Infrequent changers	Rotating changers	Habitual changers	
Pre-test and time spent on subject	Language	-0.8	1.7	0.7	1.1	-1.3	-0.5	*
	Reading	0.1	0.8	0.4	1.3	-0.4	-1.1	*
	Mathematics	-0.5	1.4	-0.1	0.3	-0.7	-0.1	NS
Pre-test and teacher age	Language	-0.6	1.4	0.3	1.1	-1.4	-0.1	NS
	Reading	0.1	0.7	0.3	1.3	-0.4	-1.0	NS
	Mathematics	-0.5	1.3	-0.1	-0.5	-0.7	-0.3	NS
Number of classes		13	9	7	6	9	14	

* significant at the 5 per cent level

In Table 5.5, where the time spent on each of the basic skills is included along with pre-test scores as an additional controlling variable in the analysis of covariance, the changes to the average residual gains are very small compared to the figures in Table 5.1 (p. 80). Style differences were still significant at the 5 per cent level for both language and reading. In mathematics the over-all difference between the mean for the *class enquirers*, the most successful style, and that for the *rotating changers*, the least successful style, was increased by only one place of decimals.

Teacher age is the next variable to be considered. Table 5.2 shows that the average age of teachers in the more successful styles was over six years higher than that of those in the less successful styles, and Table 5.3 shows that when all classrooms were included in the analysis there was a correlation of 0.25 between teacher age and residual-change score. These results immediately suggest that teacher age (or, more realistically, teacher experience, which has not been measured directly in this study) may explain the effect of teaching style. As teacher age is not a part of the teaching process in the way that, for example, the amount of class teaching is, then this result might be said to explain away the relationship between style and progress.

Nevertheless, as was argued earlier, this is not the only possible interpretation which might be placed on these findings. Rather than teacher age explaining the effects of teaching style, it may be that teaching style explains the effects of teacher age. Table 5.3 gives some support to this interpretation. If the two groups of teaching styles, those with above-average and those with below-average residual change scores, are treated separately, then the correlation between teacher age and residual-change score disappears in the case of below-average styles, and is very much reduced in the case of above-average ones. This suggests that at least part of the correlation between age and residual-change score is explained by the teaching styles, as defined by the appropriate categories of the Teacher Record, and that the effects of teacher age should therefore not be controlled in the analysis.

Nevertheless, for the sake of completeness, teacher age is introduced as an extra covariate in Table 5.5. Comparing the figures there with those in Table 5.1 (p. 80), it can be seen that the differences between the successful and unsuccessful styles in language and reading are now no longer significant. In the case of language skills the average gain of the *class enquirers*, the most successful style, is reduced, while in reading the negative residual of the *rotating changers* decreases from minus 1.11 to minus 0.40 when teacher age is taken into account. It is these changes which reduce the over-all difference between the successful and the unsuccessful styles below the 5 per cent significance level.

The final two variables to be considered in this chapter are vertical grouping and the teaching area, whether open-plan or box classroom. The last two rows of Table 5.2 show that both these factors discriminated between successful and unsuccessful styles. Only 5 per cent of the successful teachers operated in open-plan areas, compared with 38 per cent of unsuccessful ones. Eighteen per cent of successful teachers used vertical grouping, compared with 30 per cent of teachers whose classes made below average residual gains. The trend is much stronger with respect to open-plan areas than vertical grouping. All three successful styles have a higher proportion of vertically grouped classes than the *individual monitors*, whose pupils made below-average progress.

Table 5.6 Relationship between class progress (residual gains) and (a) vertical grouping, (b) open-plan areas

Subject	Vertical grouping	Single age	Open-plan area	Box classroom
Mathematics	−0.67	0.23	0.28	−0.10
Language	0.44	−0.25	0.25	−0.09
Reading	−0.74	0.26	−0.03	0.01
Number of classes	15	43	27	31

Neither of the two variables are however associated with pupil progress. In this case, because each class is coded on either one or other of two discrete categories it is easier to investigate the relationship using average residual gains rather than a correlation coefficient. The data are shown in Table 5.6. On none of the three tests of basic skills were the mean residuals between either open-plan and box classrooms or vertically grouped and single-age ones significant. While, therefore, there is a direct link between the use of certain teaching styles and both factors, it is not this association which accounts for pupil progress.

General conclusions concerning progress in basic skills

A number of conclusions, summarized in Table 5.7, emerge from the preceding discussion. Some of these are relatively tentative, while others may be more firmly asserted.

1 When class average scores rather than individual pupil scores are used as the basis for the analysis, the relative positions of the different styles remains the same and, with the exception of the mathematics test, the results are statistically significant at the 5 per cent level.

2 As in the earlier analysis, based on individual pupil scores, some styles achieve consistently higher residual-change scores than others. There is however no single 'best style', since the results vary for different subjects.

3 External factors such as socio-economic status, class size or the 11-plus do not vary between styles in a systematic fashion which could explain the observed relationship between class progress and styles.

4 Two variables closely associated with teaching style, the amount of time spent on group and class work and the proportion of lesson time the children spend working, were also considered, to see if they could explain the effects of teaching style. Although they are related to achievement to some extent, they are not principally responsible for the effects of teaching style. Class and group work were positively related to achievement only in those styles where they appeared to be important elements of the teaching approach.

5 Variables associated with the teacher, or the classroom, but not part of teaching style as defined here, had fairly complicated relationships to residual scores. The emphasis given to the basic skills as a proportion of the total observed lesson time did not correlate positively with progress. Teacher age was associated with pupil progress in the basic skills, but this relationship was stronger in classes which made above-average progress rather than in those where the residual gains were below average. This gives support to the idea that the teaching styles described here help to explain the effects of age rather than the other way round.

The aim of this section has been to look for explanations of observed differences between the residual-change scores associated with different teaching styles. Only three variables were found to have a consistent relationship with both style and pupil progress. A complete analysis of the data, however, suggests that rather than explaining away the effects of style these factors help to explain how the successful

Table 5.7 Summary of the effects of additional variables on the relationship between teaching styles and pupil progress

Variable	Status	Relationship with teaching style	Relationship with progress	Effects of controlling for variable
Socio-economic status	External	None		
11-plus	External	None		
Class size	External	None		
Proportion of time spent working	Associated	Higher in more successful styles	Positive	Effects of style remained but were reduced. Correlations were higher over all than within groups of styles. This variable explains part of the way styles achieve their effects
Proportion of class and group teaching	Associated	Higher in more successful styles	Positive	The correlation of this variable with progress only holds for teachers who emphasize these approaches. Does not explain the effects of style
Age of teacher	Problematic	Higher in more successful styles	Positive	Correlations hold between styles but not within them. The data support the view that older teachers get results by the use of certain styles
Time spent on basic skills	Problematic	Higher in more successful styles	None	
Open-plan	Problematic	Fewer in more successful styles	None	
Vertical grouping	Problematic	Fewer in more successful styles	None	

teachers achieve their effects. The value of basing a typology of teaching styles on the observed behaviours of teachers with their pupils is reinforced by these findings. None of the three associated variables can therefore totally account for the success of certain styles.

Note

1 The problem of spurious correlations is the fundamental obstacle to making causal inferences in non-experimental research, but it is not the only difficulty. Two others are concerned with the time dimension involved and the question of the direction of any causal effect. Even if the relationship between two variables is not spurious, there is still the problem of which causes which. In the present case, although the natural explanation for a relationship between teaching styles and progress is that it is the style which influences progress, an alternative explanation is that teachers behave differently with children who are doing well, and therefore that it is progress which is causally prior. However, the characteristics of the different teaching styles, and the different relationships they have with variables such as teacher age and motivation, seem to make this an unlikely explanation. In particular, the fact that teachers using the more successful styles tend to be older suggests that style is prior to any causal process.

Part III

Study skills and pupil performance

Chapter 6

The assessment of study skills

As the debate on the relative merits of traditional and progressive approaches to teaching has developed, it has come to be widely felt that conventional achievement tests are not entirely adequate as measures of pupil progress, since they do not fully reflect the aims and intentions of teachers, and in particular since they are not directly related to the skills children need in the pursuit of self-directed or independent study (Gardner, 1966; Elliott, 1978). To do justice to the aims of the many teachers who attempt to foster these activities, a process-product study should include measures of the skills of independent learning, as well as tests of achievement in the basic curricular areas.

The rapid development of interest in the concept of study skills in recent years has led to its inclusion in such measures as the Richmond Tests of Basic Skills (France and Fraser, 1975), where there is an attempt to measure children's skills at map reading, the interpretation of graphs and tables and the use of reference material. The concept of study skills, however, poses problems of both definition and assessment.

Definition of study skills

Encyclopedias and dictionaries of educational terms tend either to omit study skills or to define them in the most general terms: for example, as 'skills a student needs to develop in order to study successfully' (Page and Thomas, 1977). The authors of test batteries, as would be expected, are more specific. In the interpretive manual of the Bristol Achievement Tests, Brimer (1969) writes of 'the kind and degree of application that children can bring to bear to study the world around them and particularly within those areas of the curriculum which are normally covered by environmental studies and natural sciences'.

It seems clear that unless study skills are operationally defined, and hence directly related to the tasks students perform, they can easily become synonymous with the 'primary mental abilities' described by Thurstone (1938), or with Guilford's more recent model of the intellect (1967); and any attempts at assessment will relate more to the concept of intelligence than to the practicalities of classroom endeavour. To be of much diagnostic or predictive value, study-skill measures will need to be empirically derived and to relate to what teachers understand by independent study; or to 'intellectual initiative, independence in observation, judicious invention, foresight of consequences, and ingenuity of adaptation to them' (Dewey, 1916). They will involve the acquisition of information, its organization, its presentation and the use made of it. They will have more to do with the ways in which answers are sought than with the correctness of the answers themselves.

Individual skills will need to have unique features to justify their being regarded as independent of each other, and of scores on conventional achievement tests. They will not necessarily each relate only to isolated specific tasks, since a single skill might contribute to successful performance in a range of activities.

Within this context, an attempt was made to devise suitable exercises from which the results could be analysed for underlying characteristics, either task-specific or common to a number of activities, which might be interpreted as study skills.

Techniques for assessment

It was necessary at the outset to decide whether to direct the enquiry towards work taking place, that is, the actual activities performed by the pupils, or towards work already completed. In spite of the fact that the former approach would have fitted in well with the ORACLE emphasis on process, it was decided on several grounds to adopt the latter. An analysis of work in progress must take place *in situ*. The ORACLE programme of observation and testing was already making heavy demands on the tolerance of teachers and pupils; and in addition a large-scale investigation of performance in progress would have demanded resources of time and manpower which were wholly impracticable. Further, the aim of this particular exercise was to devise techniques for assessment; and the value of these would be maximized if they could later be used by teachers themselves to monitor the development of study skills in their pupils. For a busy teacher, upon whom demands of the day press heavily, the evaluation of products, since it can be carried out at any time whether the children are there or not, is a much more practicable proposition than the evaluation of performance in progress.

It was therefore decided to develop a number of set exercises, not restricting the enquiry to the skills of interpretation, but making it possible to evaluate the ways in which the children made graphs and other artefacts, as well as the ways in which they made use of them.

Two types of exercise were used, the first consisting of tasks specifically devised for the study, and the second consisting of structured activities which had formed part of the teacher-based assessment procedures. Although the content of the exercises was broadly similar, the underlying rationales were different.

The specifically devised exercises represented a straightforward attempt to provide pieces of work which might involve common underlying study skills. The structured activities, on the other hand, originally arose from the intention to provide techniques which would facilitate the assessment of some of the 'intellectual' aims of teachers which are not assessed by traditional measures of achievement. Here the starting point was the teacher's aim. Groups of teachers were involved in the conceptualization of some of their aims, in terms of the criteria they would use to decide whether a child was achieving in a particular area. Only after checklists of criteria had been produced were the structured activities devised to provide appropriate tasks from which teachers could make an assessment of a child's performance.

The three specially devised exercises and the three structured activities used were as follows:

Study-skill exercises
1 The interpretation of some pictorially presented data, and the construction of a block graph.
2 Making a plan of a classroom.
3 Making a model of a clock-face with movable hands.

Structured activities
4 A set of tasks involving 'listening skills'.
5 Making a picture incorporating a given geometric design, scored for originality and appropriateness.
6 A series of tasks involving the acquisition of information other than by reading.

The exercises will be described in more detail below; but first it

103

seems appropriate to make some general comment on the problems of scoring work of this kind.

Problems of scoring study-skill exercises

The scoring of pieces of work such as those collected in this study is fundamentally different from scoring of traditional tests, where some responses are right and others wrong.

Although an impressionistic approach is attractive, in that it seems to do justice to what the teacher (or scorer) feels is important about a particular child's attempt at the task, it was rejected, except in one part of the clock-face exercise. The insuperable difficulty of this approach is that without specific scoring criteria it is virtually impossible to secure agreement between scorers, and very difficult to obtain consistency even within the ratings of a single scorer. On the other hand, there is a risk that scoring from a list of criteria may in some kinds of task seem to miss the point. The whole is somehow more or less than the sum of its parts, so that a particular piece of work may be defective in many of its details and yet still give a good over-all impression which seems valid to the scorer; or conversely the over-all piece of work may forcibly strike the scorer as poor, even though its details meet many of the criteria in the scoring system.

This dilemma is probably insoluble. Attempts to resolve it have generally started from a consideration of teachers' aims and intentions in relation to particular tasks, and moved from there to a formulation of specific scoring criteria for aspects of the task which are relevant to those aims. CSE examination procedures furnish many examples of this approach; and it was used also in the three structured activities in the present study. Here the aims of teachers had already been made explicit, and the activities were devised specifically to incorporate them. It was therefore a straightforward matter to select scoring criteria which related to the initial intentions in formulating the exercises.

Nevertheless there are dangers in this approach. In the first place it must arise from a consensus of aims, and cannot deal adequately with those aspects of a task where teachers differ widely in their aims. In the second place, the scoring system arising from preconceptions about what makes a good piece of work will not take note of any aspects of the task which do not form part of the teachers' conscious framework of intentions, but which nevertheless may make a considerable contribution to the general impression upon which they rate the finished product as a good or poor piece of work.

With these considerations in mind, a different procedure was adopted for the scoring of the three specially devised study-skill exercises. The first step was to derive from a comprehensive descriptive analysis a list of all possible criteria, seemingly relevant or not, which would permit consistency of scoring. Only after this had been done was a selection made of those criteria which would be used in the scoring system.

The ease with which the preliminary descriptive analysis could be carried out varied from task to task. In the clock-face exercise the listing of scorable criteria presented some difficulties: for example, whereas the presence or absence of hands upon the clock-face was a straightforward matter, the spacing and orientation of the numbers around the face could not be scored so easily. The next step here was for scorers to work together to refine criteria in such a way that, while remaining valid, they became more objectively scorable. Two scorers repeatedly rated different batches of twenty-five models; and by discussing criteria between batches they eventually arrived at a scoring system which gave marks both for general impression and for specific features. An inter-judge reliability check after the exercise had been completed gave a Pearson r value of 0.89; and because such a small number of criteria had emerged from the analysis, all of them went forward into the final scoring system. In the other two exercises, the preliminary descriptive analysis was much more straightforward, and it was an easy matter to score each child's work for the presence or absence of each of the features which appeared anywhere in the total number of scripts.

The second step was the selection of those items which would appear in the final scoring system. Here again, the ease with which this could be done differed in the two remaining tasks. In the mapping task the demands made on the children were so straightforward that it was possible to go straight from the descriptive analysis to the selection of those scoring criteria which were, in Stake's (1967) terminology, logically contingent upon the task. In the block-graph exercise, however, many of the possible scoring criteria had more to do with custom than correctness, and here it seemed appropriate to consult teachers, not about their general aims in relation to this area of study, but about the importance they attached to each item on a comprehensive list of features of block graphs which had emerged from the descriptive analysis. The features were assembled into a questionnaire, on which teachers were asked to rate each item on a five-point scale ranging from essential to inadmissible. From this questionnaire it was possible to isolate those criteria derived from the preliminary descriptive analysis of the data which were rated as essential by the majority of the teachers consulted.

It seems likely that this general approach to scoring could be readily adapted for a much wider range of children's course work than was examined here. Its outline is summarized in Figure 6.1.

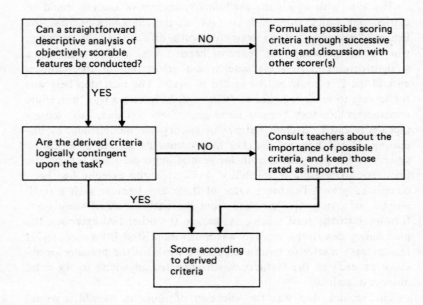

Figure 6.1 An approach to the scoring of children's coursework

In the present study the devising of scoring systems was not an end in itself, but simply a necessary preliminary to the isolation of study skills. When the descriptive analyses had been completed, the search for underlying study skills began with a factor analysis of all the scored features (items) on all the activities investigated (tasks).

Components of study-skill exercises

Factor analysis starts from the premise that if two or more variables (in this case task items) involve a common element there will be a correlation between them. The function of the analysis is to show in quantitative terms the pattern of correlations among the items, and to simplify the data in such a way that new variables, or components, are produced, each representing a cluster of inter-related items. The components themselves are mathematical constructs; and the meaning or import of the clusters of items which form them must be determined by inspection and the application of common sense. Thus the present factor analysis would not of itself yield study skills; it would simply provide a number of groups of highly inter-correlated items. Since some undoubted skills, such as accuracy, were reflected in the scoring systems of several of the tasks, the main purpose of this analysis was to discover whether children who gained points for these qualities in one task tended to gain points for them in others, so that one could validly speak of them as *underlying skills* pertaining to an individual child rather than to his score on an individual task.

It quickly became apparent that this was not so. For example, the original correlations between the accuracy items on the different tasks were uniformly very low, being generally below 0.1 and never exceeding 0.2, whereas the correlations between the accuracy items within a single task were much higher (ranging in the block-graph task between 0.3 and 0.6).

Thus the initial factor analysis of all exercises together did not suggest any underlying study characteristics which cut across the boundaries of specific tasks: the items within each task were in this respect more homogeneous than were clusters of skill-related items drawn from different tasks. However, there was a clear indication that a single task could involve two or three independent factors. It was therefore decided to carry out further factor analyses separately for each exercise. The purpose here was to discover whether the principal items in the main factors of each individual task would hang together in a way which would suggest component study characteristics or skills.

Details of the individual exercises and results of the factor analyses are given below.

The block graph

The worksheet for the block graph is shown in Figure 6.2, as an example of the kinds of materials prepared for the study-skill exercises. The instructions and the twenty-by-twenty square grid appeared on one side of a sheet of A4 paper, and the pictures of the sea creatures appeared on the other.

The sheets of instructions to teachers for all the tasks suggested that it would be better if the exercises could be presented as ordinary pieces of class work rather than as tests. It was emphasized that there was no need for all the children to do a particular task at the same time, if they would normally do such an exercise individually or in groups.

The factor analysis of the block-graph scores yielded seven main factors, two of which related to features which were not rated as important on the teachers' questionnaire responses. These two factors involved the use of colour and the presence and width of spaces between the columns on the graph. These features were not included in the final scoring system.

Of the other five factors, one related to layout, one to accuracy and one to grasp of the basic concepts involved in a graph. The remaining two factors involved different aspects of labelling, and in the final scoring system these two factors were put together to represent the

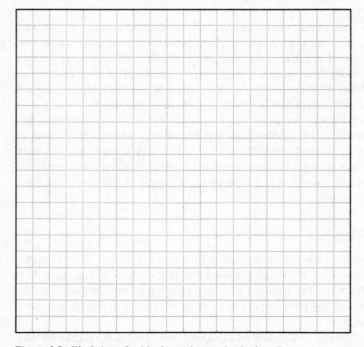

A man once studied a rockpool to see how many creatures lived in it. He tried to show what he had found by drawing the picture opposite.

In the space below make a block graph to show what there was in the pool.

Figure 6.2. Worksheet for block-graph exercise (reduced)

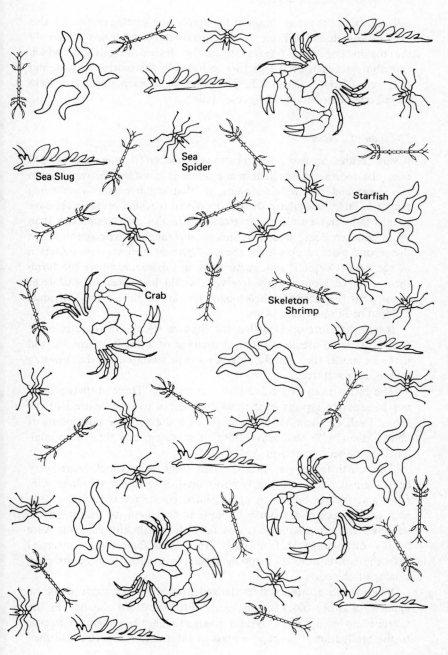

Sea Slug

Sea
Spider

Starfish

Crab

Skeleton
Shrimp

skill shown in the presentation of the graph. The scoring system for this exercise is included in Table 6.1. The maximum possible score is simply the number of items (derived from the descriptive analysis) which contribute to each of the factors included in the scoring system, and thus varies from skill to skill. The presence of each single task item scored one point, and its absence no points.

The plan of a classroom

It was decided on two counts not to ask children to draw plans of their own classrooms. In the first place, there is considerable variation in the shape and size of classrooms, so that children who were being taught in large, irregularly shaped open-plan teaching areas would have been attempting a task of far greater difficulty and complexity than those children being taught in smaller rectangular box-classrooms. In the second place, a plan must above all give an accurate representation of the area it depicts; and, particularly in classrooms where the furniture is moved around fairly freely, it would have been impossible to know what the classroom had looked like at the time when individual children had drawn their plans.

It was therefore decided that the children should be asked to make a plan from an architect's simple drawing of a small classroom, and that as a model they should be given a plan based on another drawing by the same architect.

The factor analysis yielded four factors only. Three of these related not to separate aspects of the task, but rather to specific areas of the room. Each of them had more to do with the accurate positioning of objects than with the conventions of mapping, and they were combined in the scoring system.

The fourth factor was different. The three items which loaded very heavily on it related to the symbols used to represent the door, windows and the pin-boards. A child gained points for these items if he had used in each case a symbol unique to that item, so that the door, windows and pin-boards were not only shown on the plan but were readily distinguishable from each other. This factor was concerned with the conventions of mapping rather than with the accurate positioning of objects.

Whereas the scoring system derived from the block graph could be applied to other block graphs quite different from the one in the exercise, no such general system emerged from the mapping exercise. In the production of a graph a mass of information is sorted and then

Table 6.1 Derivation of scoring systems for study-skill exercises

Task	Block graph	Plan of classroom	Clock-face
Descriptive analysis of all scorable features	Straightforward	Straightforward	Emerged from successive ratings by two scorers
Logical contingency of task and derived scoring criteria apparent	No	Yes	Yes
Selection of final scoring criteria	Made from teachers' questionnaire ratings of importance of features revealed by descriptive analysis	Straightforward	Straightforward
Scoring criteria and maximum possible scores	Grasp of concept 4 Layout 4 Accuracy 5 Presentation 6	Positioning of objects 13 Appropriate use of mapping conventions 3	General impression 3 Hands of different lengths 1 Spacing of numbers 1 Orientation of numbers 1

presented in an organized and systematic way. With mapping, however, although conventions are used and are important, the basic task is not to sort out and deal with the peculiarities of the data, but to make an accurate representation of them. The value and point of the finished map lies less in its similarities to other maps than in its differences from them. The scores obtained by the children on the ORACLE mapping task relate specifically to that exercise; and the scoring system is shown in Table 6.1.

The clock-face

The final choice for the model-making exercise was a clock-face with movable hands, previously used by Gardner (1966) for the measure of neatness, care and skill in work at the junior school level. The special materials needed consisted only of a brass fastener and a piece of printed stiff paper for each child, since scissors were readily available in all classrooms; and the finished pieces of work were easy to collect, transport and handle. It was emphasized to teachers that the instructions, which were given on a printed sheet to the children, represented merely one way in which the task could be attempted; and that children should be free to set about it in other ways if they chose to do so.

Although the scoring criteria were very similar to those used by Gardner, the allocation of points was somewhat different. For wholly practical considerations the ORACLE clock-face task had been slightly simplified so that no pasting was involved; in Gardner's scale, 2 points were given or included for pasting and cutting. Elsewhere in her scale other items which seemed disparate to the ORACLE scorers were scored together, as for example where three points were given or withheld for clarity of figures and their spacing. During their discussions of criteria the ORACLE scorers found it much easier to agree about individual models if such elements as these were scored separately. The scoring system eventually devised by two scorers is included in Table 6.1. In view of the small number of items involved, no separate factor analysis of this task was conducted.

As can be seen from Table 6.2, there was a tendency for children who scored high on general impression also to score for clock hands of different lengths. The other items did not correlate at all highly with these first two items, nor with each other, so that they could conceivably be construed as indicative of separate independent skills concerned with spacing and orientation respectively. However, since they accounted for only one point each, they were not represented as separate study skills in the analyses which follow later in the chapter: performance in the clock-face exercise is presented as a single skill.

Table 6.2 Correlation between items on the clock-face task

	Total impression	Length of hands	Spacing	Orientation
Total impression	1.00	0.39	0.02	0.05
Length of hands		1.00	−0.10	−0.07
Spacing			1.00	0.10
Orientation				1.00

Scoring the structured activities

The scoring systems for each of the three structured exercises used during the first year of the study were devised in more conventional ways than the procedures used for the specially devised study-skill exercises. Teachers discussed a series of aims, and in so doing were able to arrive at sets of criteria which could be described in terms of the presence or absence of certain kinds of pupil behaviour. The next task was for the teachers to devise exercises which reflected aspects of these behaviours, and which could be used as evidence that the criteria had been satisfactorily achieved. Finally, through discussion among themselves, the teachers determined the relative weighting to be given to each of the criteria in the scoring system.

The method is almost the reverse of that used for the graph, map-making and clock-face exercises, where the task was predetermined and the criteria allowed to emerge from a descriptive analysis of the pupils' responses. In the structured exercises, criteria were first established and only then were tasks devised which reflected those aspects of pupil behaviour deemed appropriate to the particular aspects of each study skill.

Listening with concentration and understanding

The structured activities consisted of three tasks. The teachers who devised these exercises were concerned that children with conventional learning difficulties should not be disadvantaged, so that tasks were constructed which reduced the need to read and write to a minimum. Use was therefore made of picture cartoons, taped sounds and taped instructions. The only written response required was the child's own name on one of the tasks.

The first task involved the identification of five musical instruments, recorded on a sound tape singly and in various combinations. Each instrument was identified at the beginning of the tape, and the children made their responses by marking the appropriate instruments which were pictorially represented on the answer sheet. The focus of this task was the child's ability to listen and recall content.

In the second task, a story was told on tape entirely in sound effects. It dealt with a sequence of events from the time a man was woken by his alarm clock to the time he arrived at work. There were three sections with intervals between them. At the end of each of the first two sections, the children chose one picture from each of three pairs which represented the events they had heard, placing their choices in the correct sequence. In the third section four pictures were chosen from six, and again the children recorded their choices in a similar manner. The focus of this task was the child's ability to listen and recall the sequence of events accurately. In the third task the children were required to follow a series of instructions from a pre-recorded tape. Each child was asked to write his first name inside a circle, triangle or square on a printed sheet, then to draw another shape in which he wrote his surname. The choice of shape depended on the initial letters of the child's first name and surname. The focus of this task was the child's ability to follow instructions of the type commonly given in some classrooms when pupils are told to write their names on the top of the page, draw margins of correct width and so on.

All these tasks could be scored either right or wrong. The factor analysis suggested that the first and third of the tasks were tapping a single study skill, even though they were originally designed to assess different aspects of listening with concentration and understanding. The common element was the children's ability to follow a set of pre-recorded instructions. The detailed scoring system is included in Table 6.3.

Aspects of inventiveness and creativity

The structured activity for this area was a simple picture-completion exercise. This technique has been widely used for the assessment of creativity (Foster, 1971). In this task each child was asked to draw a picture incorporating a circle and a V-shape which had been printed thus on the sheets of A5 paper which were given out to them:

Table 6.3 Derivation of scoring systems for structured exercises

	Listening with concentration and understanding	Aspects of inventiveness and creativity	Acquiring information other than by reading
Scoring system	Each task scored according to correctness of each response	Originality scored according to proportion of pupils with drawing of similar content	Comprehension exercises scored according to number of correct responses
		Appropriateness scored by independent ratings of judges	Formulating questions scored according to (i) number of questions (ii) number of themes dealt with (iii) number of 'open' questions
Maximum score possible	Following instructions 13 Sequencing 10	Originality 4 Appropriateness 3	Comprehension 12 Formulating questions no limit

O   <

The scoring system was based on two criteria identified by the teachers for this area: originality and appropriateness. The drawings were sorted so that those with similar contents were grouped together. Marks on originality were given on a four-point scale, ranging from one point for the most common response (a person, with the circle as the head and the V-shape as the legs) to four points for any picture in which the content was unique. The marking scheme for appropriateness was devised by the teachers' group through discussion of examples. A picture was judged appropriate if the child had made full use of the two printed shapes, incorporating them into a single picture. The teachers independently marked fifty examples on a nought-to-three scale. A check on inter-judge reliability yielded a Pearson r value of 0.77.

The factor analysis yielded one factor for this activity, with the originality and appropriateness items negatively correlated. This was to be expected, since the more appropriate a response, the more likely it was to be made by a large number of children and hence the less likely it was to be original. Conversely, the less common a response, the more likely it was to be inappropriate. Only in exceptional cases did a child make a response which was both original (that is, rare or unique), and appropriate, and which thus fell into the category of 'creative' as conceptualized by the teachers' group. In view of the negative correlation, scores for appropriateness and originality are presented separately in Table 6.3.

Acquiring information other than by reading

Two tasks were devised. Again the teachers' group was concerned not to penalize children with reading or writing difficulties. The instructions were therefore read by the teacher, and if a child was unable to write his response then the teacher was requested to write it down for him.

In the first task the children heard a story, and were also given a picture which illustrated it. They were then presented with a series of questions, some of which related to information appearing in the story but not in the picture, and others to information contained in the picture but not in the story. The task was intended to focus on the child's ability to acquire information from different sources. Marks were given for each correct response.

For the second task, the children were asked to write down the five questions they would most like to ask if they could meet the person in the story, but they were also encouraged to add further questions if they could think of any. The questions were scored using three criteria: first, the total number of questions; second, the range of questions, that is, whether they all dealt with one similar theme or covered a variety of topics; and third, the number of 'open' questions asked. As conceptualized by the teachers, open questions were those framed in such a way as to elicit an explanation or information rather than a one-word response such as yes or no.

Two factors emerged. The first concerned the child's ability to acquire information from the story and picture. The listening and looking component of this exercise might have been expected to load on separate factors if they represented two independent study skills, but this was not so. The other factor represented the extent to which the children were able to formulate questions. It did not differentiate between the three criteria incorporated in the marking procedure devised by the teachers. A summary of the scoring system is included in Table 6.3.

Relationship between study skills and age

Since older children enjoy more success than younger children with independent study, it is reasonable to suppose that the skills involved develop during the childhood years, although of course they do not necessarily develop evenly. At any particular age a given skill may not yet have begun to develop, or it may be static because it has reached a developmental plateau, or its development may be complete. A full investigation of the growth of study skills would require the completion of the same series of exercises by children across a far wider range of ages than was sampled in the present study.

However, it was hypothesized that within the narrow age range studied here there would be statistically significant relationships between age and the scores on the study skills derived from the foregoing factor analyses.

The mean scores of the children in the nine-plus, ten-plus and eleven-plus age groups were therefore computed separately, and are presented as percentages in Table 6.4. For the first twelve study skills the values given represent in each case a percentage of the maximum possible score for that exercise. For the final skill, formulating questions,

Table 6.4 Mean study-skill scores at different ages (expressed as percentages of maximum possible scores)†

Task	Skill	Nine plus (N = 218)	Ten plus (N = 116)	Eleven plus (N = 133)	Over-all variance	Nine plus/ ten plus difference	Ten plus/ eleven plus difference
Block graph	Concept	86	90	87			
	Layout	88	82	96	**	*	**
	Accuracy	63	74	73	**	**	**
	Presentation	33	45	53	**	**	**
Map	Positioning	52	61	65	**	**	
	Conventions	46	56	64	**	**	
Clock-face	General	44	41	47			
Sound story	Sequencing	61	70	71	**	**	
Instructions	Following instructions	81	82	81			
Picture completion	Originality	57	63	58			
	Appropriateness	54	57	58			
Picture story	Comprehension	73	75	70			
Questions	Formulating questions	22	24	28	**		**

* significant at the 5 per cent level

** significant at or beyond the 1 per cent level

† for questions, where there was no fixed maximum, scores are expressed as percentages of the highest score achieved by one child.

where the task was open-ended so that there was no maximum possible score, the values given represent percentages of the largest number of questions formulated by a single child.

Analysis of the scores shown in Table 6.4 revealed significant variations in scores at the different age levels in seven of the thirteen skills. It may be supposed that where there was no significant variation between ages, the skill in question had reached a developmental plateau; or, in the case of block-graph concept, where the scores were uniformly very high, that in so far as it was tapped by the exercise, the skill was fully developed in most children before the age of nine plus.

Where a significant variation was found, separate analyses were carried out to determine where the variation lay (and levels of significance are indicated by asterisks in the last two columns of Table 6.4).

In block-graph presentation there was a continuing development over the entire age range; in block-graph accuracy, both mapping skills and sound-story sequencing, a development between nine plus and ten plus followed by a developmental plateau; and in the formulation of questions, a plateau between nine plus and ten plus followed by a period of development.

Block-graph layout was the one skill where there was a small but statistically significant drop in mean score, followed by a significant increase (and a significant over-all increase from nine plus to eleven plus). Here the scores were all very high, and in many children of all ages the skill was fully developed. The drop between nine plus and ten plus cannot be explained in terms of chance fluctuation; nor, clearly, in terms of skill development. It may be that preoccupation with the developing skills of accuracy and presentation between nine plus and ten plus diverted the children's attention away from the layout of the block graph during that period; however, it would require a longitudinal study to test this hypothesis.

Inter-correlations between study skills

As indicated at the beginning of the chapter, study skills are conceptualized here as directly related to the tasks students perform, rather than simply as separate manifestations of some kind of underlying general ability. It was envisaged that an individual child might demonstrate some of the skills outlined above to a high degree whilst lacking others, and that consequently the skills would not necessarily correlate highly with each other.

119

The inter-correlations between the scores of the ORACLE sample on the various study skills are shown in Figure 6.3.

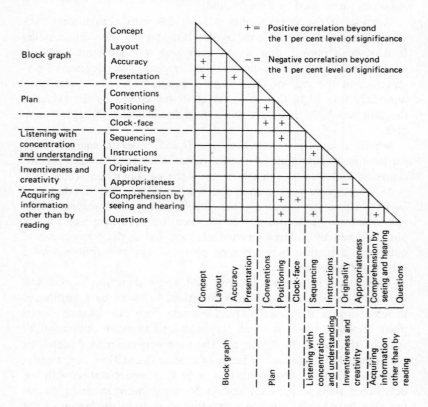

Figure 6.3 Inter-correlations between study-skill components

It will be seen that half of the significant inter-correlations were between pairs of skills derived from single tasks. However, not all the skills within each task correlated highly with each other: for example, accuracy on the block graph was related to an understanding of graphing concepts and to presentation, but not to the use of a conventional layout; indeed layout was not related to any of the other three graphing skills.

The skill which correlated highly with the most skills from other tasks was the one which involved the correct positioning of items on the mapping task. In general the children who demonstrated this skill also did well at model making, sequencing, comprehension through seeing and hearing, and asking relevant questions. Apart from these skills, however, there was no general tendency for children to be successful or unsuccessful 'across the board'. These results, together with those of the factor analysis, suggest that the scoring systems devised do reflect real component skills, associated with everyday study tasks, which although complementary do not overlap to any considerable extent.

Relationship between study skills and scores on traditional achievement tests

The correlations between scores on the thirteen study skills and the traditional achievement tests are shown in Table 6.5.

Table 6.5 Correlations between study skills and scores on standardized achievement tests

Study skills		Maths	Language	Reading
Block graph	Concept	.15	.16	.13
	Layout	.07	.08	.09
	Accuracy	.32**	.31**	.30**
	Presentation	.32**	.29**	.26**
Plan	Conventions	.28**	.27**	.30**
	Positioning	.35**	.38**	.40**
	Clock-face	.24**	.17	.23**
Listening with concentration and understanding	Sequencing	.32**	.27**	.27**
	Instructions	.13	.15	.17
Inventiveness and Creativity	Originality	−.04	−.11	−.09
	Appropriateness	.09	.06	.09
Acquiring information other than by reading	Comprehension	.21*	.19	.23**
	Questions	.30**	.25**	.26**

Achievement-test scores heads the Maths, Language, Reading columns.

* significant at the 5 per cent level
** significant at or beyond the 1 per cent level

The preponderance of small and moderate correlations lends support to the view that the overlap between the two kinds of measure is not large, and that the inclusion of study-skill exercises alongside more traditional tests is justified in a process-product study of this kind.

The smallest degree of overlap was found in the originality and appropriateness aspects of the inventiveness and creativity task, and in the three skills where most children of all three age groups achieved very high scores. It is by now well established that measures of creativity, which are in general open-ended, tend to correlate poorly with tests which seek correct answers, such as traditional attainments and intelligence tests (Cropley and Maslany, 1969; Kogan, 1971). The relevance of inventiveness and creativity to the carrying out of independent study is much more apparent than is their value in giving the correct answer to a closed question on a test of maths, language or reading. With regard to the three tasks where the skills in question tend to develop at an earlier age than was here investigated, a detailed study of their relationship with achievement-test scores would more appropriately be conducted with a younger age group than any in the ORACLE sample.

It should perhaps be emphasized that the presence of statistically significant positive correlations of the magnitude found here does not in any sense imply that the two measures used are very similar, or that they are measuring the same thing, but merely denotes a tendency for children who do well on one measure to do well on the other, and reflects the fact that for many children success, or lack of it, is something which is experienced across the full range of classroom activities.

Relationship between study skills and progress in basic subjects during the year

A further analysis was conducted, to investigate the relationship between the study skills and improvement in performance on the standardized achievement tests during the year. In view of the pitfalls of a simple statistical comparison of raw scores 'before' and 'after', the measure of progress used was the residual-change score, that is to say, the extent to which each child's actual score at the end of the year exceeded or fell short of what would be predicted on the basis of his score at the beginning of the year. (A fuller description of this procedure is given in Chapter 4, p. 58.)

In no case did the correlation coefficient between study skills and test gains reach statistical significance.

Thus, although in the long term there was a tendency for children who scored high on study skills to do better on traditional measures of achievement (to be 'good students' across the board), nevertheless over a short period of time the study skills outlined above were sufficiently specific to the types of task investigated not to relate closely to increased scores on tests of a very different nature. In so far as the tasks investigated were characteristic of some of the activities of children engaged in independent study, the scores obtained from them provide a source of information about the skills involved in such study to complement the data derived from traditional achievement tests.

Chapter 7

Teaching styles and study skills

As explained in the previous chapter, the various study-skill exercises were given on only one occasion, so that it is possible to describe only the pupils' performance at the time when the exercises were administered. It is not possible to talk of *progress* in study skills, as was the case when dealing with the results of the Richmond Tests. The present results must be interpreted more cautiously than those obtained for reading, mathematics and language skills, since here there is no way of estimating the extent to which the pupils' initial achievement on entering the class may have influenced their performance under the teaching style to which they were subjected there.

Two further problems complicate the analysis. It was shown in the previous chapter that for some of the study skills there appeared to be a 'plateau affect', so that the greatest increase in scores occurred over a limited part of the age-range of the ORACLE sample. In Chapter 6 of *Inside the Primary Classroom*, certain teaching styles were also found to vary with pupil age. The *individual monitors*, for example, tended to work in the schools which had the oldest children in the sample. The effect of these differences in age on both teaching and study-skill achievement must therefore be allowed for when examining the variation of pupil performance across styles of teaching.

The main reason for developing 'study-skill' exercises was to tap those qualities which enable pupils to work independently of the teacher on such activities as topic and project work. However, the fact that the study-skill scores correlated moderately but significantly with scores on the Richmond Tests of Basic Skills suggests that some pupils may do well on study skills simply because they are successful students, rather than because of the influence of a particular teaching style. It is therefore important in the analysis to allow for the effects of proficiency in the basic skills (Richmond Test scores) upon study-skill scores.

Using the technique of analysis of covariance, which was explained in Chapter 4, it is possible to control for the effect on study-skill scores of the relative success of each pupil on the Richmond Tests. For this purpose a total score from the pre-test administration of the Richmond Test was obtained by adding together each individual pupil's score on the tests of mathematics, language skills and reading. By determining the regression line between this total pre-test score and the scores on the various study skills it is possible to allow for the effects of successful performance in basic skills by adjusting the study-skill scores. In effect, the pre-test score on the basic skills is used to predict the study-skill score which may be attributed to 'all round success'. The difference which remains between the observed and predicted scores can then be attributed to the different teaching that pupils experience in the classroom. Similarly pupil age may be correlated against each study-skill score and the latter adjusted to allow for any age effects.

Calculating the adjusted means

In the analysis of covariance procedure described in Chapter 4, residual-change scores were used. These showed the difference between a pupil's observed post-test score and the score predicted by the regression line, which was derived from the pupil's performance on the pre-test. The idea of a change score of any kind, however, is inappropriate when considering the pupils' scores on the study-skill exercises, since these were given on only one occasion. Here it is more straightforward to talk about the adjusted mean study-skill scores of groups of pupils taught by each teaching style. These adjusted means are obtained directly from the residual change scores of the individual pupils.

The calculation and interpretation of these adjusted means can best be explained by referring back to Figure 4.1 and the accompanying discussion (p. 58). In the present context, each pupil's pre-test score is the sum of his scores on each of the three tests of basic skills, while the post-test score is the score obtained on a particular study skill. M_1 is the average total score for all the pupils on the pre-test, while M_2 is the study-skill mean. The regression line will always pass through the point where these two means intersect. It is for this reason that the sum of the positive residual-change scores in Chapter 4 was balanced by the sum of the negative ones. All comparisons between groups of pupils, for example, those taught by a particular style, are relative to these two sample means.

In the present case, the difference y − z obtained for pupil A in Figure 4.1 represents the extent to which this particular pupil has performed better on the study skill than would have been predicted from the result of his combined pre-test score on the basic skills. To obtain the adjusted mean, the average of all these pupil differences for a particular teaching style is added to the over-all post-test mean M_2, taking account of the sign of these differences. Thus a group of pupils who, on average, perform less well on a particular study skill than would have been predicted from the results of the pre-tests of basic skills will have an adjusted mean which is less than the post-test mean for the over-all sample.

Since all means are adjusted in relation to the point on the regression line where the pre-test and post-test means intersect, the adjusted study-skill means for the six teaching styles in the following tables are calculated on the basis that they all have the same pre-test mean on the Richmond Tests.

Analysis of covariance makes use of statistics to do what random assignment does in an experiment, namely to obtain groups of pupils who receive different styles of teaching but who are matched initially on certain variables. The adjusted post-test means can be used to estimate the extent to which one style is more successful than another in developing the study skills, irrespective of the groups' Richmond pre-test scores. In a similar manner, when age is used as a covariate, the adjusted means are used to compare groups of pupils as if the mean age of pupils taught by each style was in fact the same. Seen in this light, covariance analysis is a useful statistical technique for controlling those factors which are usually kept constant in experimental research, but are unlikely to be so in naturalistic studies such as ORACLE.

Pupil performance on study skills

For each study-skill area three sets of means are given for the six teaching styles. In each case, the first row gives the raw-score means with no adjustment for the effect of either age or Richmond pre-test scores. The second row gives the adjusted means when the effect of the pre-test is taken into account while the third and final row controls for both age and pre-test. It is this final row which is used to examine the over-all difference between teaching styles through a comparison of the highest and lowest adjusted mean scores. Each study-skill area will be considered in turn, but detailed discussion will be confined to the dimensions on which significant differences were established.

Pupil performance on the block-graph exercise

The block graph yielded scores on four dimensions: grasp of concept, layout, accuracy and presentation. The method of scoring these dimensions was set out in the previous chapter. Table 7.1 gives the mean scores for groups of pupils taught by each teaching style. In each class, the means were obtained from the scores of the eight target pupils on whom observation data were also obtained. They therefore can be directly compared with the scores relating to progress in the basic skills which were discussed in Chapter 4. On only two of the dimensions, layout and presentation, did differences in the adjusted means of pupils taught by the different styles remain significant after both pre-test and age were introduced as controlling variables. In both cases the *individual monitors* and the *habitual changers* were the two teaching styles who had the highest adjusted means (row 3). On the accuracy dimension there were significant differences due to style when raw-score means were examined (row 1); however, when the effects of both pre-test and age were taken into account the differences between the adjusted means were no longer significant.

For each dimension, the effect of age and pre-test can be seen by comparing the raw-score mean and the adjusted means for each of the teaching styles. In the case of the *individual monitors* and the concept dimension in Table 7.1 the raw-score mean was 3.62. When the scores were adjusted to allow for the effects of the pre-test this value was reduced to 3.52. When age was introduced as an additional controlling variable the adjusted means score moved back slightly to 3.54. Repeating this inspection for the other columns in the table shows that for most of the teaching styles the largest adjustment in the means occurred when the pre-test was introduced as the controlling variable. Table 7.1 also indicates significance levels for the effect of age, the Richmond pre-test scores and teaching style respectively. It can be seen that for all dimensions the Richmond scores account for a significant proportion of the variation in study-skill scores.

Table 7.1 Relationship between teaching style and mean scores on block graph

Study-skill dimension	Controlling variable	Teaching style						Significance level		
		Individual monitors	Class enquirers	Group instructors	Infrequent changers	Rotating changers	Habitual changers	Age	Pre-test	Style
Concept	1 None	3.62	3.46	3.50	3.52	3.64	3.44			
	2 Pre-test	3.52	3.51	3.59	3.53	3.69	3.42		**	
	3 Pre-test and age	3.54	3.44	3.52	3.50	3.64	3.48		**	
Layout	1 None	3.83	3.49	3.05	3.67	3.27	3.75			**
	2 Pre-test	3.79	3.51	3.09	3.68	3.29	3.75		**	**
	3 Pre-test and age	3.86	3.50	3.07	3.67	3.26	3.76			**
Accuracy	1 None	3.67	3.41	2.88	3.52	3.61	3.48			**
	2 Pre-test	3.34	3.56	3.18	3.56	3.76	3.42		**	
	3 Pre-test and age	3.39	3.54	3.08	3.53	3.71	3.52		**	
Presentation	1 None	3.17	2.35	2.14	1.93	2.13	2.73			**
	2 Pre-test	2.95	2.45	2.34	1.96	2.22	2.69		**	**
	3 Pre-test and age	2.78	2.52	2.44	2.00	2.24	2.81	**	**	**
	N =	94	62	50	40	64	93			

** significant at or beyond the 1 per cent level

Pupil performance on mapping skills

For this exercise pupils obtained two scores, one for the correct use of conventions and another for accurate positioning of objects on the map. Once again, under each teaching style means are given for each of the two dimensions of the study skill. These are presented in Table 7.2. The data in the table show that on both the dimensions there were significant differences due to style. Again, as with the block-graph exercise, the Richmond pre-test scores also accounted for a significant part of the variation in the study-skill scores. The analysis of covariance (Appendix C, Table C.4) revealed that the variation in study-skill scores due to age was not significant. Examination of the adjusted means in row 3 of the table shows that while for conventions the *habitual changers* were again the most successful style, for positioning it was the *infrequent changers* who had the highest adjusted mean.

Pupil performance on the clock-face exercise

The results for the clock-face are given in Table 7.3. Only a total score was given for this exercise. None of the differences between styles in either the raw-score or the adjusted means reached statistical significance. The analysis of covariance tables in Appendix C (Table C.4) indicated that the Richmond pre-test accounted for most of the variation in the scores on this particular study skill. Since the scoring of the clock-face exercise strongly reflected the accuracy with which pupils marked out and constructed the model, this result is not surprising. Success on the Richmond Tests also calls for a degree of accuracy, particularly in working towards recognition of the correct answer to mathematical problems and numerical computations. This result therefore confirms the evidence presented in the previous chapter where scores on the clock-face were shown to be positively correlated with pupils' scores on the mathematics test.

Pupil performance in listening

Two scores were given on this exercise, one for recalling and following a set of instructions and the other for placing the events of a sound story in the correct sequence. The data are presented in Table 7.4. To master each of these tasks pupils needed to concentrate carefully in order to

129

Table 7.2 Relationship between teaching style and mean scores on mapping task

Study-skill dimension	Controlling variable	Teaching style						Significance level		
		Individual monitors	Class enquirers	Group instructors	Infrequent changers	Rotating changers	Habitual changers	Age	Pre-test	Style
Conventions	1 None	1.75	1.55	0.95	1.74	1.36	2.05			*
	2 Pre-test	1.58	1.63	1.10	1.76	1.43	2.01		**	**
	3 Pre-test and age	1.58	1.68	1.15	1.93	1.47	1.98		**	**
Positioning	1 None	7.84	7.61	6.68	7.41	6.81	8.43			*
	2 Pre-test	7.11	7.94	7.32	7.50	7.11	8.29		**	
	3 Pre-test and age	6.73	8.30	7.81	8.48	7.29	8.17		**	*
	N =	94	62	50	40	64	93			

* significant at the 5 per cent level
** significant at or beyond the 1 per cent level

Table 7.3 Relationship between teaching style and mean scores on clock-face exercise

Study-skill dimension	Controlling variable	Teaching style					Significance level		
		Individual monitors	Class enquirers	Group instructors	Infrequent changers	Rotating changers	Habitual changers	Age	Pre-test	Style
Clock-face	1 None	2.81	2.78	2.77	2.33	2.56	2.60			
	2 Pre-test	2.67	2.85	2.89	2.34	2.61	2.58			
	3 Pre-test and age	2.60	2.99	2.99	2.56	2.67	2.54	**	**	
	N =	94	62	50	40	64	93			

** significant at or beyond the 1 per cent level

recall the events described in the sound tape. Since the power of concentration is a prerequisite of all successful study, it is not surprising that a significant part of the variation in the two sets of listening scores was accounted for by the pupils' Richmond scores. There were no significant teaching-style differences in following a set of instructions. For sequencing, the major influence was again the pupils' Richmond scores. Differences in the raw-score means (row 1) between the teaching styles were significant at the 5 per cent level, and when allowance was made for both the pre-test scores and for age, the effect due to teaching style remained. *Group instructors* and *class enquirers* had the highest adjusted mean score and *rotating changers* the lowest.

Pupil performance in acquiring information

This exercise required pupils to acquire information by means other than reading. Marks were given for two tasks. The first was a comprehension exercise in which pupils had to find the answers to questions by listening to a story and studying a picture; in the second they were asked to write down suitable questions which would allow them to extract even further information from the story and picture. The data are presented in Table 7.5. In both cases the scores of pupils on the Richmond pre-tests accounted for a significant proportion of the variation in the study-skill scores. Differences between the style means were not significant for the comprehension exercise, but were significant for the task in which pupils were required to pose suitable questions. Examining the raw score means (row 1), it can be seen that the *group instructors* had only the fourth highest average score. After making allowance for the differences in the Richmond scores, however, the value rose to 5.13, and there was a further increase to 5.52 when age was also taken into account. This made them second only to the *class enquirers*, the most successful style.

Pupil performance in originality and appropriateness

The final series of study-skill scores concerns two aspects of creativity; originality and appropriateness. Pupils were scored both for the uniqueness of their response on a picture-completion exercise and for its appropriateness. The mean scores for these two dimensions are listed in Table 7.6. For neither of these exercises were the differences in the

Table 7.4 Relationship between teaching style and mean scores on listening exercises

Study-skill dimension	Controlling variable		Teaching style						Significance level		
			Individual monitors	Class enquirers	Group instructors	Infrequent changers	Rotating changers	Habitual changers	Age	Pre-test	Style
Instructions	1	None	10.41	10.84	10.91	10.85	9.69	10.75			
	2	Pre-test	10.25	10.98	11.17	10.89	9.81	10.70		**	
	3	Pre-test and age	10.25	11.06	11.17	11.12	9.83	10.74		**	
Sequencing	1	None	6.90	6.88	7.04	6.30	5.66	6.83			*
	2	Pre-test	6.54	7.07	7.44	6.36	5.85	6.74		**	*
	3	Pre-test and age	6.53	7.25	7.31	6.41	5.77	6.77		**	*
		N =	94	62	50	40	64	93			

* significant at the 5 per cent level
** significant at or beyond the 1 per cent level

Table 7.5 Relationship between teaching style and mean scores on acquiring information exercises

Study-skill dimension	Controlling variable	Teaching style						Significance level		
		Individual monitors	Class enquirers	Group instructors	Infrequent changers	Rotating changers	Habitual changers	Age	Pre-test	Style
Comprehension	1 None	8.40	8.81	8.80	8.09	8.73	9.07			
	2 Pre-test	8.01	8.98	9.14	8.13	8.88	9.00		**	
	3 Pre-test and age	8.10	9.35	9.19	8.91	8.90	9.30	**		**
Questions	1 None	5.01	5.57	4.70	3.61	4.27	5.20			**
	2 Pre-test	4.54	5.78	5.13	3.66	4.47	5.10		**	**
	3 Pre-test and age	4.26	6.25	5.52	4.06	4.73	5.31	**	**	**
	N =	94	62	50	40	64	93			

** significant at or beyond the 1 per cent level

average raw scores between the teaching styles found to be significant. For appropriateness, neither the Richmond pre-test scores nor age accounted for a significant proportion of the variation in study-skill scores. For originality, when the means were adjusted to take account of the equalities in both pre-test and age, there were significant differences between styles.

The result is interesting because of its relationship to the findings of Haddon and Lytton (1968). These researchers gave various creativity tests in which pupils were required to think of unusual uses for common objects, as well as a picture-completion exercise similar to that used in this study. Classes were identified as either traditional or progressive, largely in terms of the use made of class teaching and individualized instruction. The progressive classes, where there was less class teaching, were found to do better on the creativity tests. Barker Lunn (1970) also used some of the same tests, and found that the pupils of her Type 1 teachers, who were less traditional than her Type 2, also performed significantly better. The ORACLE result is therefore in keeping with the trend of previous research. The *individual monitors*, as their name implies, engaged in the highest levels of individualized instruction. There appears, therefore, to be something about the use of an individualized approach to learning which helps performance on such exercises. Neither Haddon and Lytton nor Barker Lunn observed any of their teachers in the classroom. Until now the assumption has been that teachers using an individualized approach are more successful in fostering skills of originality because they encourage pupils to discover things for themselves. The observational data from the ORACLE research, however, show that teachers favouring an individualized approach are far less likely to indulge in activities designed to develop enquiry skills among their pupils. Indeed, the classes of the *individual monitors* were mainly characterized by silent monitoring of task work. Nor in such classes did the pupils engage in high levels of work interaction among themselves.

It may be that it is the relative isolation of the *individual monitors'* pupils, rather than certain kinds of teacher-pupil interactions, which made them successful on this kind of creative task. The *individual monitors* required their pupils to spend more time working on their own and gave less oral feedback, of either a positive or a negative kind. In such classes there were no pressures on the pupils to conform to the teacher's expectation of how work should be presented. There was, and this is borne out by the observers' accounts, less tendency for pupils to copy from one another. The usual practice was to take work to the

Table 7.6 Relationship between teaching style and mean scores on creativity exercise

Study-skill dimension	Controlling variable	Teaching style						Significance level		
		Individual monitors	Class enquirers	Group instructors	Infrequent changers	Rotating changers	Habitual changers	Age	Pre-test	Style
Originality	1 None	1.92	1.77	2.13	1.59	1.71	1.69		*	
	2 Pre-test	1.92	1.56	1.65	1.41	1.57	1.57			
	3 Pre-test and age	1.95	1.61	1.55	1.37	1.50	1.50		**	
Appropriateness	1 None	1.71	1.73	1.63	1.86	1.55	1.69			*
	2 Pre-test	1.69	1.74	1.65	1.88	1.56	1.69			
	3 Pre-test and age	1.64	1.73	1.72	2.00	1.62	1.58			
	N =	90	57	41	39	61	89			

* significant at the 5 per cent level
** significant at or beyond the 1 per cent level

teacher for marking as soon as it was completed. In contrast, the *class enquirers* made very clear to the pupils what was expected of them. Pupils therefore tended to check with one another before putting up their hands to attract the teacher's attention so that she could come and mark the work.

In the picture-completion exercise there were no predetermined expectations on the part of the teacher. Children were simply told to complete the picture and, as is usual with such exercises, given no instruction to make their picture as different as possible from those of other children. Pupils taught by the *class enquirers* would probably have been more likely to check with each other before finishing their pictures, whereas children taught by the *individual monitors* would have tended to carry out the task on their own.

A summary of study-skill performance

The previous discussion has been concerned with over-all differences between the teaching styles. The test of significance was used only to compare the styles giving the highest and lowest adjusted means; there is no indication that these differences also hold in respect of the remaining four teaching styles. To obtain further information on this point, it is necessary to examine in turn the differences in means between the most successful group of teachers and each of the remaining styles. A summary of these significant differences is presented in Table 7.7. As with Table 4.4 (p. 70), in any column the teaching styles are listed in rank order, the highest adjusted mean being listed first. Study-skill dimensions without over-all significant differences are omitted.

The similar table of differences for the Richmond Tests was dominated by the *class enquirers* and the *infrequent changers*, whose pupils made the greatest progress (Table 4.4, p. 70). However, these teaching styles do not enjoy a monopoly of success here. The one case where the *class enquirers* emerged as the most successful teachers was in their pupils' ability to pose suitable questions. This result seems very appropriate, given the fact that, as shown in *Inside the Primary Classroom*, these teachers engaged their pupils in the greatest level of 'higher-order interactions', involving open and closed questions and statements of ideas. Their pupils were relatively unsuccessful at block-graph layout, mapping conventions and at making original drawings. *Infrequent changers,* whose pupils also made considerable progress in the basic skills, were the most successful style in terms of their children's ability

Table 7.7 Summary of results for teaching style and achievement in study skills

Study-skill exercise	Most successful style	Not significantly different from most successful style	Significantly different at or beyond 5 per cent from most successful style	Significantly different at or beyond 1 per cent from most successful style
Block-graph layout	Individual monitors	Habitual changers Infrequent changers		Class enquirers Rotating changers Group instructors
Block-graph presentation	Habitual changers	Individual monitors Class enquirers	Group instructors	Rotating changers Infrequent changers
Mapping conventions	Habitual changers	Infrequent changers	Class enquirers	Individual monitors Rotating changers Group instructors
Mapping positioning	Infrequent changers	Class enquirers Habitual changers	Group instructors Rotating changers	Individual monitors
Sequencing	Group instructors	Class enquirers Habitual changers	Individual monitors Infrequent changers	Rotating changers
Questioning	Class enquirers	Group instructors		Habitual changers Rotating changers Individual monitors Infrequent changers
Originality	Individual monitors			Class enquirers Group instructors Rotating changers Habitual changers Infrequent changers

to position objects in the mapping exercise. However, their pupils were among the least successful on block-graph presentation, sequencing the sound story, posing suitable questions and originality.

An interesting feature is that the *habitual changers*, whose pupils performed relatively unsuccessfully on the Richmond Tests, emerged as the most successful style for study skills. Only on posing suitable questions and on originality did their pupils perform significantly less well than the best style. In contrast, the pupils of the *rotating changers*, who were also unsuccessful on the Richmond Tests, did no better on the study-skill exercises. These pupils performed relatively poorly on all the study skills. Given that the analysis of the pupil observation data, presented in *Inside the Primary Classroom*, showed that this particular style had a number of unsatisfactory features, such as relatively high amounts of time wasting and distraction, these results suggest that there is little in this particular teaching approach to commend it.

An interesting feature of the *habitual changers* was that on most of the categories of the observation schedule they were found to have some of the lowest levels of teacher-pupil interaction. The main exception to this was the small-talk category. They also devoted less time to basic skills than any of the other teaching styles (Chapter 5, p. 85), preferring to spend their time on topic work and on activities which make use of the kinds of skills assessed in these exercises.

The use of a relatively large proportion of small talk is an interesting finding. It was shown in *Inside the Primary Classroom* that the *habitual changers* were very quick to respond to the first sign of disruption by changing their classroom organization. They would revert to class teaching if the noise became too great when pupils were working in topic groups. The use of small talk can be indicative of a relaxed, friendly atmosphere, and the observers' reports reflected this. Such an atmosphere is of help when pupils are involved in independent study, since it enables the teacher to encourage persistence without seeming to nag.

Further discussion of the *habitual changers* will be found in the concluding chapter, when successful and unsuccessful teachers within each style are compared. Before that, however, it is necessary to consider the part played by the pupils' behaviour and their personal characteristics in determining the relative effectiveness of each style. Details will be given of the levels of both motivation and anxiety among the pupils involved in the ORACLE study. When considered alongside the observation data derived from the Pupil Record this will present a much fuller picture of classroom life, permitting a more complete evaluation of each teaching style in the penultimate chapter.

Part IV

Pupil behaviour and progress

Chapter 8

Personality and classroom behaviour

Among the process variables so far considered, the major emphasis has been upon the activities and the observable behaviour of teachers, and the relationships between these variables and pupil achievement. It is now time to give more direct consideration to the pupils themselves, and to deal with the different ways in which they meet the demands which are placed upon them in the classroom. Differences of behaviour dependent upon the age and sex of the pupils will also be described, and patterns of anxiety and motivation will be examined.

In spite of the inaccessibility of explanatory concepts such as anxiety and motivation to direct observation, there are strong grounds for including them in a study of classroom processes and products if suitable techniques can be found. At a very basic, common-sense level, both qualities seem to be important components of what the child brings with him to his school experience, and they are seen as relevant concepts by teachers, who frequently make use of them in their comments on the children they teach. Both have figured in earlier classroom research (Nisbet and Entwistle, 1969; Trown and Leith, 1975; Bennett, 1976). Bennett found that in analysing changes between pre-test and post-test in a wide range of personality variables, under his three general teaching styles, only motivation and anxiety showed a marked effect, both of them increasing in informal classrooms. Finally, in the context of the over-all ORACLE research programme, both qualities might be expected to have particular influence on the ease with which children face the emotional and intellectual demands of their transfer from primary to secondary school.

The pupil types

A major objective of the research was to identify the relative effectiveness of different teaching styles for different types of pupils, both in general, and across the different subject areas (particularly language and mathematics). As with the teachers, the identification of groups of pupils having different behavioural characteristics was carried out by cluster analysis. The data were provided by the Pupil Record, upon which the observers coded a wide range of information about individual pupils. They noted the pupil's activity, indicating whether he was, for example, working at his task, working on a routine activity such as pencil sharpening or collecting a book from his locker, distracted, disrupting others and so on. They also recorded the size and composition of his work base (for example, two children of the same sex), and indicated whether at the time of the signal he was in his base or out of it, and, if he was out of it, whether he was static or mobile. If the pupil was interacting with other pupils, the observers recorded information about the interaction. They noted who started it, the number and sex of the other pupils involved, and their tasks and work bases. The observers also noted where the teacher was at the time signal; and if she was interacting with the pupil under observation, they recorded information about the setting and content of the interaction, noting whether it involved questions, statements or other forms of communication (showing, marking and so on); and whether it related to tasks, supervision or routine.

The cluster analysis of this mass of data yielded four pupil types which, on the basis of their most characteristic behaviour, were called (i) *attention seekers*, (ii) *intermittent workers*, (iii) *solitary workers* and (iv) *quiet collaborators*. In general, it is the children in the first two groups who have the most intense relationship with the teacher. Those in the first group seem to seek her out, while those in the second group persistently avoid her. The pupils in the third and the fourth group on the other hand seem to fade into the background for much of the time, the main difference between them lying in the extent to which they work on their own or with other pupils.

The attention seekers

The typical *attention seeker* quickly and persistently makes his presence felt in the classroom. Although he is busily occupied on his task or on associated routine activities for two-thirds of the time, he will seek out the teacher far more frequently than will the typical member of any other group. This means that he spends a comparatively large amount of time moving about the classroom or waiting at the teacher's desk. When he has caught her attention, he is more likely to want to talk about his work than to have an idle chat; thus he is not trying to avoid work, but rather to seek constant feedback, whether it be re-assurance, praise or even blame. He will return again and again for each bit to be checked, discussed and re-worked if necessary.

Within this general pupil type there is a smaller sub-group of children whose behaviour in most ways closely resembles that so far described, but who differ from the main group in that they respond to, rather than initiate, the large amount of teacher-pupil interaction in which they are involved. In terms of their conversations with the teacher, they might be more accurately described as attention getters than *attention seekers*. In terms of their more general behaviour, however, it seems valid to retain the label *attention seekers*, since the teacher's opening words are often a response to the kind of overt behaviour which looks remarkably like a bid for the teacher's attention; and the observers' descriptive accounts furnish many examples of this kind of non-verbal attention seeking. A child may ostentatiously do nothing, for example, when he is supposed to be working; or he may cause some disturbance in the classroom, thereby provoking the teacher into asking him to bring out his work so that she can see what he has been doing.

An *attention seeker* of either of the two kinds described is likely to have a much less intense relationship with his fellow pupils than he does with the teacher; he neither pursues them nor avoids them, and his level of interaction with them is average. His type is somewhat under-represented in the classes of *group instructors*, and one can see that his way of dealing with life in the classroom is poorly adapted to the routines of a teacher whose style is to treat small groups of children as a teaching or learning unit. He thrives and is over-represented in the classes of *infrequent changers*, whose way of changing their approach seems to be a response to the perceived needs of the particular children who happen to be in the class, rather than a temperamental need for variety or the mechanical following of a pre-arranged plan. With this kind of teacher, the hard-working *attention seeker* might be expected to experience a particularly tolerant hearing, followed by a change of teaching method designed to bring out the best in the class as a whole. About one-fifth of all the pupils in the study are in the group labelled *attention seekers*.

The intermittent workers

Intermittent workers are more numerous, and account for just over a third of the pupils. Unlike his attention-seeking classmates, the typical *intermittent worker* avoids rather than seeks or provokes the teacher's attention. He characteristically spends most of his time in his work base, and rather more time than other children in watching what the teacher and the other pupils are doing. If the teacher looks in his direction she is likely to see him working; but the moment her back is turned he will probably continue talking with his neighbours. Given the choice he will prefer children of his own sex, from his own work base; and his conversation is more likely to be about the previous evening's television programmes, or some such topic, than about the task in hand. It must not be supposed, however, that he is an unremitting time waster. Although he spends more time talking to other pupils than do children of any other type, he still manages to spend almost two-thirds of the time working on his task or on associated routine activities. His conversations are sporadic and brief; during a creative-writing period, for example, he will generally write two or three words and then chat briefly to a neighbour before writing a bit more. The observers' accounts suggest that he particularly enjoys lessons such as painting, where he can work and talk about other things at the same time. The over-riding impression one gets when observing him is that he lacks application. However, in some cases this masks the fact that the work is not sufficiently demanding to require much effort.

Intermittent workers are over-represented in the classes of *individual monitors* and *rotating changers*, where they account for 48 per cent and 45 per cent of the pupils respectively. Both of these teaching styles involve a kind of fragmentation of the teacher's attention, which provides an ideal setting for an *intermittent worker* to remain unnoticed for comparatively long periods of time. In the classes of *class enquirers*, however, on average only 9 per cent of the pupils are of this type. Here there is a strong tendency for the teacher to remain at the front, or at some other vantage point, and to scan the class for incidents which need her intervention. One might hypothesize that under this kind of surveillance, many pupils who would be *intermittent workers* under a looser supervision become *solitary workers* instead. Certainly with *class enquirers* that third pupil type is massively over-represented.

The solitary workers

About a third of the pupils are *solitary workers*. They are characterized by the infrequency of their interaction with other pupils and the teacher, and by the high proportion of time they spend working. The typical *solitary worker* spends most of his time in his work base, and is busy with his work or with associated routine activities for more than three-quarters of his time (a higher proportion than in any of the other pupil types). He has very little conversation with his fellow pupils, and will sometimes irritably brush aside a classmate who is trying to intrude upon his privacy while he is working. Even with the teacher his interactions are limited. He rarely seeks a conversation with her, and is rarely singled out for her individual attention. Most of his dealings with her are as a member of the whole class, or of the group to which she is talking, and most of his feedback is from simply listening, rather than asking questions. At first glance he may seem an ideal pupil: hard-working, rarely distracted, quiet and unobtrusive; making few demands on the teacher and thereby releasing her to turn her attention to other pupils whose needs in the classroom are more overtly demonstrated. However, he can be construed as ideal only if the teacher's aim is a single-minded emphasis on diligence in the pursuit of the more formal curricular activities. For the many teachers who attach great importance to the fostering of social skills and general oral fluency, the extreme *solitary worker* is a curiously one-sided pupil, purchasing his undoubted success at the expense of a kind of isolation within the group.

Solitary workers seem to thrive best in the classrooms of *class enquirers*, where they make up about two-thirds of the pupils. It is clear that they are temperamentally well suited to that particular teaching style where bouts of class instruction are followed by periods of individual work, with the teacher acting as monitor and general supervisor. They are under-represented in the classes of *habitual* and *rotating changers,* where the constant intrusion of new organizational demands might be expected to inhibit or interrupt private individual study, and where less than a quarter of all pupils are of this particular type.

The quiet collaborators

The fourth pupil type is the smallest in numbers, constituting only one-eighth of the total sample. In many ways the *quiet collaborators* resemble *solitary workers.* Their work output is almost as high, and their verbal contact with the teacher and their fellow pupils almost as low. The teacher spends more of her time with these pupils than with those of the other three types, but this is because most of her contact with them is in a group or a whole-class setting. She tends to tell them things rather than developing ideas or encouraging discussion, and then leaves them to carry out a task together. Once she has gone, however, they show a tendency to revert to the work patterns of *solitary workers*. When they do co-operate it is likely to be at the non-verbal level of sharing apparatus and materials rather than through conversation. They spend more time on routine activities than the other types, and more time waiting for the teacher to return with further instructions. Some of the observers formed a clear impression that for many of these children their pattern of work was something imposed upon them rather than something they would have chosen. They are very rare in the classes of *individual monitors*, accounting for only 2 per cent of the pupils. In the classes of *class enquirers* they are only slightly more common, still representing well under a tenth of all pupils. The style changers have rather more of them, depending largely on the extent to which the changes of style include phases of group instruction. Here they range from about one child in twenty-five with the *infrequent changers*, to about one child in six with the *habitual changers*.

With the *group instructors*, as one might suppose, they are much more heavily represented. Here, 38 per cent are *quiet collaborators*. It should be noted that even in this setting, where the pupil type so closely matches the teacher's style, these children are still a minority. They do not dramatically outnumber either *intermittent workers* or *solitary workers*, who account for 32 per cent and 25 per cent of the class respectively.

Distribution of pupil types across teaching styles

A piecemeal indication has already been given of the extent to which the distribution of the four pupil types differs across the six teaching styles. The question of the relationship between teaching style and pupil behaviour is clearly a complex one, and a fuller, more technical account is given in *Inside the Primary Classroom*. For immediate reference, a diagrammatic summary of the differences in distribution can be seen in Figure 8.1, similar to that in the previous volume (p. 149).

The attempt in the present chapter has been to present a more descriptive account of the four pupil types, not only for its own sake but also as a background to the analysis which follows of other pupil variables, such as age, sex, anxiety and motivation.

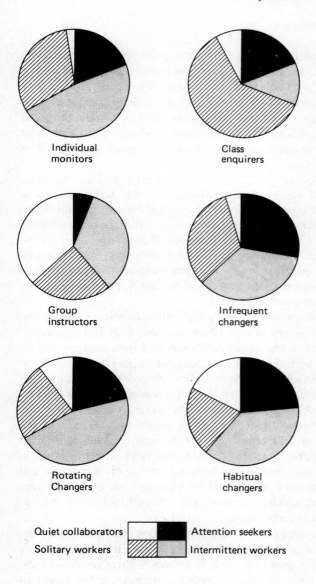

Figure 8.1 Distribution of pupil types across teaching styles

Anxiety and motivation

The classroom behaviour from which the pupil types are derived was directly observed: a child can be seen to be looking at a book or moving about the room, and because of the low level of inference involved, two independent observers would be very unlikely to disagree about whether the child was engaged in those activities or not. There would be greater scope for disagreement about the reasons behind them, since that question would demand from the observers a much higher level of inference.

A consideration of pupils' levels of motivation and anxiety takes place within this realm of high inference. A child seems anxious or highly motivated because of certain things that he does or fails to do; and there is a real danger of circular thinking, in that the observed piece of behaviour may be seen as both the *result of* and the *evidence for* the inferred construct. An unwary teacher or observer may reach the conclusion, for example, that Wayne is poorly motivated because he never does any work, and thereafter be confident that Wayne never does any work because he is poorly motivated.

The main problem in researching such characteristics as anxiety and motivation is to secure ratings which are free from this circularity. Teachers, who get to know their pupils very well from intensive day-to-day interactions with them, will gain valuable insights into such dimensions of their personalities. Nevertheless, if anxiety and motivation ratings are to be compared with children's scores on tests of achievement and study-skill exercises, it is clearly inappropriate to use ratings which may themselves have been made largely on the basis of the children's levels of achievement. If, for example, a group of children were rated as poorly motivated because their levels of achievement in class were low, the correlations between ratings of motivation and scores on achievement tests would be high, and the conclusion that poorly motivated children achieve little, though seemingly demonstrated, would be entirely circular.

An alternative approach is to assess motivation and anxiety from the children's own responses to questionnaire items. Here too there is a problem, in that a questionnaire is in no way a direct measure of the qualities under investigation, but rather a measure of the extent to which the respondents are willing or able to make them known. It must not be supposed, however, that questionnaires are less valid than other techniques in this respect. Like all theoretical constructs, anxiety and motivation cannot be directly observed and measured. They are derived from the interpretation of behaviour or feelings. Teachers' ratings of children's anxiety, and the children's own questionnaire responses, are both based on such interpretation, and will both contain some misjudgments. Children's questionnaire responses were preferred to teacher ratings in the ORACLE study because of their independence from other measures, and their lack of circularity.

The ORACLE questionnaire was derived and adapted from that used by Bennett (1976) in the Lancaster study. The shortened version (W) used in the ORACLE research was based only on the anxiety and motivation sub-scales of the Lancaster instrument, which was called WIDIS.[1] A factor analysis of the ORACLE items gave five factors, as follows:

Factor 1   Pupil-oriented anxiety
Factor 2   Teacher-oriented anxiety
Factor 3   Extrinsic motivation (competitiveness)
Factor 4   Intrinsic motivation (conformity)
Factor 5   Contentment

The full results of this factor analysis are shown in Appendix A, Table A.4.

As a check, the analysis was repeated after the second administration of the questionnaire in June 1977, and a virtually identical pattern emerged. To obtain individual scores for the purposes of constructing the various anxiety and motivation scores, the items which loaded on each factor were simply added together.

Pre- and post-test differences

A summary of an analysis of differences between mean scores at the beginning and end of the school year is presented in Table 8.1. There was a statistically significant drop in the pupils' anxiety about other children (beyond the 5 per cent level of significance), in their anxiety about the teacher (beyond the 1 per cent level) and in their contentment or adjustment (beyond the 1 per cent level). There were no significant differences between mean pre- and post-test scores on either intrinsic or extrinsic motivation. It seems that whereas motivation, as measured by this instrument, may be a trait within the child, both anxiety and contentment so measured may more often be reactive states. At the beginning of the year, when the children move to a new class, usually with a new teacher, the very novelty of the situation could generate both anxiety and positive feelings. By the end of the year the novelty has worn off: there is presumably less to be anxious about, and at the same time less to provide actively experienced contentment within the classroom.

Table 8.1 *Pre-test and post-test mean scores on W questionnaire* (*N = 402*)

Variable	Pre-test	Post-test	Significance level of difference†
Teacher-oriented anxiety	13.7	12.7	**
Pupil-oriented anxiety	11.5	11.0	*
Intrinsic motivation	17.2	17.3	
Extrinsic motivation	15.5	15.8	
Contentment	7.6	6.9	**

 * significant at the 5 per cent level
** significant at or beyond the 1 per cent level
 †   using t-test for matched samples

The drop in anxiety about the teacher was more dramatic than the drop in anxiety about other pupils. Here again, teacher-oriented anxiety may be a reaction to the unknown, heavily reinforced by the tales which often circulate at the end of a school year about how ferocious next year's teacher is going to be. In most cases the anxiety is soon discovered to have been unnecessary. Anxiety about one's fellow pupils, however, is much more likely to be realistic. In most schools the children move up as a group, so that on the whole they know their classmates well at the beginning of the year. The anxiety they express about them at that time is rather more likely to be based on past experience than on fear of the unknown future.

Pupil types and W-questionnaire score differences

The mean scores on anxiety, motivation and contentment of pupils of the different types described earlier in this chapter are shown in Table 8.2. There were no statistically significant differences between pupil types on either the pre-test or the post-test.

On both administrations of the questionnaire, *solitary workers* had the highest mean score on contentment, both kinds of motivation and

Table 8.2 Pre-test and post-test mean scores of pupil types on W questionnaire

Variable	Pre-test				Post-test			
	1	2	3	4	1	2	3	4
Teacher-oriented anxiety	13.9	13.4	13.9	13.7	12.8	12.8	12.6	13.1
Pupil-oriented anxiety	11.9	10.9	12.0	10.9	10.9	10.5	11.4	11.1
Intrinsic motivation	16.7	17.1	17.5	17.0	16.9	17.3	17.5	17.3
Extrinsic motivation	15.3	15.2	15.9	15.7	15.7	15.5	16.3	15.4
Contentment	7.3	7.6	7.8	7.5	6.9	6.7	7.2	7.0
N =	74	143	136	46	74	143	136	46

Type 1 = Attention seekers
Type 2 = Intermittent workers
Type 3 = Solitary workers
Type 4 = Quiet collaborators

pupil-oriented anxiety. Their mean pre-test score for teacher-oriented anxiety was joint highest with *attention seekers*, but by the time of the post-test their score had dropped, and was at that time lower than the mean score of any other group. One cannot here be confident that these were not chance findings. If they were replicated in further studies this would argue for a very close involvement in work demands on the part of *solitary workers*, coupled with a high degree of realistic sensitivity to threat from outside. This picture certainly tallies with the descriptive accounts of the classroom observers, who tended to see *solitary workers* as more likely to have difficulties in their relationships with other pupils than in their dealings with the teacher.

The *intermittent workers*, on the other hand, were among the lowest-scoring children on pupil-oriented anxiety at pre-test, and were the lowest scoring of all on this dimension at post-test. During the times when they were not working, these pupils would characteristically chat with their neighbours; it was perhaps their lack of pupil-oriented anxiety which to some extent accounted for the intermittent nature of their work effort.

By the end of the school year the *quiet collaborators* became the highest-scoring group in teacher-oriented anxiety, and the lowest scoring in extrinsic motivation. It has already been noted in the description of the pupil types (p. 147) that this is a group of children whose behaviour is clearly affected by the teacher's strategy, and that in the absence of teacher support they tend to work individually. It must be emphasized that their pattern of scores on teacher-oriented anxiety and extrinsic motivation did not reach statistical significance; nevertheless it raises the possibility that these particular children are in some way at cross purposes with their teachers, and that they would be more at ease in a situation where they could spend more of their time working individually.

The *attention seekers* began the year as one of the groups with the highest level of teacher-oriented anxiety, and as the group with the lowest level of contentment. At the end of the year they were closer to the mean for all groups on both of these dimensions. It seems reasonable to suggest that this shift was brought about by the fact that to a great extent their teachers responded to their apparent need to be at the centre of attention for much of the time.

Teaching-styles and W-questionnaire score differences

The mean scores of pupils subjected to each of the teaching styles are

Table 8.3 Pre-test and post-test mean scores on W questionnaire of pupils subjected to differing teaching styles

Variable	Pre-test						Post-test					
	1	2	3	4a	4b	4c	1	2	3	4a	4b	4c
Teacher-oriented anxiety	13.8	13.6	13.7	13.3	14.2	13.3	13.4	12.6	11.7	13.0	12.4	12.5
Pupil-oriented anxiety	11.2	11.5	12.1	11.0	11.8	11.3	11.3	11.0	10.9	10.8	10.7	11.1
Intrinsic motivation	17.0	17.2	17.0	17.3	17.8	17.0	17.1	17.5	17.4	16.9	17.9	17.0
Extrinsic motivation	16.0	15.5	15.3	15.2	15.7	15.3	16.2	16.3	15.2	15.3	15.6	15.5
Contentment	7.5	7.3	7.9	8.2	7.4	7.6	7.1	7.0	7.0	7.0	6.9	6.8
N =	96	64	47	41	61	87	96	64	47	41	61	87

Style 1 = Individual monitors
Style 2 = Class enquirers
Style 3 = Group instructors
Style 4a = Infrequent changers
Style 4b = Rotating changers
Style 4c = Habitual changers

shown in Table 8.3. None of the differences between styles was statistically significant.

Whereas the scores of the different pupil types fell into patterns which could be readily interpreted in terms of the information gained from classroom observation of the children, the scores of children subjected to each of the differing teaching styles did not fall into any such clear patterns. In view of this, and of the fact that none of the differences were statistically significant, no detailed recital will be given here of the highest- and lowest-scoring groups on each of the dimensions.

In the context of the over-all ORACLE study, the importance of the findings summarized in Tables 8.2 and 8.3 lies in the absence of a strong systematic relationship between anxiety, motivation and contentment on the one hand, and the pupil types and teaching styles on the other. When, in the next chapter, comparisons are made between the achievements of different pupil types, or between those of pupils subjected to differing teaching styles, the effects of anxiety, motivation and contentment on these variables can be discounted with confidence. Although pupils differ widely in these qualities, they do not differ in such a way that, for example, a significantly high proportion of the anxious children fall in one pupil type, or in the pupils subjected to one teaching style. If this had been so, any apparent relationship between the pupil type or the teaching style and the pupils' achievement might have been attributable to the anxiety, rather than to the type or the style in question. As it turns out, however, this problem does not arise.

Age differences in motivation, anxiety and contentment

Analyses of the mean scores on the questionnaire were carried out separately for children in the nine-plus, ten-plus and eleven-plus age groups. An interpretation of the results of these analyses cannot be straightforward, since in the ORACLE sample the age of the pupils was strongly related to other factors. For example, all the children in the eleven-plus age group came from local authority C, all those in the ten-plus age group and two-thirds of those in the nine-plus age group from local authority B, and one-third of those in the nine-plus age group from local authority A. All the eleven-plus children were attending junior middle schools, the ten-plus and two-thirds of the nine-plus children were attending junior or infant and junior schools, and the remaining third of the nine-plus children were attending lower schools.

Table 8.4 Age differences in mean scores on W questionnaire

	Pre-test				Post-test			
Variable	9+	10+	11+	Significance level of difference	9+	10+	11+	Significance level of difference
Teacher-oriented anxiety	13.9	13.6	13.3		12.9	12.6	12.4	
Pupil-oriented anxiety	12.1	11.1	10.7	**	11.3	10.4	10.8	
Intrinsic motivation	17.3	17.0	17.0		17.7	16.9	17.0	*
Extrinsic motivation	15.8	14.4	16.1	**	16.1	14.9	16.1	**
Contentment	7.8	7.6	7.2		6.9	7.2	6.7	
N =	192	103	107		192	103	107	

* significant at the 5 per cent level
** significant at the 1 per cent level

A further complicating factor was that the children attending lower schools were in their final year before transfer to middle school, a situation which might be expected to influence their anxiety, their motivation and their general contentment at school. Thus in no sense can it be said that children of different ages were randomly distributed among the sample. The purpose of this particular analysis was to see whether any effects on anxiety, motivation and contentment arising from the age of the pupils would be so strong as to over-ride the confounding variables just mentioned. The mean scores of the different age groups are presented in Table 8.4.

It will be seen that at the time of pre-test, three of the five measures showed systematic drops in score with increasing age, and one more showed a drop followed by no subsequent increase. Only in the case of pupil-oriented anxiety did this trend reach statistical significance. With extrinsic motivation, however, the ten-year-olds scored lower than either the nine-year-olds or the eleven-year-olds; and this non-linear trend was echoed in four of the five post-test measures. With the fifth, contentment, the pattern was reversed, and the middle age-group scored highest.

Thus, no powerfully age-related trends emerged from this analysis, although it may be valid to suggest that, with the exception of extrinsic motivation or competitiveness, there is a slight tendency for the variables under investigation to decrease within this age range.

It may be of interest to compare these findings with the results of the standardization sample on the Junior Eysenck Personality Inventory. The N dimension from that questionnaire is to some extent comparable with the W anxiety scales, in that 'we may describe the typical high N scorer as being an anxious, worrying individual . . . [whose] main characteristic is a constant pre-occupation with things that might go wrong, and a strong emotional reaction of anxiety to these thoughts' (Eysenck and Eysenck, 1975). The standardization manual shows that, over the age-range seven to fifteen years, 'for N there is an increase in score for the girls only; for boys the scores are irregular, and do not indicate any trend.' Thus, for neither sex is there the decrease in anxiety with age suggested by the ORACLE findings. A likely explanation for this difference is to be found in the suggestion by Bennett and Youngman (1973) that in a setting such as the classroom, where the 'institutional demands are sufficiently strong to swamp the effects of individual differences in personality,' a general inventory such as the JEPI is of less use or validity than a measure specifically designed for the particular social situation encountered. The W questionnaire is just such a measure. It makes no statements about generalized anxiety or motivation in the child's over-all style of life, but attempts rather to tap these qualities in the specific situation under investigation.

Sex differences in behaviour, motivation, anxiety and contentment

An investigation of sex differences in response to the questionnaire is much more straightforward than an investigation of age differences, since from the outset an equal number of boys and girls was observed in each of the classes which participated in the study. Thus the research design allows one to be confident that any differences which appear between the responses of boys and girls are indeed sex differences, rather than artefacts of some confounding variable. Preliminary analysis of the data established that there were marked sex differences in response to the W questionnaire, and these are summarized in Table 8.5.

It will be seen that both at the beginning and at the end of the school year girls tended to express much more anxiety than boys about the teacher and about the other pupils. This finding is parallel to that of the JEPI standardization data, where girls scored higher than boys on the N scale at all ages from seven to fifteen. Girls also emerged as more contented with school, and more strongly motivated to do their best and please the teachers. When it came to competitiveness (extrinsic motivation), however, there was no statistically significant difference between the sexes (although here there was a slight tendency for the boys to score higher than the girls). In an earlier study, Nisbet and Entwistle (1969) found that boys showed a lower degree of 'academic motivation' than girls in a large sample of children between the ages of eleven and thirteen. A comparison between the W questionnaire and the Aberdeen Academic Motivation Inventory used in the earlier study shows that the AAMI contains no items which are similar to the extrinsic motivation items on the W questionnaire. Many of its items resemble those on the W intrinsic-motivation scale; for example, 'Is it important for you to do well at school?' Other AAMI items resemble questions from the W teacher-oriented anxiety scale; for example, 'Do you worry about not doing well in class?' It will be seen that in so far as the two measures overlap, their findings are in agreement with each other. The element of competitiveness in the W extrinsic-motivation scale is not covered by the AAMI, and does not play a part in Nisbet and Entwistle's concept of academic motivation.

In considering sex differences in questionnaire responses, it must again be emphasized that the questionnaire is not a direct measure of

159

Table 8.5 Sex differences in mean score on W questionnaire

	Pre-test			Post-test			Significance level of pre-test/post-test difference	
Variable	Boys	Girls	Significance level of difference	Boys	Girls	Difference	Boys	Girls
Teacher-oriented anxiety	12.4	14.9	**	11.4	13.9	**	**	**
Pupil-oriented anxiety	10.5	12.4	**	9.7	12.2	**	*	
Intrinsic motivation	16.6	17.7	**	16.6	17.9	**		
Extrinsic motivation	15.8	15.3		15.9	15.6			
Contentment	7.0	8.2	**	6.3	7.6	**	**	**
N =	195	207		195	207			

* significant at the 5 per cent level
** significant at the 1 per cent level

anxiety, motivation and contentment, but rather a measure of the extent to which the pupils are willing or able to make their anxiety, motivation and contentment known. It could be that girls are more likely than boys to perceive some or all of the qualities under examination as socially acceptable. If this is so, then even if the levels of anxiety, motivation and contentment were equal in boys and girls, the greater willingness of the girls to admit that they were anxious, highly motivated and contented in school might be expected to have led to their achieving a higher mean score than the boys. However, there is nothing in the data at hand to enable this hypothesis to be tested.

In view of the finding that girls and boys differed considerably in their responses to the questionnaire, both at pre-test and post-test, analyses of the differences between mean scores at the beginning and end of the school year were carried out separately for each sex. The results of these analyses also appear in Table 8.5.

The one area of marked difference here was pupil-oriented anxiety. It has already been reported that, taking both sexes together, there was a significant drop in mean score, and an explanation has been offered. It can be seen now, however, that the drop in mean score was peculiar to the boys; the mean score of the girls at the end of the year was almost the same as their mean score at the outset. If anxiety about one's fellow pupils is likely to be realistic and based on past experience, it could be that girls are indeed more likely than boys to be harassed by their classmates during the course of the school year. An alternative explanation (and perhaps a more convincing one) is that in both sexes levels of anxiety in this area remain stable throughout the year, but that as the children get older the boys find it increasingly difficult to admit to their anxiety, because it is not 'manly', whereas the girls are not troubled by this, since our society still allows them to be anxious while keeping their self-esteem. These particular questions might be clarified through the use of depth interviews of a type which were not used in the ORACLE study, but which could provide a useful avenue of research for a team with a specialist interest and the necessary expertise.

However, the immediate task is to consider the relationship between the pupil and his achievement. A rather complex picture of the pupil has emerged, in which his age, sex, manner of working, anxiety, motivation, contentment, and the style of teaching to which he is subjected, all play a part. It has been seen that anxiety, motivation and contentment are not systematically related either to pupil type or to teaching style, a finding which permits a direct examination of the relationship between pupil type and teaching style on the one hand, and achievement on the other.

Teachers who recognize examples of the four pupil types among their own classes may find themselves faced with an interesting series of problems. Those who place hard work and academic achievement at the top of their hierarchy of values may feel that the *solitary workers* represent their best pupils; nevertheless it must be acknowledged that these children tend to shut themselves off from much of the cut and thrust of everyday classroom life, and that in some ways they may be the worse off for that. Conversely, teachers who value social relationships very highly might find themselves wishing to encourage the undoubted sociability of the *intermittent workers* in their classes, yet be somewhat puzzled about how at the same time to deal constructively with the tendency of these pupils to develop the skills of avoiding the teacher's eye and making a small amount of work go a long way. Each pupil type has its inbuilt strengths and weaknesses, which the teacher will want to evaluate for herself.

To assist this evaluation, a detailed picture has been assembled of the progress of the different pupil types. The network of relationships among pupil progress and the pupil characteristics discussed here is the subject of the next chapter.

Note

1   In its original version, the Lancaster questionnaire (WIDIS) has two parallel forms consisting of sixty items each, and was devised to throw light on fourteen pupil characteristics, including distractability, sociability and so on. Four of the scales are concerned with different aspects of anxiety, and four more with aspects of motivation.

Chapter 9

Pupils' characteristics and their progress

The strategy for analysing pupil progress discussed in Chapters 1 and 4 involves considering the effects of characteristics of the pupils themselves on their progress, as well as analysing the impact of teaching methods on them. This goes beyond most previous studies of teaching styles, as it allows for the possibility that the effects of these styles are not necessarily uniform. Such an analysis can become fairly complicated, as it must allow for the independent effects of both teaching styles and pupil characteristics, and for the possible effects of interactions between them.

The term 'interaction' is used here in the statistical sense, rather than in the more general sense of the earlier discussions of, for example, pupil-teacher interaction. In this statistical usage, interaction is a description of the process whereby the joint effects of two variables on a third variable cannot be derived from knowledge of their separate effects. In the present analysis the effect of teaching style on pupil progress has been considered; this is a main effect. Later in this chapter the effect of pupil type on progress will be considered; this is also a main effect. But it is also important to consider the possibility that a particular style may achieve better results with one type of pupil than with another; that, for example, pupil type A may achieve below-average results over-all, but achieve above-average results when taught by style X. As data have been gathered not only on teachers and classrooms but also on individual pupils, it is possible to look at the effects on progress of pupil characteristics as well as of teaching styles, and to consider the possibility that a particular teaching style may be more effective for one type of pupil than for another.

This analysis will concentrate on the relationship between pupil characteristics and progress in the basic skills, rather than dealing with the types of skills considered in Chapters 6 and 7. There are two reasons for this. First, the availability of scores on the basic skills at the beginning and end of the year make the notion of progress more appropriate. Second, when considering the ways in which different teachers deal with different groups of pupils, the latter's performance in basic skills is likely to be more relevant than performance in other areas.

One pupil characteristic which has been widely used in the analysis so far is initial achievement. This has been used as the covariate in the comparison of the progress of pupils taught by different styles. The additional pupil variables to be considered here have been described in Chapter 8. They include pupil motivation and anxiety, and the data from the direct observations of pupil behaviour. These last variables were used in the cluster analysis which produced the four pupil types described in Chapter 8.

Pupil types and progress in basic skills

From the description of the characteristics of these four clusters of pupils, there are reasons to anticipate that differences will be found in their performance on the tests of basic skills. Children classified as *attention seekers* spend very much more time than the other pupils in interaction with the teacher, and most of this interaction is concerned with work. The members of the cluster of *solitary workers* spend more time on work than any other pupil type, and although they receive relatively little individual attention from the teacher they are particularly likely to be members of the class audience. On the other hand, members of the cluster of *intermittent workers* seem successful in avoiding interaction with the teacher, and are also the lowest of the four types in the proportion of their time they spend working.

With these differences in mind, the results presented in Tables 9.1, 9.2 and 9.3, for the four types of pupil in the three tests of basic skills, are somewhat surprising. The top two rows of each table give the pre- and post-test score in each test. The relative achievements of the four pupil types in all three tests, and at the beginning and end of the year, follow a remarkably stable pattern. This pattern is for *solitary workers* to have the highest scores and *intermittent workers* the second highest. These are followed by the *quiet collaborators*, with the *attention seekers* having the lowest scores. The only exception to this pattern is for the post-test reading scores, where the positions of the *attention*

Table 9.1 Pupil types and progress in mathematics

	Pupil types				
Variables	Attention seekers	Intermittent workers	Solitary workers	Quiet collaborators	
Pre-test score	10.4	12.2	12.5	10.6	**
Post-test score	15.5	17.1	17.6	15.9	*
Residual-change score	−0.25	−0.30	0.54	−0.21	
Residual change controlling for teaching style	−0.18	−0.02	0.13	−0.01	
N =	77	144	138	47	

* significant at the 5 per cent level
** significant at or beyond the 1 per cent level

Table 9.2 Pupil types and progress in language skills

	Pupil types				
Variables	Attention seekers	Intermittent workers	Solitary workers	Quiet collaborators	
Pre-test score	7.6	9.0	9.3	8.7	*
Post-test score	11.2	13.2	14.0	12.8	**
Residual-change score	−1.06	−0.06	0.75	−0.22	*
Residual change controlling for teaching style	−0.79	0.18	0.48	−0.67	
N =	77	144	138	48	

* significant at the 5 per cent level
** significant at or beyond the 1 per cent level

seekers and *intermittent workers* are reversed. These differences between the pupil clusters are statistically significant in the case of mathematics and language skills, but not in the case of reading. However, the raw scores of the pupil types are not, in themselves, of great interest, as the clusters differ with regard to age composition and the schools and classes from which they come. In accordance with the strategy adopted throughout this volume the main focus of interest is on progress made.

All four groups of pupils have made progress on the three tests, and the absolute amount of progress (the raw-score gain) is very similar for all four groups. This can be calculated for each style by taking the simple differences between scores on rows 1 and 2 of Tables 9.1 to 9.3.

Table 9.3 Pupil types and progress in reading

Variables	Pupil types			
	Attention seekers	Intermittent workers	Solitary workers	Quiet collaborators
Pre-test score	11.7	12.8	13.2	12.4
Post-test score	18.1	18.5	19.8	17.9
Residual-change score	0.28	−0.57	0.69	−0.69
Residual change controlling for teaching style	0.30	−0.67	0.64	−0.34
N =	79	145	138	47

However, an alternative comparison, taking into account the initial scores, makes use of an analysis of covariance in the same way as in Chapter 4. As before, this involves using the two sets of scores on each test (that is the scores at the beginning and end of the year, summarized in the first two rows of Tables 9.1 to 9.3) to calculate how much progress a pupil would be expected to make on the basis of his score at the beginning of the year. This expected progress is then compared with his actual progress in order to obtain a residual-change score. This score is the extent to which a pupil has made more or less progress than would have been expected.

It should be noted that this concept of expected or predicted gain is a statistical one, and is calculated with respect to the progress of other pupils taking the test. For some pupils to perform better than predicted from their initial score, others must perform less well than predicted. Consequently the average residual-change score for the whole sample must always be zero. However, individual pupils and particular groups of pupils can have positive or negative residual-change scores, and these are presented in the third row of Tables 9.1, 9.2 and 9.3. These figures show the average residual-change score for the members of each pupil type. A positive value for residual change means that members of a pupil type have, on average, done better than pre-dicted, and a negative score means that they have done less well. A negative score of, for example, —0.5 means that members of a pupil type have scored, on average, half a mark less than expected.

The differences between pupil clusters in the amount of progress made are rather less substantial than are the differences between teaching styles presented in Chapter 4 and 5. The only case of a residual-change score of one mark above or below zero is the score of —1.06 of the *attention seekers* on language skills. Most of the scores are much lower than this, indicating that the pupil clusters do not differ much in the extent of progress made. Only in the test of language skills do the differences reach statistical significance at the 5 per cent level, despite the relatively large size of the sample. The *solitary workers* have the largest residual score on all three tests, and are the only cluster to have consistently positive scores across the tests. The *attention seekers* do particularly badly on the language test, but score above average on reading. The other two clusters score a little below their predicted scores on all the tests.

The differences between the pupil types are not, in general, very substantial. However, they decrease still further when the effects of teaching style are taken into account. It is necessary to control for teaching style because, as shown in Chapter 8, the pupil types are not distributed evenly among the various styles. Consequently, the possibility that the apparent effects of the pupil clusters are really the effects of the teaching styles, or vice versa, must be tested. This is the kind of problem which has been discussed in Chapter 5, when alter-native explanations for the apparent effects of teaching styles were being considered. Another problem arises when considering the effects of more than one variable at a time, even if they are not inter-related. This is the question of interaction between the variables; the possi-bility, discussed at the beginning of the chapter, that the effects of teaching style may differ between boys and girls, or between different pupil types.

The appropriate analysis to control for the relationship between teaching style and pupil type is a two-factor analysis of covariance, in which the covariate is, as before, the pre-test score, and the joint effects of pupil types and teaching styles on the adjusted post-test scores are considered. The procedures followed are those given in *Statistical Package for the Social Sciences* (Nie *et al.*, 1975, pp. 405-8). Briefly, the approach used is the *classic experimental design* in which no causal order between the two variables (style and type) is assumed, and the main effects of these variables are given higher priority than interactions. The test for the main effects of each variable only attributes to it those effects not accounted for by the other variables.

A summary of the full analysis, also controlling for the pupils' sex, is presented in Table 9.5, and is discussed later. However, in the fourth row of Tables 9.1, 9.2 and 9.3 the residual-change scores for the four pupil types after the effects of teaching styles have been removed are presented. The rankings of the four types relative to one another are not affected by this procedure, but the size of the differences are still further reduced. In addition, for none of the tests do the differences now reach statistical significance. This shows that part of the differences between the pupil clusters can be explained by their unequal distribution between the teaching styles, and that after this has been taken into account the possibility that such differences as remain are a consequence of random sampling fluctuations cannot be safely discounted.

Sex differences and pupil progress

Differences between boys and girls in behaviour and achievement in school have not figured largely in this volume, or in the earlier report on classroom processes, *Inside the Primary Classroom*. In that volume it was shown that boys and girls are very similar in terms of the amount and type of interactions with the teacher and with other pupils (p.66). Data for involvement in work were not presented separately for boys and girls. However these figures are also very similar. Girls spend 58.5 per cent of their time directly on task, 12.5 per cent on routine activities connected with work and 4.4 per cent of their time waiting for the teacher. This adds up to 75.4 per cent of lesson time involved with work in some way. The equivalent figures for boys are 57.7, 11.3 and 4.3 per cent, adding up to 73.3 per cent involved time, 2 per cent below that for girls.

The figures for achievement on the tests of basic skills presented in Chapter 3 of this volume show that boys and girls are also very similar in this respect. Girls do slightly better on the test of language skills, boys slightly better on mathematics and both score equally on reading. This pattern holds for both pre- and post-test scores (Table 3.3, p. 50). As both boys and girls start and finish virtually level over the year, it is not necessary to conduct an analysis of covariance to know that their rates of progress must also be virtually identical. However, possible interactions between sex and pupil types and teaching styles will be considered later in this chapter.

The similarity between boys and girls in terms of behaviour and achievement may be surprising, in view of previous evidence that girls are better adjusted to primary schools, achieve better and are better regarded by their teachers (Douglas, 1964; Plowden Report, 1967, Vol. 2, Appendix 10). However, this contrast is more apparent than real. In the first place, other studies have not based their conclusions on direct observation of primary pupils, and it is on this that the comparisons of the activities and interactions of pupils is based. With regard to the similarity of behaviour between boys and girls, it should be noted that the observation was of lesson time in classrooms, and it is only to this that the conclusions apply. The data do not relate to possible differences in 'outdoors' behaviour of the kinds noted by the Newsons (Newson and Newson, 1976, Chapter 3).

Studies which have compared the achievement of boys and girls have emphasized that the differences which occur are very susceptible to changes in the content of the tests, and this probably accounts for such differences as there are between ORACLE and other studies. The slightly better performance of boys in mathematics is in line with the findings of the National Child Development Study (Plowden Report, 1967, Vol. 2, Appendix 10), and the small advantage that girls have in language skills match the results obtained in *The Home and the School* (Douglas, 1964, pp. 69-76) that girls have an advantage in verbal skills. The equal scores on the reading test of the two sexes is at variance with the results of the two studies quoted above, where girls performed better than boys. However, these studies relied in part on word-recognition tests, while the ORACLE tests were of vocabulary and comprehension. The Douglas study found that boys did better than girls on vocabulary items, and differences in the balance of test content make exact comparisons between the studies impossible.

In addition to comparing boys and girls and looking for interactions between sex and pupil type or teaching style (see below), it was also decided to compare the performance of boys and girls when taught by male and female teachers. It has sometimes been suggested that one of the reasons that the performance of girls falls off relative to that of boys in secondary school, and especially falls off in scientific and mathematical subjects, is that primary schools tend to be dominated by female teachers, and secondary schools, and especially science subjects, by male teachers. For example, Douglas (1964, p. 71) writes; 'It is noticeable that girls excel in subjects that are taught by women and boys in subjects that are taught by men. . . . The subjects taught in primary school mainly by women may come to be thought of as "girls subjects". . . .' The extent to which primary school teachers are predominantly female should not, of course, be exaggerated. In the age range of the pupils in the present study, well over a third of teachers in England and Wales are men, and this is reflected in the ORACLE sample (*Inside the Primary Classroom*, p. 27). Nor is a simple comparison over one year an adequate test of the possibility of interactions between the sex of the pupil, sex of the teacher and orientation towards school work. Nevertheless, it is worth investigating differences in achievement between boys and girls taught by male and female teachers.

As Table 9.4 shows, Douglas's suggestion cannot be supported by the present data. Differences between the achievement of boys and girls taught by men or women are very small and, as the details of the analysis of covariance in Appendix C5 show, in no case anywhere near statistical significance, despite relatively large sample sizes.

Table 9.4 Sex of pupils and teachers and progress on the basic skills

Residual-change scores	Male teachers		Female teachers	
	Boys	*Girls*	*Boys*	*Girls*
Mathematics	0.04	−0.04	0.06	−0.05
Language skills	−0.42	0.38	−0.17	0.16
Reading	0.20	−0.19	0.23	−0.14
N =	77	77	131	142

Interactions between teaching styles, pupil type and pupil sex

Earlier in this chapter the effect of pupil types on progress was considered, at first on its own, and then together with the effect of teaching style. The results of tests for statistical interactions were not presented in the earlier discussions. They are, however, important, because if there are statistically significant interactions then to present the separate effect of each main variable will be misleading. Although boys and girls perform equally well on the pre- and post-tests, and there is therefore no obvious effect of sex on performance, the possibilities of interactions cannot be discounted. This would mean, for example, that boys performed particularly well when taught by one style and girls particularly well when taught by another. Therefore, pupil sex as well as pupil type has been included in the analysis.

The analysis performed was a three-way analysis of covariance using the procedure described above. It considers the significance of all inter- actions: three-way interactions (sex × style × type) and three sets of two-way interactions (sex × style, sex × type, style × type). If these interactions are not significant, the significance of the effect of each of the three variables is considered. In the procedure used here, effects are only assigned to a variable if they are not accounted for by either of the other two variables. A variable is only considered to have those effects which are independent of other variables. In the results pre- sented in Tables 9.1 to 9.3 it was shown that the independent effect of pupil type was reduced when teaching style was included in the analysis.

Details of the three-way analysis are given in Appendix C (Table C.5) and the results are summarized in Table 9.5. In this table it can be seen that none of the interactions, two-way or three-way, are significant for any of the three basic skills. It is therefore possible to consider the in- dependent effect of each of the three variables. For each of the basic skills, the pattern is that neither sex nor pupil type has a statistically significant effect when the effects of the other variables have been re- moved. Teaching style, on the other hand, has significant effects in all three areas.

Table 9.5 Progress in the basic skills: results of a three-way analysis of covariance with teaching styles and pupil sex

	Mathematics	*Language skills*	*Reading*
Main effects:			
Teaching style	Significant at or beyond 1 per cent	Significant at or beyond 1 per cent	Significant at or beyond 1 per cent
Pupil types			
Sex	Not significant	Not significant	Not significant
Two-way interactions:			
Style and type			
Style and sex	Not significant	Not significant	Not significant
Sex and type			
Three-way interactions:			
(Style × sex × type)	Not significant	Not significant	Not significant

Pupil behaviour and progress

Motivation, anxiety and pupil progress

Other pupil characteristics to be considered in relationship to pupil progress are levels of motivation and anxiety, measured by the attitude questionnaire described in Chapter 8. There are obvious reasons to expect that levels of motivation will be related to pupil progress, although such a relationship, if found, will not necessarily be easy to interpret. It may be that high levels of motivation increase a child's progress, but it is also possible that children who are doing well at school are more likely to express high levels of motivation than are other children. It is less easy to predict a relationship between anxiety and progress, but, should one be found, similar problems of interpretation remain. A child might, for example, do badly because he was anxious, or he might be anxious because he is doing badly.

The simple correlations between motivation and anxiety, and the combined residual-change scores (the extent to which a child does better or worse on the three post-tests together than would have been expected from his pre-test score), are given in Table 9.6. There is, as expected, a positive correlation between motivation and residual gain of

Table 9.6 Correlations between residual gains and motivation and anxiety

	Motivation	Anxiety	N
All pupils	0.16**	−0.11*	407
Teaching style:			
Individual monitors	0.31**	−0.06	97
Class enquirers	0.05	−0.21	67
Group instructors	−0.05	−0.18	49
Infrequent changers	0.04	−0.06	43
Rotating changers	0.37**	0	59
Habitual changers	0.29**	−0.09	92

 * significant at the 5 per cent level
** significant at or beyond the 1 per cent level

a fairly modest but statistically significant 0.16. Anxiety correlates negatively with gain at a lower but still statistically significant value of −0.11. These results show that well-motivated pupils do better than less well-motivated ones, and anxious pupils less well than less anxious ones. Although these may seem obvious conclusions, the interpretation to be put on them is not at all obvious. In particular, they raise the question of whether pupils are successful because they are well motivated or well motivated because they are successful.

One approach to the question of the direction of the relationship is to consider the correlations in relation to other variables, and in particular to teaching styles. It has been established that teaching styles are related to progress, but not to levels of anxiety and motivation. In Chapter 8 it was shown that pupils taught by different styles do not differ in levels of anxiety or motivation at the beginning or end of the year. This means that these attitudinal variables cannot account for the effects of teaching styles on progress.

Although the levels of anxiety and motivation are about the same across the six teaching styles, this uniformity does not extend to their relationship with progress. This is shown in Table 9.6, where the correlations between the attitudinal items and the total residual-change scores are given for pupils within each teaching style. While the correlations between motivation and residual gain is 0.16 for the whole sample, for pupils in three of the styles it is virtually zero, and for the other three styles it is about double the whole sample figure. This shows that motivation and progress have a relatively high correlation among pupils in certain teaching styles, but are uncorrelated in others. Specifically, among pupils taught by the less successful styles (*individual monitors, rotating changers* and *habitual changers*), the correlations are 0.31, 0.37 and 0.29 respectively, all of which are statistically significant, while among pupils taught by *class enquirers, group instructors* and *infrequent changers* the correlations are 0.05, −0.05 and 0.04.

The suggestion that in the less successful classrooms individual pupil motivation is important for progress fits in with the other findings of this study. The styles in which motivation is related to progress are those in which the pupil has to draw most on his own resources. These styles are high on individualized work, and the constant changes of setting imposed by *rotating changers* and *habitual changers* require high levels of pupil commitment if learning is to be maintained. In contrast, in the classrooms of the *class enquirers* and *group instructors* pupils have less choice with regard to taking part in lessons, as they spend a higher proportion of their time as part of the class or group being taught. Although the *infrequent changers* do not have high proportions of group or class work, the description of this style in Chapter 2 and in *Inside the Primary Classroom* shows that these were classes in which teachers exercised high degrees of control.

Thus the analysis of the relationship between motivation and progress, separately for the different styles, shows how an apparently obvious correlation is the result of a much more complex set of relationships, and gives an extra perspective on the association between teaching style and progress. This sort of analysis is similar to that conducted in Chapter 5. By introducing extra variables, alternative explanations for the observed correlations can be evaluated.

The discussion has been concerned so far with motivation and progress, where the differences between the correlations within different teaching styles is clear and explicable. The situation with regard to anxiety and progress is rather less clear. As stated earlier, there is a small but statistically significant negative correlation between anxiety and progress. Taking the teaching styles separately, none of the equivalent correlations reach statistical significance as the relevant sample sizes become smaller. However, there are differences between the teaching styles. In particular the *class enquirers* and *group instructors* have much larger negative correlations than the other styles. The correlations are −0.21 and −0.18 for pupils taught by teachers from these clusters. The correlations within the other clusters are −0.09, −0.06 and zero. Although none of the correlations within the groups reach significance, it is possible to offer a tentative explanation for the findings. It may be that anxiety acts to reduce performance in classes like those of the *class enquirers* and *group instructors*, where performance is more public, but not in more individual settings. On the other hand, the reversed form of this hypothesis, that poor performance creates anxiety in the class and group settings but not in individual settings, cannot be ruled out.

It must be emphasized that the above discussion is very tentative. The possibility that the observed relationships on which it is based derived from chance sampling fluctuations cannot be dismissed. However, research by Trown and Leith (1975) has also found negative relationships between anxiety and learning. Their study also found that this relationship held for certain teaching methods but not for others, although differences in the way that teaching methods were classified make it impossible to compare their result directly with the ORACLE findings.

Class size, pupil-teacher interaction and pupil progress

In *Inside the Primary Classroom*, the relevance of class size to the amount and type of pupil-teacher interaction was emphasized. These results, which are repeated in Table 9.7 of the present volume, can now be extended, in order to investigate the relationship between these variables and pupil progress. Research on the relationship between class size and pupil achievement has typically started from the expectation that smaller class sizes will lead to improved pupil achievement. This is an assumption which fits a common-sense view of teaching; the fewer children there are to make demands on the teacher the more she can help them. Nevertheless, these studies have failed to find a straight-forward relationship of this kind, and some studies have suggested that children make more progress in larger classes. A recent review of work in this area shows that this latter argument cannot be sustained, and quotes the conclusions of a 'meta-analysis' of research on class size which suggests that children do indeed learn more in smaller classes (Burstall, 1979). This review shows the complexity of the question of the effects of class size, and emphasizes the need to look at the conse-quences of various class sizes for a wide range of classroom activities and relationships, as well as for achievement.

One consequence of larger classes is that the teacher spends more of her time working with pupils. The second column of Table 9.7, based on data from the Teacher Record, shows the correlations between the class size and different types of pupil-teacher interaction measured by observing the teacher. There is an over-all correlation of 0.16 between class size and all pupil-teacher interaction. This comes about mainly through increased teacher interaction with groups, and also with in-dividual pupils. Teachers with large classes in our sample do not react by increasing their interaction with the whole class: the correlation between class size and class interaction is a negative one (Table 9.7). But, as the figures presented in Chapter 2 show, teachers already spend the great majority of their time interacting with pupils, and so it is impossible to compensate fully for increased class size by increased rates of interaction. The first column of Table 9.7 based on data from the Pupil Record shows the correlations between class size and pupil-teacher interaction from the pupils' point of view. These correlations are negative: −0.27 for total pupil-teacher interaction. Despite the increase in the teacher's interaction with pupils in large classes, indi-cated by the positive correlations in column 2 of Table 9.7, individual pupils receive less attention in these classes.

Large classes result in higher teacher work-loads and lower levels of teacher-pupil contact, but in the classrooms in the present study they do not result in lower rates of progress in the basic skills. In Table 9.8

175

Table 9.7 Class size and pupil-teacher interaction

	Pupil Record	Teacher Record
Correlation between class size and:		
Individual interaction	−0.21**	0.12
Group interaction	−0.06	0.23
Class interaction	−0.21**	−0.13
All pupil-teacher interaction	−0.27**	0.16
Time on task	−0.03	−0.05
N =	489	58

** significant at or beyond the 1 per cent level

the correlations between class size and class average residual change scores are given. In all three areas of the basic skills, and for the three together, the correlations are negligible. This result accords with the results of other studies mentioned above, but does not match the common-sense view of effective teaching. Nevertheless the detailed observational data from the ORACLE research enables it to be put in

Table 9.8 Class size and pupil progress

Correlation between class size and class average residual-change scores for:	
Mathematics	−0.05
Language skills	0.04
Reading	0.06
Total residual change	0.02
N =	58

perspective. The sizes of the fifty-eight classes in the study related closely with the variations in class size nationally. It is clear from the observational data that, for the most part, the additional teacher time available to pupils in the smaller class is very limited. Moreover, as Burstall suggests, teachers accustomed to large classes may not be equipped to take advantage of such extra time as is available in a smaller one (Burstall, 1979). This matter will be referred to again in Chapter 11.

Class size, pupil-pupil interaction and pupil progress

The final aspect of pupil behaviour to be considered in relation to progress is pupil-pupil interaction. Plowden suggested that the opportunity to work together with other children is beneficial for pupils' learning (Plowden Report, 1967, p. 274). Table 9.9 gives some support to this view. Among the ORACLE sample of pupils there is a negative (although non-significant) correlation of −0.09 between the amount of interaction a pupil engages in with other pupils and his residual-change score. But there is a positive correlation of 0.11 between the amount of work-oriented interaction and residual change. These figures suggest that co-operating on work is related to progress, although only weakly. It must be remembered that co-operative work of this kind was not an important feature of the classrooms in this study. As Appendix B shows only 5 per cent of a pupil's time in the classroom is spent in this way.

Table 9.9 Correlations between class size, pupil-pupil interaction and pupil progress

Residual change and all pupil-pupil interaction	−0.09	n = 410
Residual change and work-oriented pupil-pupil interaction	0.11	n = 410 *
Class size and all pupil-pupil interaction	0.04	n = 489
Class size and work-oriented pupil-pupil interaction	0.17	n = 489 **

* significant at the 5 per cent level
** significant at or beyond the 1 per cent level

Table 9.9 also presents the correlations between class size and levels of pupil-pupil interaction. Over-all levels of interaction are not associated with class size, but there is a positive correlation of 0.17 between work oriented pupil-pupil interaction and the size of class. It may be that in larger classes, where pupils see less of the teacher, they are more likely to turn to one another for help with their work, and, as Table 9.9 also shows, such co-operation is positively related to progress.

These correlations, between class size and co-operation between pupils, and between such co-operation and progress, are fairly small ones, although they do reach statistical significance. They suggest that, just as teachers compensate for large classes by increasing the amount of time they spend working with pupils, so pupils can themselves compensate to some extent by working together.

Summary

The main conclusion from the results presented in this chapter is to re-emphasize the importance of teaching style with regard to pupil progress. When the effects of pupil sex, pupil type and teaching style are considered together, only teaching style has an independent effect on progress. Moreover, this effect operates uniformly across the sexes and pupil types. Class size did not affect progress in our sample of classrooms; and pupil types, despite the fact that they differ considerably in the amount of time their members spend working, also did not have independent effects. The implications of this last point will be considered in the next chapter.

The relevance of teaching styles emerges again in the analysis of the relationship of pupil attitudes to progress, and, in particular, in the analysis of pupil motivation. The over-all correlation between progress and motivation disguises considerable differences between the teaching styles. In the more successful teaching styles, individual pupil motivation does not affect progress. But in the less successful styles, well-motivated pupils make more progress than less well-motivated ones.

Part V

Effective teaching in the primary classroom

Chapter 10

Effective teaching in the primary classroom

It is a curious fact that, just as there appear to be cycles of fashion in the advocacy of certain teaching methods, the language used by those reflecting these different approaches draws heavily on imagery associated with nature's 'annual cycle'. Thus as Bernstein and Davies (1969) comment, the Plowden Report appears to be 'committed to a particular horticultural view of child nature' favouring spring-like images associated with growth and development. At the moment, however, the imagery is autumnal. The talk is of the need to prune drastically and to get rid of dead wood in teaching, as a prelude for a prolonged winter period of retrenchment.

Good and bad teaching

Throughout these seasonal changes there has naturally been no shortage of advice directed at teachers, and those responsible for training them, regarding ways and means of improving the system. For example, a prominent polytechnic director has recently argued that the supposed fall in standards is due to the poor quality of entrants into the profession during the late 1960s and early 1970s. Looking back over his period in office prior to retirement, he gave a newspaper interview (*The Times*, 22 November 1979) in which he recommended drastic pruning at all levels of the teaching profession. Citing the parallel of Montgomery's decimation of the 8th Army Officer Corps before the battle of El Alamein, he claimed that the problem of the educational system would be easily solved if only all the bad teachers were weeded out.

Such critics, of course, seem quite confident that there would be no difficulty in distinguishing between good and bad teachers. This in spite of the evidence acquired as far back as 1929, when Charters asked 'educational experts' to list the characteristics of 'good' teaching. These eminent members of the profession put together a list consisting of eighty-three separate traits. Only six of these obtained a wide measure of support, including such characteristics as adaptability, honesty and imagination. Such descriptions are so general as to be useless for diagnostic, remedial or selective purposes (Charters and Waples, 1929).

The *Times* interview is indicative of the prominence given by the press to any criticism of modern teaching practice. During the 1970s there has been continual sniping by critics at recent innovations, such as secondary reorganization and the associated changes at primary school level. A return to more traditional practices is usually advocated as a panacea for the supposed ills within the system. The critics seem endowed with remarkably short memories. They forget the strains inflicted on children and teachers by the demands of the 11-plus, and ignore studies of the effects of the selective system on those who failed the examination (Hargreaves, 1966) as also on some of those who gained grammar school places (Lacey, 1970).

Even a casual visitor to a modern primary classroom must be struck by the fact that many of the suggestions which come from such critics seem to have little immediate relevance to the issues confronting a teacher with, for example, a class of thirty lively ten-year-olds. The accommodation, particularly if it is of recent origin, is likely to be cramped and inadequate; there may well be a shortage of stimulating materials. There may be a constant stream of interruptions by pupils from other classes who have mislaid property, or perhaps by the head teacher coming to check on a point before dealing with some issue with a local authority or parent. Such happenings are well documented in the accounts of the typical primary teacher's day (Hilsum and Cane, 1971). In the face of these difficulties, it is not surprising that many teachers have become convinced that the debate taking place in the educational media has little of practical value to offer. Since from time to time the flames of controversy are fanned by the publication of yet another research report, the profession has also come to regard the evidence presented by researchers in much the same light. In this situation, teachers have tended to concentrate on the issues relating to everyday life in the classroom, attempting to get through each day as best they can while shielding themselves from criticisms directed from the outside.

Though understandable, this position has its dangers. To cease to talk about issues can mean ceasing to do anything about them. When this happens, individual teachers may become very isolated, with little incentive to evaluate and improve their teaching. In extreme cases the need for such continuous evaluation is not even admitted. Some schools seem remarkably confident that they know what is best for their pupils. This attitude can lead to a position where teachers tend to excuse the indefensible, or to pretend that certain practices are either rare or never happen. Researchers whose findings indicate anything to the contrary are sometimes pilloried, or told that they ought to get back into a class-room to deal with real problems.

During the course of the ORACLE research, the observers have spent well over 1,000 days in classrooms. For the most part, the pupils seemed to have been hard-working and well disciplined. Although teachers, too, worked hard, in a number of cases the observers reported that the teaching, particularly of number and language skills, was often repetitive and somewhat boring. The observation data support this view. Teaching basics took up nearly two-thirds of class time, with pupils working silently on their own for most of this period. When a teacher did inter-act with a pupil about work, it was likely to be at a very low intellectual level. A quarter of the sample in the first year of the study were *habitual changers*, who had low levels of interaction on most of the categories of the Teacher Record.

One such lesson took place in a mixed-ability class of twelve-year-olds in an eight-to-twelve middle school, and is worth attention here. To relieve the monotony of number work, the teacher designed a numerical crossword puzzle where the clues consisted of multiplication and division sums. The children, however, spent most of the period drawing the crossword grid and shading in the appropriate squares. In other classrooms, the observers saw numerous examples of copying from the board, once to the accompaniment of music from a record player, while in many classes the only art consisted of drawing and colouring a picture after completing a piece of writing. There seemed to the observers, who were experienced teachers, little of educative value in these activities. For the most part they seemed a device for filling in time. Perhaps more surprising was the fact that the children, although not enthusiastic, tackled such tasks with quiet resignation. Given the obvious difficulties involved in the management of lessons where the pupils are more actively involved, it may be that young teachers, in particular, preferred to avoid these challenges by setting 'safe', intellectually undemanding tasks. Similar experiences have been described at the top end of the secondary school by Willis (1977), and are reflected in the guarded comments of the inspectors in both the primary and secondary reports (HMI survey, 1978; HMI survey, 1979).

Research in the primary classroom

Researchers who seek to observe and record events in the classroom, therefore, have a difficult and delicate path to tread. Almost certainly the media will tend to stress any negative aspects of their findings. Teachers who read such accounts will thereby become convinced that the researcher is not on their side. They are then likely to ignore the results or to respond in a defensive manner. While responsible researchers, who seek to influence classroom practice, cannot suppress unpleasant findings, they must seek ways of presenting them which will allow subsequent discussion to take place in terms which can be of help to teachers. Only by doing so can they hope to interest the profession in what they have to say.

The previous reference to dull repetitive lessons was not intended as a direct criticism of the teachers concerned. The purpose of including these observer accounts was to stress how inappropriate are many of the suggestions for improving teaching, put forward in the media by supporters of traditional methods. In the light of evidence presented in this book, a call for a return to basics, with the emphasis on rote learning and factual recall, would seem a particularly ineffective remedy. Both the observers' accounts and the evidence from the observation data suggests that already too much time is spent on such activities.

It is reasonable to assume that most teachers aim to provide pupils with a stimulating learning environment. Primary teachers face considerable difficulties in seeking to achieve this goal. Unlike specialists at secondary level, they are expected to be experts and enthusiasts in a whole range of subjects. It would not be surprising if on occasions their interest flagged, or if, faced with the problem of coping with relatively large classes, they sought a respite by turning to 'time-filling' activities.

The value of observational research is that, having identified successful teachers, it can then go on to describe for the benefit of the less successful what it is that such teachers do in their classrooms, and the effect this has on pupils. It provides a mass of evidence with which to evaluate the claims made for particular practices in terms of the observed behaviours of both teachers and pupils. As such, it adds an extra dimension to the debate, which has previously been conducted almost solely in terms of pupil progress on various tests. Detailed analysis of the results both in this and in the previous book, *Inside the Primary Classroom*, suggests that whatever criteria are used to evaluate present teaching methods, they are likely to lead to the over-all conclusion that no single approach can claim to have a monopoly of desirable characteristics. Nor do the successful approaches fit easily into the rather simplistic descriptions based on the notion of a dichotomy between traditional and progressive methods. The hope is that the more detailed descriptions of teaching which emerged from the ORACLE study will shift the debate away from the acrimonious exchanges of the past, and encourage teachers to become more involved in the continuing debate about modern primary practice.

To assist this process, the remainder of the chapter summarizes the results presented earlier in the book, particularly the important conclusions relating to teaching style. An attempt will then be made to identify some of the classroom behaviours which serve to distinguish the successful teachers in the sample from the less successful ones. In the concluding chapter the practical consequences of these results will be discussed, and particularly their implications for those who are responsible for inducting students into the profession.

Essential elements in the teaching process

In *Inside the Primary Classroom*, a descriptive model was used to facilitate discussion of the relationship between different aspects of the teaching process. The model was partly derived from the psychological theories of Piaget, as developed by Taba (1966) and subsequently modified by Strasser (1967). Other elements in the model were introduced as a result of the emphasis given to certain variables in recent reviews of classroom research (Dunkin and Biddle, 1974; Harnischfeger and Wiley, 1975). An important distinction was made between *teaching strategies* and *teaching tactics*. The former are the result of the teacher's over-all attempt to translate her aims into practice, while the latter consist of the minute-by-minute exchanges which take place between teacher and pupil once the lesson has commenced. In particular, the ORACLE research has concentrated on the use of different organizational strategies, and the use of consistent sets of tactics which are defined as the teaching style. In this research the tactics were monitored using two observational systems, which focused mainly on the cognitive and managerial transactions between teachers and pupils. Teaching style, as defined in the study, does not take account of differences in the affective behaviour of teachers.

Teaching tactics both mediate and are themselves mediated by the pupil's behaviour. Each of these factors might be expected to play a part in predicting pupil progress, as measured in the short term by the gains on various tests of achievement. An important issue in developing the model concerns the relative influence which both the teaching style and pupil behaviour have on progress. Although this question can be satisfactorily answered only when the results of the process data for all three years of the ORACLE study have been examined, it is possible to draw some tentative conclusions from the present analysis.

The results for the tests of basic skills are summarized in Table 4.4 (p. 70). One method of simplifying the data, to gauge the relative success of each style, is to construct a league table based on a points system. Here the system used gives three points to the most successful style on each test. Progressively less points are given to others, according to the level of statistical significance attached to the difference of pupils' average residual gains from that for the successful style. Two points are awarded to a style which does not differ significantly from the most successful style, one point to a style differing at the 5 per cent level and no points to a style differing at the 1 per cent level or beyond. The final league positions are shown in Table 10.1. *Infrequent changers* are placed top rather than *class enquirers*, who have the same points total, because on none of the three tests did their pupils' average residual differ significantly from the most successful style. In reading, the *class enquirers* were not as successful as either the *infrequent changers*, the top style, or the *individual monitors*. Although the *group instructors*, who were third, scored three points fewer than the *class enquirers*, they too made above-average progress on the tests of mathematics, language skills and reading.

In looking for common characteristics among the top three styles which might explain their success, the most striking and perhaps most important feature was that the teachers all achieved above-average levels of interactions with their pupils. The actual nature of these exchanges will be considered later, but it is necessary to say something of the manner by which the teachers achieved these higher levels.

The *class enquirers* engaged, as their name implies, in the highest levels of class teaching. In such classrooms the teacher tended to talk to the whole class for about one-third of the time, and then go from child to child checking on the progress of work. Consequently, much of the interaction of the pupils in such classes consisted of listening and watching what the teacher was doing or saying to other pupils. *Group instructors*, on the other hand, had the highest levels of interaction with groups of children. When, however, the teacher moved away from a group to deal with a problem elsewhere, then the children who were left tended to behave in a similar fashion to those taught by the *class enquirers*. They either worked on their own, or watched and listened to the teacher talking to the children in another group.

Table 10.1 League positions in basic skills

	No. of tests	MS	NSD	S5	S1	Total points
Infrequent changers	3	1	2	0	0	7
Class enquirers	3	2	0	1	0	7
Group instructors	3	0	1	2	0	4
Individual monitors	3	0	0	1	2	1
Habitual changers	3	0	0	0	3	0
Rotating changers	3	0	0	0	3	0

KEY: MS   Most successful style   3 points per test

NSD   Not significantly different from most successful style   2 points per test

S5   Significantly different from most successful style at the 5 per cent level   1 point per test

S1   Significantly different from most successful style at 1 per cent or beyond   0 points

The nearest and most successful approach to total individualization of the learning process was achieved by the *infrequent changers*, who nevertheless still had the second-highest level of class instruction. Children in these classes interacted more frequently with the teacher because of the teacher's extremely high work rate. The most successful *infrequent changers* were interacting with children for nearly 90 per cent of the day, leaving little time to spare for other activities to do with housekeeping and monitoring. Such teachers only managed to achieve such rates by dint of very effective organization, which allowed them the extra time for dealing with pupils. They appear very similar to the 'super teacher' described by Wragg (1978).

In terms of over-all progress in basic skills, there was no one particular organizational strategy which succeeded more than others. Although there was a tendency for the use of class teaching to be associated with success in mathematics, this approach seemed less effective over-all for below-average achieving pupils (Table 4.5, p. 75). Above-average achievers who were taught by the *individual monitors* did particularly well, compared to the remaining pupils who were taught by that style. When this latter result is considered in the light of the finding in Chapter 9 that highly motivated pupils who were taught by this style were also very successful, it would suggest that such children survive many of the disadvantages of these classrooms where there are upwards of thirty children. The use of one-to-one contact between teachers and pupils does, however, seem to be important in developing the skills measured by the tests of reading and comprehension. Here the *individual monitors* made the second highest amount of progress after that of the *infrequent changers*. These two styles had the highest levels of interaction with individual children.

Teaching and pupil behaviour

The second issue which arises from the descriptive model used in this study concerns the relationship between teaching style and pupil behaviour, together with the relative influence of each of these factors on pupils' progress. When taken together, the findings suggest that it is the teaching style which is the more important factor. Contrary to Harnischfeger and Wiley's (1975) view, none of the results support the notion that the time pupils spent working was the most important determinant of pupils' progress. The time-on-task variable never accounted for more than 3 per cent of the variation in pupils' scores on the Richmond Tests.

It could be, however, that previous findings which are claimed to support this thesis used tests which measured less complex activities than those which the Richmond Tests assessed. If a class spends considerable time learning multiplication tables, then it is logical to expect pupils to do particularly well on items which ask them, for instance, to find the missing number in a multiplication sum. It is less likely (though possible) that knowing one's tables will result in superior performance on items which call for the use of multiplication procedures in solving a problem. In this context, the most important aspect may be, as Taba (1966) suggests, the strategies that have been learnt about tackling problems. Indeed, there is evidence from a recent American study (Solomon and Kendall, 1979) that the time-on-task variable does not correlate very well with success in problem-solving activities. The Richmond Tests were 'objective' referenced, in the sense defined in Chapter 1. All the tests included a range of items attempting to test higher-order cognitive skills as defined by Bloom (1956) and his co-workers.

There is further evidence from this study suggesting that teaching style is the dominant influence. In Chapter 5, analysis of pupil progress in basic skills using the class average as a unit of analysis yielded almost identical results as when individual scores of target pupils were used in Chapter 4. This points to some of the effects of teaching style operating across the class, irrespective of individual pupil differences within it. Additional support for this view comes from the analysis of the differential rates of progress of each pupil type in Chapter 9. The *solitary workers* do well on the Richmond Tests, as might be expected since 64 per cent of the pupils taught by one of the most successful teaching styles, the *class enquirers*, are of this type. But if being a *solitary worker* is the more important determinant of success, then pupils of this same type who are taught by other teaching styles should also do well. When this hypothesis was tested, however, it was found that controlling for teaching style reduced the differences between pupil types until they were no longer statistically significant (Tables 9.1 to 9.3).

Solitary workers are relatively successful only because they belong to a class taught by a *class enquirer*. Similarly, being an *attention seeker* in the class of an *infrequent changer*, or for that matter a well-motivated pupil in the class of an *individual monitor*, is also more likely to bring success. In Chapter 8 it was shown that the distribution of the pupil types for each style varies considerably. When the teaching tactics used by each style are examined, there appears to be a logical explanation in each case of why this should be so.

The result for the *intermittent workers* is of particular interest. It was shown in *Inside the Primary Classroom* that these pupils used up on average one day each week chatting to their neighbours and generally avoiding work. They might have been expected to do less well than the *solitary workers*, who in terms of their application were model pupils. In fact, both types of pupils did equally well. As Tables 9.1 to 9.3 show, they made identical progress in terms of the difference between their pre- and post-test scores (raw-score gains), and there were non-significant differences in their mean residual-change scores. This demonstrates very clearly that, for the ORACLE pupils, progress is not strongly related to the time that children spend at their task. However, the finding also provides some confirmation for the observers' comments about the nature of work which is done in mathematics, language and reading.

The evidence indicates that these *intermittent workers* are not just lazy pupils with low levels of concentration. Indeed, it would appear that some are able to cope easily with the work, and that, rather than collect another worksheet with similar examples, they seek to eke out the time in conversation with their fellow pupils. This suggests that what is needed is not just a greater emphasis on basics, as some critics recommend, but more varied and exciting activities across the curriculum to stimulate these pupils. Ways and means of achieving this aim will be discussed in the final chapter.

Further evidence of the impact of teaching style on pupil behaviour will emerge from the complete analysis of the second- and third-year observation data. It will be possible to see what happens to an *intermittent worker* in the class of an *individual monitor* when he moves to a new teacher who is, say, a *class enquirer*. This issue will be taken up again in a future book reporting on the effect of transfer to secondary school.

Teaching style and related variables

The final source of evidence suggesting that the teaching style is an important determinant of pupils' progress is derived from the analysis in Chapters 5 and 9 of the ways in which styles achieve their effects. In Chapter 5, a wide range of variables that might be expected to influence pupil performance were considered, alongside the effect of teaching style, in an effort to reduce the differences produced by the latter. These variables ranged from the social-class mix of the pupils to some of the organizational characteristics of the school, such as the use of vertical grouping and the existence of open plan areas. A similar analysis was carried out in Chapter 9 in relation to various aspects of pupil behaviour, such as anxiety and motivation. Only two of these variables appeared to exert an appreciable effect on teaching style. To some extent, the differences attributable to style could be explained away by the fact that the successful teachers engaged in higher amounts of either group or class teaching. These differences can, however, be put down to the earlier finding that these organizational strategies are means by which teachers increase the amount of teacher-pupil interaction, the main ingredient of style as defined in this study.

By far the greater influence appeared to be the age (or experience) of the teacher. Here again, common sense would suggest that a teacher's age in itself was not a sufficient reason for the pupils' success. It seems logical to suppose that it was what these older teachers did that made the difference. The best illustration of this explanation concerns the contrast between the *individual monitors* and the *infrequent changers*. In many respects, both these groups of teachers appear to have similar aims. Both wish to maximize the amount of time they spend with individual pupils. Unlike the *infrequent changers*, the teachers who are *individual monitors* did not in practice achieve this aim. Much of their time was spent keeping the children at work, so that their predominant characteristic was silent monitoring, the handing back of work, marked without any oral comment.

In *Inside the Primary Classroom* it was shown that the *individual monitors* included some of the younger teachers in the sample, while the average *infrequent changer* was in her mid-thirties. The most plausible explanation for these differences is that, with experience, the *infrequent changers* have been able to increase their work rate, to the point where they can overcome many of the difficulties experienced by the younger *individual monitors*. In the same way, the *rotating changers* appear to be a less successful version of the *group instructors*. Both of these styles make use of groups for teaching purposes. The *rotating changers*, however, do not increase the levels of group interaction, and the descriptions of the observers suggested that there were considerable organizational problems involved in these regular changes from one curriculum group to another. Again, it is the *rotating changers* who, of the two styles, have the younger teachers. If differences in age can be accounted for in this way, then it raises important questions for those responsible for initial training. This issue will be taken up again in the next and final chapter.

Teaching and study skills

Although the emphasis given to the basic skills, in evaluating the effectiveness of different teaching styles in this study, reflects the general concern about such measures within the national debate on primary school practice, there are also strong grounds for including some assessment of the pupils' capacity for independent study. The study-skill exercises used in this research were designed to achieve this objective. As with the basic skills, the results on the study-skill exercises can be expressed as league positions using the same points system allocated earlier. This time the relevant data were obtained from Table 7.7 (p. 138).

Study-skill exercises were somewhat more complex to analyse than basic skills. Each exercise had several dimensions, and in Table 7.7 only the seven where over-all significant differences were found between the most and least successful style were included. As with basic skills, three points are awarded to the most successful style on each of the seven dimensions, giving a maximum possible score of twenty-one. Table 10.2 shows the final order. It was shown in Chapter 6 that, in terms of over-all differences, the pupils of the *habitual changers* and *individual monitors* were the most successful, having the highest adjusted means on four out of the seven dimensions. However, it can be seen from Table 10.2 that the *class enquirers* are now second to the

Table 10.2 League positions in study skills

	No. of tests	MS	NSD	S5	S1	Total points
Habitual changers	7	2	3	0	2	12
Class enquirers	7	1	3	1	2	10
Individual monitors	7	2	1	1	3	9
Infrequent changers	7	1	2	1	3	8
Group instructors	7	1	1	2	3	7
Rotating changers	7	0	0	1	6	1

KEY: MS   Most successful style   3 points per test
       NSD   Not significantly different
                from most successful style   2 points per test
       S5   Significantly different from most
                successful style at 5 per cent level   1 point per test
       S1   Significantly different from most
                successful style at 1 per cent or beyond   0 points

habitual changers. The pupils of *individual monitors* did particularly badly on the mapping exercise, and it is this fact which accounts for their position below the *class enquirers.* These differences are very slight, since the points margin between second and fifth positions is not so marked as with basic skills in Table 10.1. The *group instructors,* in fifth position, are only three points below the *class enquirers* who came second, but six points above the *rotating changers* who are bottom.

The result is interesting, because the two styles at the bottom of the league for the basic skills obtained totally dissimilar results on the study-skill exercises. The *habitual changers* compensate for their previous poor performance, but the *rotating changers* again find themselves at the bottom of the table, by a considerable points margin. Part of the success of the *habitual changers* must be attributed to the fact that they devote more time to these aspects of pupil learning. In Chapter 5 it was shown that this particular teaching style gave the least time to basic skills, and correspondingly additional periods to topic work and other similar activities. The observational data from *Inside the Primary Classroom* showed that this group also made the lowest use of most of the categories on the Teacher Record involving telling and questioning. They were known, from the observers' accounts, to make frequent changes of organization from class to group to individualized work, particularly reverting to class teaching whenever they detected a drop in the level of activity among the pupils. Much of the instruction was by means of demonstrating, and showing pupils how to perform tasks. Apart, therefore, from the emphasis which the *habitual changers* give to practical activities such as graphing and map making, there is little in the observational data which suggests reasons for their success.

The *rotating changers* appeared to be the one style which, over-all, had little to commend it. Here groups of pupils sitting at the same table all worked on the same curriculum area. When the time came to change from, say, mathematics to English, all the pupils in the group either moved to the table which was reserved for English work, or stayed in the same place but exchanged their mathematics books for English ones with another group. This strategy appeared to be a device for easing problems of organization, rather than for increasing the levels of teacher and pupil interaction. Although the children were working on similar tasks, the teacher seldom interacted with them as a group, preferring to deal with individuals. It was rare to find the pupils co-operating over work when the teacher was not present. Often the timing of these changes from one subject area to the next appeared to the observers to be somewhat arbitrary, causing breaks in concentration in some pupils who were happily working at the task. This in part explains why, along with the *individual monitors*, this style had the second highest number of *intermittent workers*, having the highest levels of distraction in the sample.

It is of interest that the *rotating changers* are joined at the bottom of the study-skill league by the *group instructors*, who also make use of groups. The data from *Inside the Primary Classroom* indicated, however, that the *group instructors* also function in a manner very dissimilar from that recommended by Plowden. The use of group work as a medium for facilitating independent study skills should not therefore be considered a failure as a result of the findings presented here. More research is needed into the working of such groups and, if the difficulties involved in getting them to function correctly can be overcome, there are grounds for suggesting that there should be a greater stress on the use of this particular strategy.

The nature of the interactions involved in successful teaching

The conclusion drawn in the earlier part of this chapter was that teaching style, here defined in terms of the categories on the Teacher Record observation schedule, was the most important influence on the pupils' progress in the basic skills. Both the *class enquirers* and the *infrequent changers* did relatively well on the study-skill exercises also, although here the evidence is not sufficient to suggest that teaching tactics are an important element in the level of pupils' performance.

The question arises as to the nature of the interactions between teachers and pupils which contribute to the latter's success. Each style has its own set pattern in the use of certain categories. However, it may be that over and above this there are certain behaviours which are characteristic of *all* successful teachers from within the three groups. To examine this issue, the most successful teachers from the *group instructors, class enquirers* and *infrequent changers* (in terms of overall pupil progress in basic skills) were extracted from the sample, and the profile of their use of the categories on the Teacher Record examined. Examination of the combined score on the three tests of basic skills for the eight target pupils in each class shows that for the *group instructors*, the third most successful group in Table 10.1, there were three teachers whose pupils achieved almost identical highest scores. In the *infrequent changers* there were two teachers whose pupils had scores above this figure, while among the *class enquirers* there were six more successful teachers, on this criterion. Average use of the categories of the Teacher Record by each of these three groups of successful teachers is shown in Table 10.3, together with the average values for the whole sample.

With so few teachers it is not possible to make valid statistical comparisons, but it is interesting to look for categories where all the successful teachers are either above or below the average value for the whole sample. In addition, it should be expected that, where there is a trend for successful teachers to score, for example, above the average value, then *infrequent changers* and *class enquirers* should have higher group averages than *group instructors*, who are below them in the league.

The profiles of each of the three styles in Table 10.3 reinforce the

Table 10.3 Interaction patterns of successful ORACLE teachers:
Teacher Record (percentage of total observations)

	All teachers	Successful class enquirers	Successful group instructors	Successful infrequent changers
Questions:				
Fact	3.5	3.4	2.7	4.4
Closed solutions	2.2	2.4	1.7	3.4
Open solutions	0.6	0.9	0.6	1.3
Task supervision	3.9	4.3	2.8	3.2
Routine	1.8	2.7	1.9	3.5
Task Statement:				
Fact	6.9	8.3	11.4	7.1
Ideas	2.5	3.6	1.0	1.9
Telling	12.6	10.4	9.4	11.2
Praising	1.0	1.6	0.4	0.9
Feedback	9.6	12.1	18.7	14.3
Routine Statement:				
Information	6.5	8.9	7.3	6.9
Feedback	2.0	3.2	2.0	3.3
Critical control	2.3	1.6	2.9	2.9
Small talk	1.3	2.1	0.4	1.5
Silent interaction:				
Marking	10.1	3.3	9.0	12.0
Audience:				
Individual	55.8	41.5	50.7	66.0
Group	7.5	7.0	15.6	5.5
Class	15.1	33.2	14.3	18.1
Summary:				
Total interaction	78.4	81.7	80.6	89.6
Total questions	12.0	13.7	9.7	15.8
Total task	15.7	18.6	17.4	18.1
Total higher-order	5.3	6.9	3.3	6.6
Total number	58	6	3	2

descriptions provided for these groups in Chapter 2. The *infrequent changers* have the highest levels of questioning over-all, and the *class enquirers* have the highest level of statements of ideas, give more praise and appear highly organized in the way they supply routine information. The *group instructors*, as their name implies, have the highest number of statements of fact, and although this was not an important characteristic of the style over-all, these two successful teachers also gave nearly twice the amount of feedback compared to the whole sample, presumably because the increased activity of the pupils demanded a response on the part of the teacher. The features in Table 10.3 which show a consistent trend across all three groups of successful teachers are higher than average proportions of routine questions, the number of factual statements and the amount of feedback given. The three groups of successful teachers are less likely to engage in task-supervision statements, where pupils are told what to do.

Although the use of statements of ideas, closed and open questions is relatively low when these categories are grouped together in the final four rows of the table, both the *class enquirers* and the *infrequent changers* are above average in the use of the total number of higher-order interactions. The fact that the *group instructors* fail to reach similar levels has been commented on in Chapter 4, and in *Inside the Primary Classroom*. This style is less successful than the other two, but the data from the second year of the study reveal that there is no intrinsic reason why use of a grouping strategy should preclude the use of higher-order interactions. As indicated in Chapter 2, *group instructors* in year two of the study in fact increase the number of such exchanges.

Of some significance may be the fact that all three groups of successful teachers had more task interactions than the typical teacher in the sample. This follows from the earlier point that the successful styles have the highest levels of interactions over-all. Nevertheless, it is interesting to see that the two most successful teachers from the *infrequent changers* style were interacting with pupils for nearly 90 per cent of the time in which observation was carried out. Within this high rate of working, they engaged not only in higher levels of questioning but also, like the *individual monitors*, in more silent marking than the typical teacher. This reinforces the view of them as special examples of the *individual monitors*, who, by dint of extremely hard work, are able to compensate for the difficulties of using an individualized approach in large-sized classes.

Successful teaching and organizational and curricular strategies

A further aspect of these successful teachers concerns their relationship with the classification used by Bennett, in the Lancaster study, to describe formal and informal teaching (Bennett, 1976). In Chapter 8 of *Inside the Primary Classroom* it was shown that the characteristics of the two ORACLE teaching styles, which in terms of their organization appeared most similar to Bennett's extremes, showed little relationship to the nineteen variables from which the informal-formal dichotomy was derived. Data on these variables were collected by the observers using the various instruments listed in Table 1.2 (p. 22), particularly the teacher questionnaire (TQ) and the grouping instrument (GI). The small number of teachers involved here makes it inappropriate to look at the actual percentages across each of the successful styles, as in the original Bennett study. It is of some interest, however, to examine the key variables which Bennett argued were important characteristics of formal teaching.

The figures for the eleven successful teachers are interesting, and reveal no systematic tendency towards either the formal or informal ends of Bennett's continuum. Five out of eleven teachers allowed a choice of seats. Nine out of eleven did not seat by ability. While the majority set regular tests (nine out of eleven), none set homework or gave marks, and only two of the eleven teachers awarded stars. Five out of the eleven teachers had above-average levels of integrated subject teaching. Three of these five were *class enquirers*, whereas none of Bennett's formal teachers favoured an integrated approach.

Apart from regular testing, the only other variable showing consistency among the successful teachers concerned the need for quiet in the classroom. Ten out of the eleven teachers insisted that the noise level should be minimal. While supporters of traditional methods will express satisfaction at this result, seeing it as evidence of a need for old-fashioned discipline and control, the data acquired from the observation of these classrooms suggest an alternative explanation as to why quiet was so important.

A striking finding from *Inside the Primary Classroom* concerned the amount of time pupils spent working on their own. Even in the classes of teachers who preferred an individualized approach to learning, pupils engaged in most of their interaction with the teacher in a class rather than a group or individual setting. Much of this interaction was therefore as part of an audience, listening and watching the teacher engage in conversation with another pupil. One possible way of compensating for these low levels of interaction with the teacher is for pupils to pick up snatches of conversation dealing with problems of other children elsewhere in the classroom. Thus, successful pupils may become adept at getting on with their work, but at the same time keeping one ear open for the kind of information which is of help to them in completing the worksheet or exercise. Such a strategy could only be employed if there was comparatively little background noise in the classroom. Most of the observers found it easy to code conversation for the Teacher Record without needing to move from a permanent position in the classroom. If these instructions could be recorded by our observers without moving from their seats, then they could also be overheard by any pupils who wished to listen.

Some of Bennett's findings receive support from the American study by Solomon and Kendall (1979); for example, that low-achieving boys prefer informal classrooms, while anxious children do best in formal ones. The American research also supports Bennett's suggestion that, whatever the teaching approach, the structuring and correct sequencing of the lesson is an important ingredient of pupil success. Solomon and Kendall also collected observation data of a similar kind to that obtained in this study. However, their method of analysis involved combining this data with a large number of other variables. After fifteen separate factor analyses, the resulting scales were clustered to produce descriptions of teaching styles and pupil types. It is difficult to compare these descriptions with the ones obtained in this study. In obtaining the ORACLE teaching styles, only the observational data were clustered. Other variables were then examined in turn, using analysis of covariance to control for their effects. This made it possible to explain how particular styles achieved their success. In Solomon's and Kendall's clusters, so many variables are combined together that it is difficult to seek out clear-cut explanations of this kind. Comparison of the two approaches to the analysis of classroom data suggests considerable advantages for the procedures used in this research.

The study has shown that, although there are common elements in the practice of successful teachers, different styles achieve these effects in different ways. *Class enquirers* use more statements of ideas by way of raising the level of intellectual activity, whereas the *infrequent changers* use open-ended questions to similar effect. *Infrequent changers* prefer pupils to work out their own tasks rather than telling them what to do, whereas the *class enquirers* usually give instructions once to the whole class with enough clarity to ensure that they do not need repeating. Both styles, therefore, for different reasons, make less use of task-supervision statements than do the less successful teachers. The observers' descriptive accounts of lessons bear out these findings. One observer commented on the most successful *infrequent changer's* aim that his pupils should take increasing responsibility for the management of their own learning tasks as the year progressed. Another observer described the exposition given by the most successful *class enquirer* on converting fractions to decimals as so lucid that she understood the procedure clearly for the first time in her life.

Thus, in summary, the successful teachers all engage in above-average levels of interaction with the pupils. They appear to devote considerable effort to ensuring that the routine activities proceed smoothly; they engage in high levels of task statements and questions, and provide regular feedback. At the same time, they also encourage the children to work by themselves towards solutions to problems. The majority make above-average use of higher-order interactions, including statements of ideas and more open-ended types of questioning. They also manage to avoid the need to provide children continually with instructions on how to carry out the set tasks. This comes about either because they prefer pupils to find out for themselves or because their initial instructions are so clear that there is little need to follow up by further exchanges. These teachers, while using different organizational strategies, and emphasizing certain other specific characteristics of their particular style, nevertheless have in common that they interact with the pupils more frequently than teachers using the less successful styles. Increased levels in the above kinds of teacher and pupil contact appear to be an important determinant of pupils' progress.

Chapter 11

Implications of ORACLE
findings for teaching

Before turning to consider·the implications of these results for those
involved with initial and in-service programmes, it is perhaps important
to examine the criticisms directed at the use of systematic observation
for these purposes. There are those who doubt that the findings obtained from studies using observation schedules such as the Teacher
and Pupil Records have much relevance for the practising teacher.
Among them is Professor Stenhouse, who argues that interaction
analysis is something of a 'cul-de-sac' in developing ideas about teaching
(Stenhouse, 1975, p. 148). While systematic observation provides
'mirrors of behaviour' (Simon and Boyer, 1970), for Stenhouse 'they
are distorting mirrors'.

He sees teaching as an art rather than a science. For him, the closest
parallel to the classroom is the stage, with every lesson a new performance. Attempts to make generalizations about classroom practice on the
basis of a number of randomly selected visits are therefore doomed to
failure, since the classroom observer, like the theatre audience on
different nights, undergoes a different experience on each occasion.
Stenhouse argues that the only feasible way to improve practice is to
engage in a type of research where the researcher works closely with a
teacher over an extended period, and where the subject of the research
arises from the problems identified by the teacher, rather than the
researcher. In this way, the study which emerges is 'vivid and generally
speaks directly to teachers', in a way which frequency counts are unable to do (Stenhouse, *ibid*., p. 151).

There are a number of issues which arise from these criticisms. In
the theatre such research is perhaps closely paralleled by the rehearsal period of a play. Here the actor will seek to interpret his character, and in discussion with the director and his fellow players will try

to refine his performance until it is in tune with the demands of the play. A final evaluation then takes place after the reaction of the audience is known.

In a similar manner, the teacher who takes part in this kind of research begins by reflecting on her aims, and describing the actions which she carries out in the classroom to achieve them. Working closely with the researcher, she attempts to evaluate her performance. Where videotapes or sound recording with stop-frame film are used to make a permanent record of these lessons, fellow teachers and sometimes pupils will help to enlarge the teacher's awareness of what is happening.

Just as actors value the closeness of the working relationships which are established during the rehearsal period, so too teachers should experience similar benefits when participating in these activities. This should lead not only to an enhanced awareness of the problems arising from the use of particular teaching methods, but also to a greater realization of their possibilities. What is not clear is whether it would lead a teacher to abandon rather than simply modify her classroom procedure so that, for example, a *rotating changer* might become a *class enquirer*. There is also evidence from other types of study that where teachers are doubtful about the success of their methods, recording and discussing transcripts of lessons can be counter-productive, causing a hardening of attitudes against the use of such aids (Salomon and McDonald, 1970). This suggests that the approach may work best where teachers are reasonably confident of the esteem of their colleagues, their pupils and the researcher. It may be less attractive to practitioners who are uncertain of themselves or who, like the *rotating changers* in this study, are seen to be unsuccessful.

A further difficulty is that in order to achieve the close relationships which the method demands, the numbers involved at any one time must be kept relatively small. As a large-scale approach concerned with improving teacher effectiveness this would seem to be a severe drawback, although it could be argued that once a teacher has come through the experience she can then take on the role of the researcher. The system is therefore seen to be self-perpetuating, although relatively slow moving in its advance.

It is, however, possible to draw some different conclusions from the analogy of teaching with acting. Theatre directors recognize that there are certain styles of acting which interact with an individual's own special qualities to determine how he approaches the demands of a specific part. Although no one would wish to describe an actor's performance solely in terms of these elements of style, nevertheless they can make an important contribution to his success. In some cases where an actor is uncertain of his ability to succeed in the part, the director may even concentrate on a small number of specific techniques in the hope that by mastering these the performer will gain confidence. Sometimes it is also the case that in the process of achieving these more limited goals an actor comes to change in other ways, which also improve the performance.

Those who support the use of systematic observation as an aid to improving teaching also argue that when teachers concentrate on improving one or two aspects of their classroom behaviour, this may in turn lead to even more dramatic changes. For example, the use of more open-ended questions, an ingredient of the successful ORACLE teachers, will not by itself guarantee greater effectiveness. A teacher who attempts to increase the number of such interactions, however, may find that she needs to question other aspects of both her teaching strategy and tactics. It may be that she needs to organize her classroom and her teaching time to allow for lengthy discussions, and in the process her relationship with her pupils may change so that the children become more open in their response. Indeed, the evidence from experiments designed to monitor the effect of using micro-teaching or interaction analysis in teacher training suggests that these techniques do result in an improvement in general performance (McIntyre *et al.*, 1977). Micro-teaching concentrates on improving a limited number of specific behaviours. Nevertheless, students who take part in such activities are generally rated more highly on all aspects of teaching practice by assessors than those who have not received this type of training.

The observers' descriptive accounts contain numerous comments supporting the view that their over-all impression of a classroom as workmanlike and productive was dependent on the presence or absence of certain kinds of interaction. For example, during the lesson described in the previous chapter where pupils shaded in crossword squares, the teacher's interaction with pupils consisted mainly of low-level class supervision statements telling children what to do, or paraphrasing the instructions already given. In Chapter 10 it was shown that a distinguishing feature of the unsuccessful teachers was their relatively high use of this category. The observer also noted that while pupils were drawing the numerical crossword there were few reasons for questioning or giving feedback, because the intellectual demands of the task were minimal.

Yet the same pupils were seen in another lesson where the regular teacher was absent, and had left a series of questions for the pupils to begin in class and complete for homework. At the start of the lesson the pupils were slow to settle. They were reluctant to set about the task, and the substitute teacher, instead of getting on with his own work, was forced to walk up and down and encourage the pupils repeatedly to 'get on with it'. At one point he asked one pupil a question about the work, which concerned simple ideas on wave motion. It appeared that the pupil had little understanding of what was involved. The teacher disappeared to return with a number of 'slinky' coil springs. He began to get the pupils in groups to experiment with the springs by shaking them and creating different wave patterns, and called for suggestions about ways of altering the number of waves, their length and width, without using technical terms with so young an audience. The pupils were asked to suggest a variety of hypotheses and then to test these out with spring coils.

Gradually a transformation overtook the classroom. What had earlier been an uninterested and bored class of pupils suddenly became actively involved and enthusiastic, as the teacher's own enthusiasm for the subject transferred itself to them. By the end of the period, the pupils had completed the set work successfully, tackling it with a sense of purpose, if not with quite the same enthusiasm with which they carried out the experiments.

Using the Teacher Record to code this lesson yielded a pattern with relatively high levels in the use of the higher cognitive categories. In addition, the higher level of pupil involvement and interest led to increased demands on the teacher for feedback. Pupils also began to have their own ideas about further experiments, and the teacher had to arrange for pupils with similar ideas to work together, and tell them where to find additional materials. The busier the class became, the more routine interactions of this sort took place. Teachers may care to examine their own practice in the light of these descriptions of the same pupils in two lessons. The teacher's enthusiasm and interest in the subject of waves meant that he was keen to pass on his ideas to the pupils. This in turn meant that the pupils had to respond in different ways, and this led to an increase in other kinds of interaction. But these changes appeared to initiate other changes in the teaching approach. In particular, organizational strategy changed, so that the pupils were working in the kinds of co-operative group recommended by Plowden. The groups formed and then reformed according to whether particular children had a common interest. At the same time, the more formal outcomes of the task were not neglected. The pupils completed the set work, which in most cases was checked by the teacher and approved.

Thus in this example, the increased level of interactions in the categories most used by the successful teachers was, for the observer, a key factor. We see value in teachers seeking to monitor their use of these categories and in attempting to increase their number. This, however, should be seen not as an end in itself, but as a means by which they can examine every aspect of their classroom practice. Where this is done, then the evidence from the ORACLE findings suggests that pupil performance is likely to be enhanced.

Implications for teacher training

Apart from the problems of individual teachers adapting their own particular style characteristics to match more closely the interaction patterns of the most successful teaching styles, there is a more important task facing many of them. This concerns the organizational strategy needed to increase the number of interactions during class time. This appeared to be a particular problem for young teachers in the sample who had the lowest levels of interaction with pupils. It has been shown that the more successful styles find extra time either by increasing the amount of class teaching, working with individuals at a frenzied pace, or, in fewer cases, by the use of grouping strategies. In spite of the evidence from *Inside the Primary Classroom*, that pupil groups experienced difficulty in working co-operatively together when the teacher was elsewhere, the use of grouping and of group work would seem to be the best strategy for new teachers to concentrate upon. This does not, of course, exclude the use of other organizational forms required to complement co-operative group working, but certain constraints operate which limit their feasibility.

If we consider first the solution adopted by the *class enquirers*, that is, increasing the amount of class teaching, this certainly appears the most economical way of increasing the amount of teacher-pupil interaction. As we have seen, it also maximizes the proportion of higher-order interactions across *all* styles. However, this solution is likely to prove impossible in many schools. In the ORACLE sample, some of the work areas in open plan schools were built to a specification which assumed that not all children in a register group would be in the area at the same time. Until numbers in these classes are drastically reduced it is impossible to find enough space for all the children. Again, for administrative or other reasons, many classes are vertically grouped by age. If such classes were to be split in two and each half taught as a separate unit, the problems occurring when children are left for long periods to work alone would remain.

Nevertheless, in many classes an increase in the use of whole-class teaching would be a practicable proposition. It may be remembered that, while the Plowden Report threw its weight behind individualization and argued that there was 'still too much' whole-class teaching, it conceded that there was a place for using this form. The ORACLE evidence reinforces this to some extent, though it should be remembered that the style which maximizes its use, the *class enquirers*, only used this approach for one-third of the time. It may be noted that whole-class teaching is still the form most widely used in Scandinavia,* the Soviet Union and Poland, for example, where primary-age classes are of 'mixed ability', as the great majority are now in Britain. The same is generally true of such classes in the United States.

In *Inside the Primary Classroom* it was suggested that, with the move to mixed ability classes, the whole-class teaching option tended to be rejected by teachers in this country (Chapter 3, p. 54). However, the ORACLE evidence suggests that the swing towards total individualization may have been misconceived, while the almost total rejection of class teaching by the *individual monitors* presented them with an insoluble problem. At its lowest level, whole-class teaching increases dramatically the amount of teacher-pupil interaction, though admittedly largely of a passive kind for individual pupils. The extent to which this is the case clearly depends on the teacher; a skilled teacher, for example, able to involve a class of pupils in thinking alongside her, using probing, querying techniques, as the *class enquirers* tended to do in our sample, can make a whole-class teaching lesson a stimulating experience, actively involving a high proportion of the children. Observations by one of the authors in Sweden and Denmark suggest that this is a more practicable solution than is commonly realized. However, one factor contributing to the relative success of this approach in Scandinavia is the relative smallness of class size. In Sweden there is a statutory *maximum* of twenty-five pupils in grades 1 to 3 (six to nine years), and of thirty in grade 4 and above (age nine upwards). In Denmark, by a Parliamentary Act of 1976, the maximum for grades 1 to 3 is only seventeen pupils, in grade 4 (nine to ten years) twenty-five and in grade 5 (ten to eleven years) twenty-nine. In practice, it appears that *average* class sizes are well below this in both countries; a series of sixteen

---

* Sweden has individualized schemes for mathematics. Otherwise whole-class teaching is generally used in primary classes.

lessons for primary-age children in several different schools observed in Lund (Sweden) recently yielded an average class size of seventeen (though in most cases desks were provided for twenty children); in Denmark the average size of observed classes was even lower.

A radical reduction in class size, of course, opens up various new strategies in terms of teacher-pupil interaction. It would certainly make class teaching easier, since a smaller class allows more individual pupil involvement in terms of direct interaction with the teacher.

A return to a new form of whole-class teaching, as an accepted component of teaching strategies, would imply a deliberate attempt by teachers both to bring the whole class along together, in terms of mastery of the basic skills (numeracy and literacy), and to develop class-management techniques, providing for the active involvement of all the pupils in the proceedings (or 'process'). While retaining this objective, the teacher must also learn ways of encouraging pupils to contribute at their own level in lessons. The 'slower' as well as the more advanced need to be given scope for self-expression, and each need to be challenged at his or her appropriate level. Such teaching is by no means impossible, as the *class enquirers* in this study have clearly found, and as the practice of skilled teachers on the continent indicates. It is therefore suggested that training in the skills of mixed-ability class teaching, the management of the whole class as a unit, should be a component of primary teachers' training. This point is made because it would appear, from the ORACLE evidence, that the *individual monitors,* who in general were the more recent products of the colleges, may lack these skills, and indeed were perhaps never introduced to them.

Turning now to individualization, we have seen that the problem here is that the amount of time which can be given to each individual pupil is on average so small that the vast majority of the interactions are necessarily purely didactic in character. This was one of the main conclusions of *Inside the Primary Classroom*, where it was suggested that the Plowden prescripts stressing discovery learning and the probing, questioning character of the teacher's role appear, at least with present class sizes, impossible of achievement (Chapter 9, pp. 157–8). If classes were reduced to Scandinavian average levels, say to an average of twenty rather than thirty as at present in this country, then clearly the Plowden prescripts might become more practicable. To achieve this should surely be a major objective. In the meantime, however, total individualization must be ruled out as an option. Indeed, if the amount of class teaching is increased, as suggested above, the time available for one-to-one teacher-pupil interaction is inevitably reduced. The only way of increasing the time available for individualized interaction at present is by increasing the proportion of over-all teacher-pupil inter-action, as the *infrequent changers* manage to do (90 per cent of lesson time compared to an average of 80 per cent); but it is probably too much to expect beginning teachers to reach such levels, and in fact the ORACLE evidence indicates that the *individual monitors* (largely young teachers) have the lowest percentage of teacher-pupil interaction of all teacher categories.

We return, therefore, to the original question of enhancing the extent of group work in the primary classroom, as the most practical, and probably the most rewarding means of increasing the level of teacher-pupil interaction, and of raising its quality. The Plowden Committee, it will be remembered, recommended the use of grouping both on the grounds that it economized teacher time and for positive reasons: the pupil gains from the 'cut and counter thrust of conver-sation', and from formulating hypotheses (*Inside the Primary Class-room*, pp. 46-7). One of our most striking findings was that, on average, our sample teachers spent very little time interacting with groups of pupils, and that many of the pupils in our sample never ex-perienced *co-operative* group work at all. Among the teaching styles identified, the *group instructors* maximized interaction with groups, but again the nature of that interaction was overwhelmingly didactic.

This, it seems to us, presents a genuine challenge both to teacher trainers and to researchers. At present, very little is known about the nature of the interactional process in small groups of children at the primary stage. Preliminary research carried out in connection with ORACLE has reached certain tentative conclusions (Tann, 1980). For 'successful' group work certain conditions appear to be necessary. These concern both intellectual and social aspects of such work. Of primary importance is the children's capacity to challenge each other's contributions, to raise questions and also to reason. These are intellectual skills which can be learned, but of course, they will (or may) not be learned unless teachers regard them as important. Then, for the main-tenance of self-sustaining groups, the tasks set need to be structured so as to demand co-operative working, and relevant resources must be provided (Worthington, 1974). Finally, there are certain social skills, for instance a degree of tolerance of each other's idiosyncrasies, a willingness to listen to each other and a certain level of responsible behaviour in the absence of an adult; in short, the skills needed to work co-operatively with others on a common task. Such skills, and they are complex, need to be learned, and so taught.

There will be, and are, difficulties with such a strategy. The research already mentioned has indicated that mixed-sex grouping is, at present, unproductive (unless carefully monitored); that all-girl groups tend to be very consensus oriented, that is, are primarily concerned to seek agreement and to reduce tension, and so do not probe and challenge each other. Interestingly, the groups that seem to gain most from co-operative work are those defined in the research as low-achieving boys. These appear to have found the group context one in which they were able to articulate their ideas, to challenge each other and to arrive at mutually acceptable solutions, providing the task did not require much writing. This research was carried out with children who had not, of course, received any training in the skills of small-group interaction, either intellectual or social.

In the training of student-teachers, it is suggested, particular attention might be given to familiarizing them with the techniques and skills involved in promoting small-group work in the classroom, and in changing pupils' attitudes so that they come to value the process of discussion as well as its end product. It is not only that a deliberate attempt needs to be made by teachers to develop the necessary skills and attitudes on the part of pupils, but there is also a problem for the teacher in the simultaneous management of a number of small groups. Clearly, many teachers today do utilize management skills of this kind, since spatial grouping is the normal practice, at least in the schools in the ORACLE sample. But our evidence indicates clearly that what might be called the pedagogic or educational value of existing small-group activity is relatively small. The level of pupil-pupil interaction was found to be low and the exchanges typically of very short duration; few of the pupils' conversations had anything to do with the set task.

The fact that, in the second year of classroom observation, as indicated in Chapter 2, the proportion in the sample of *group instructors* increased substantially, and that their interaction with pupils reached higher cognitive levels, indicates that this strategy is both practical and has further potential for development. Our conclusion is that training in group work and functioning should form an important aspect of teacher education, and that an effort should be made, through research in the classroom, to gain systematized knowledge about group functioning at the primary age.

The use of groups as a medium for instruction may be seen as something of a compromise between total individualization, on the one hand, and class teaching on the other. However, it is important to bear in mind that co-operative group work was strongly recommended, for instance, by Dewey and others, who saw it as a means of developing social attributes necessary in a democratic society. In this sense, such an approach has its own justification; its rationale lies not so much in economizing teachers' time as in its own intrinsic value.

There is, therefore, a sense in which grouping procedures may be seen as central to the techniques available to the teacher. If this is accepted, then appropriate organizational strategies would involve, first, a focus on whole-class teaching, utilized primarily as a means of sparking relevant group work, sustaining it over time, and bringing a given stage of work to a close. At the same time, co-operatively working small groups carry through carefully structured related tasks. Within this over-all system, individual one-to-one contact or interaction falls into place as a necessary adjunct, taking a subordinate but still essential role. Feedback to individual pupils will, of course, still be necessary, and this may prove to be the essential and remaining function of individualization, which is no longer regarded as being the central, even the single, mode of teacher-pupil interaction.

A deliberate shift in the distribution of teacher attention along these lines has, of course, considerable implications, the investigation of which was beyond the scope of the ORACLE programme. The thrust towards individualization, as practised in the majority of the classes in the ORACLE sample, finds its rationale in the theoretical stance adopted by the Plowden Committee, clearly much influenced by Piaget (*Inside the Primary Classroom*, Chapter 3). A move towards class teaching and co-operative group work, as suggested here, carries with it the implication that the Plowden theory, or rationale, is inadequate as a base or support for primary school teaching in practice. The fact is that the actual problems of class management, which Plowden tended to leave out of account, require that, for effective teaching, the teacher should relate more specifically to children in the whole-class or group situation, rather than in the individualized, one-to-one manner. A shift of practice of this kind implies reliance, to a greater extent than in the Plowden prescripts, on the characteristics that children have in common, rather than on those that differentiate them one from another.

Further important issues arise in relation to the patterning of the content of instruction, or of the children's learning activities, as already suggested. In a totally individualized situation, structure or pattern may be minimized. The objective here is that each individual child proceeds 'at his own pace', and the content of his activities is chosen so that it is 'appropriate' to his level of development, as perceived by the teacher. This, as we have seen, puts an immensely difficult burden on the teacher, the demands on whom are described by the Plowden Committee itself as 'frighteningly high' (para. 875). In our view, as stated in *Inside the Primary Classroom*, these demands are in fact impossible of achievement. It is simply not possible to structure and monitor the activities of thirty individual children simultaneously, in such a way as to ensure that the level of work of each is consistently 'appropriate', in Plowden's terms.[1] The net outcome is not only a lack of structure, or pattern for most of the pupils in the class, but also a lack of probing or challenging either by the teacher or by other pupils.

A shift towards some class teaching organically related to group work as the main mode, on the other hand, requires careful structuring on the part of the teacher. The purpose, objectives and procedures appropriate to whole-class teaching sessions therefore need careful definition. But the relation of co-operative group activities to the class teaching sessions also requires thought and determination, while each individual task itself requires definition both as to its purposes and procedures. Similarly, the *sequencing* of tasks is crucial, as there must be a clear relation between the succeeding tasks in a series. All this implies a much more precise and careful ordering of children's experiences in the main teaching and learning sessions in the junior school than is the case, generally speaking, at present. Some of the planning and resources available in recent curriculum projects, for instance *Science 5 to 13*, represent an attempt to develop procedures of the kind suggested, but this is only a beginning. There is no reason why groups of teachers in different areas should not begin to work out techniques and resources relevant to the approach suggested here, and indeed some are already doing so.[2]

Another area relevant to teacher training is that of assessment; specifically what we have called teacher-based assessment in the ORACLE project. The central feature here is the definition of criteria relating to the evaluation of skills and abilities required in learning, both in the field of literacy and numeracy and in the wider field of study skills, leading to the capacity for independent learning and so autonomy. Related to this is the enhancement of the teacher's ability, through careful and sustained observation of individual children's activities, to assess the level at which the pupil operates. The use of structured exercises, as on the ORACLE programme, could provide relatively standardized situations where the development of such skills could be assessed in a more systematic way than in the past. Specific proposals for this area will be included in a later publication.

Finally, there is the question of sensitizing students (and practising teachers themselves) to enhanced awareness of the variety of options open to the individual teacher, in terms of patterns of interaction and class management. Observation of actual classroom practice under skilled guidance, perhaps utilizing simplified observational schedules, is one technique now increasingly used in teacher education. This has obvious value, but is time-consuming and perhaps disturbing for pupils and teachers, while the events observed are also contingent (that is, there is little control over what may happen in the observed classroom). For this reason, the systematic induction of student-teachers into procedures for observing and analysing classroom events, using videotaped incidents and materials, has a great deal to be said for it. An example here is the Primary Teachers Induction Programme developed at the Moray House College of Education in Edinburgh (Cameron-Jones, 1979). This sets out systematically to make students aware of the nature and implications of different patterns, to introduce them to different procedures for conducting their own observations and so on. Such programmes or packages represent an economic and systematic approach to the induction of the student into important issues raised in teaching. Another major help is the development of micro-teaching as part of teacher-training procedures. Since micro-teaching almost always involves the student-teacher with between four and six pupils, it lends itself admirably to developing the relevant skills, and allows experiment in the use of different techniques or approaches with small groups of pupils. Indeed, accumulating evidence indicates that micro-teaching, together with its evaluation by means of interaction analysis, is one of the most effective methods of training (Brown, 1975; Mc-Intyre *et al.*, 1977). These techniques can and do emphasize training in those aspects of teaching which the ORACLE findings suggest are vital determinants of pupil progress, for instance, the use of higher-order questioning.

All that is said here about the training of student-teachers applies generally also to in-service training. While it is clearly desirable that young teachers entering the profession should examine carefully, practise, discuss and evaluate the different options open to the class teacher, in terms of varieties of interactional patterns, so teachers already in the profession could only gain from sensitizing themselves also to these different patterns, now identified through systematic classroom observation of the kind carried through on the ORACLE programme. The forms that in-service training can take are many and various, but this approach lends itself to discussion among teachers, either in individual schools, or grouped by area. Videotape material illuminating the practice of different teaching styles — for instance, focusing on the teacher's interaction with small groups working co-operatively — is one form such in-service education can take, though there are, of course, many others. The main point to make, however, is that practising teachers should by no means be excluded from such re-training programmes, since what is required, it seems, is a shift from some aspects of current practice across the board.

In calling for these changes, we are not simply advocating another revolution of the 'cycles of fashion' in teaching. It has sometimes been argued that, in the immediate post-Plowden era, when the last upheaval took place, certain colleges pressed new students to adopt individualized approaches to teaching in too prescriptive a fashion. In this book we have sought to point to problems in some areas of current practice, and proffer some suggestions for overcoming them. A correct balance be-tween different forms of organization, which will permit an increase in the use of those interactions emphasized by successful teachers, will still need to take account of an individual's personal qualities and the context in which she teaches. Thus we are offering suggestions for dis-cussion and appraisal, rather than preaching a new orthodoxy.

Notes

1 This point is well and clearly made by Eleanor Duckworth, an edu-cationist and psychologist who has worked with Piaget for many years. In a recent article on the application of Piaget's findings to education, she writes that 'a current interpretation of Piaget is that one should diagnose children's intellectual levels and tailor individual instruction accordingly'. She goes on (Duckworth, 1979):

> This has always seemed to me an impractical aim. To begin with, in any class we can assume there are thirty children. A minimum number of Piaget notions that are pertinent to teaching at any age would surely include number, length, area, volume, causality, time, spatial co-ordinates, and proportion. This is only a beginning, but let's say modestly that a dozen tasks might serve to diagnose a child's intellectual level. That adds up to three hundred and sixty tests for one class of children. And, of course, tests should be carried out periodically to assess progress during the year — let's say thirty-six tests, four times a year. Even with a full-time psycho-logist assigned to each teacher, this pace could probably not be maintained.

2 It is suggested that careful structuring of children's learning activities, as proposed here, applies more specifically to those areas of the curri-culum which embody linear (or logically sequential) conceptual develop-ment. Time can also be provided during the day for activities structured by the pupils themselves.

Appendices

Appendices

Appendix A

Data-gathering instruments

Table A.1 *The observation categories of the Pupil Record*

Category	Item	Brief definition of item
Coding the pupil-adult categories		
1 *Target's role*	INIT	Target attempts to become focus of attention (not focus at previous signal)
	STAR	Target is focus of attention
	PART	Target in audience (no child is focus)
	LSWT	Target in audience (another child is focus)
2 *Interacting adult*	TCHR	Target interacts with teacher
	OBSR	Target interacts with observer
	OTHER	Target interacts with any other adult such as the head or secretary
3 *Adult's interaction*	TK WK	Adult interacts about task work (task content or supervision)
	ROUTINE	Adult interacts about routine matter (classroom management and control)
	POS	Adult reacts positively to task work (praises)
	NEG	Adult reacts negatively to behaviour, etc. (criticizes)
	IGN	Adult ignores attempted initiation
4 *Adult's communication setting*	IND ATT	Adult gives private individual attention to target pupil
	GROUP	Adult gives private attention to target's group
	CLASS	Adult interacts with whole class
	OTHER	Adult gives private attention to another child or group or does not interact
Coding the pupil-pupil categories		
5 *Target's role*	BGNS	Target successfully begins a new contact
	COOP	Target co-operates by responding to an initiation

Category		Item	Brief definition of item
		TRIES	Target unsuccessfully tries to initiate
		IGN	Target ignores attempted initiation
		SUST	Target sustains interaction
6	*Mode of interaction*	MTL	Non-verbal, mediated solely by materials
		CNTC	Non-verbal, mediated by physical contact or gesture (with or without materials)
		VRB	Verbal (with or without materials, physical contact or gesture)
7a	*Task of other pupil(s)*	STK	Same as target's task
		DTK	Different to target's task
7b	*Sex and number of other pupil(s)*	SS	Target interacts privately with one pupil of same sex
		OS	Target interacts privately with one pupil of opposite sex
		SEV SS	Target interacts publicly with two or more pupils having same sex as target
		SEV OS	Target interacts publicly with two or more pupils, of whom one at least is of the opposite sex to the target
7c	*Base of other pupil(s)*	OWN BS	From target's own base
		OTH BS	From another base

Coding the activity and location categories

8	*Target's activity*	COOP TK	Fully involved and co-operating on approved task work (e.g. reading)
		COOP R	Fully involved and co-operating on approved routine work (e.g. sharpening a pencil)
		DSTR	Non-involved and totally distracted from all work
		DSTR OBSR	Non-involved and totally distracted from all work by the observer
		DSRP	Non-involved and aggressively disrupting work of other pupil(s)
		HPLY	Non-involved and engaging in horseplay with other pupil(s)
		WAIT TCHR	Waiting to interact with the teacher
		CODS	Partially co-operating and partially distracted from approved work
		INT TCHR	Interested in teacher's activity or private interaction with other pupil(s)
		INT PUP	Interested in the work of other pupil(s)
		WOA	Working on an alternative activity which is not approved work
		RIS	Not coded because the target is responding to internal stimuli

Category	Item	Brief definition of item
	NOT OBS	Not coded because the target is not observed for some reason
	NOT LIST	Not coded because the target's activity is not listed
9 *Target's location*	P IN	Target in base
	P OUT	Target out of base but not mobile
	P MOB	Target out of base and mobile
	P OUT RM	Target out of room
10 *Teacher activity and location*	T PRES	Teacher present with target through interaction or physical proximity
	T ELSE	Teacher privately interacting elsewhere with other pupil(s) or visitor
	T MNTR	Teacher not interacting but monitoring classroom activities
	T HSKP	Teacher not interacting but housekeeping
	T OUT RM	Teacher out of room

Reproduced from *Inside the Primary Classroom*, pp. 12–13.

Table A.2 The observation categories of the Teacher Record

Questions	Task	Q1	recalling facts
		Q2	offering ideas, solutions (closed)
		Q3	offering ideas, solutions (open)
	Task supervision	Q4	referring to task supervision
	Routine	Q5	referring to routine matters
Statements	Task	S1	of facts
		S2	of ideas, problems
	Task supervision	S3	telling child what to do
		S4	praising work or effort
		S5	feedback on work or effort
	Routine	S6	providing information, directions
		S7	providing feedback
		S8	of critical control
		S9	of small talk
Silence*	'Silent' interaction, i.e., interaction other than by question or statement		Gesturing Showing Marking Waiting Story Reading
			Not observed Not coded
	No interaction between teacher and any pupil in the class		Adult interaction Visiting pupil Not interacting Out of room
	Audience		Class, group of individuals
	Composition		Identification or pupils involved
	Activity		E.g., Creative writing, practical maths etc.

* While it was recognized that the term 'Silence' was in some instances a misnomer, its use for everyday purposes was preferred to the cumbersome term *silence or interaction other than by question or statement.*

Table A.3 Richmond Tests items used in the long and short forms of the ORACLE tests of basic skills

ORACLE reading tests		Richmond Tests of Basic Skills		ORACLE maths tests		Richmond Tests of Basic Skills		ORACLE language skills		Richmond Tests of Basic Skills			
R	SR	V	R	M	SM	M-1	M-2	L	SL	L-1	L-2	L-3	L-4
1	1	1		1	1	1		1	1	1			
2	2	4		2	2	3		2	2	12			
3	3	8		3	3	6		3	3	22			
4	4	15		4	4	8		4	4	31			
5	5	23		5	5	18		5	5	43			
6	6	31		6	6	23		6		52			
7	7	39		7	7	30		7		62			
8	8	46		8	8	36		8		73			
9		54		9	9	39		9		84			
10		62		10	10	47		10	6		1		
11		69		11		53		11	7		14		
12		77		12		56		12	8		27		
13		85		13		64		13	9		41		
14	9		6	14		73		14			55		
15	10		7	15		77		15			64		
16	11		8	16		84		16			80		
17	12		9	17		90		17	10			1	
18	13		10	18	11	94	1	18	11			12	
19	14		11	19	12		2	19	12			22	
20	15		37	20	13		18	20	13			32	
21	16		38	21	14		19	21	14			47	
22	17		39	22	15		23	22				53	
23	18		40	23	16		32	23				67	
24	19		41	24	17		36	24				79	
25	20		42	25			43	25	15				1
26			132	26			49	26	16				14
27			133	27			53	27	17				27
28			134	28			59	28	18				39
29			135	29				29					53
30			136	30			62	30					62

Table A.4 Factor analysis of ORACLE W questionnaire* (1,400 pupils: September 1976)

	Teacher-oriented anxiety	Extrinsic motivation	Intrinsic motivation	Pupil-oriented anxiety	Contentment
1 Do you try your hardest to get your work right?			0.49		
2 Do you play noisy games in the playground?					
3 Do you worry a little that other children might pick on you?				0.47	
4 Do you enjoy being at school?					0.74
5 Are you scared you might do badly on tests?	0.49				
6 Is it very important to you to please the teacher?			0.40		
7 Do you ever forget your swimming or P.E. kit?					
8 Are you a bit afraid of being bullied?				0.45	
9 Would you like to do very much better than the others in tests?		0.53			
10 If you get told off do you worry about it afterwards?	0.63				
11 When your teacher is talking do you pay attention?			0.50		
12 Are you a bit afraid of getting into arguments?				0.49	
13 Is is especially important to you to get good marks?		0.44			
14 At playtime do you play with children who are not in your class?					
15 Are you frightened of being told off by the teacher?	0.66				
16 Do you try very hard to do your best?			0.64		
17 Are you scared of being made fun of by the other children?				0.49	
18 Are you happy when you are at school?					0.62
19 Do you worry that the teacher might get cross?	0.56				

		Teacher-oriented anxiety	Extrinsic motivation	Intrinsic motivation	Pupil-oriented anxiety	Contentment
20	Do you ever lose things at school?					
21	Do you try to be top of the class?		0.51			
22	Do you worry a little in case others gang up on you?				0.57	
23	Do you like to think of answers to the teacher's questions before the others?		0.50			
24	Do you worry about getting into trouble in class?	0.56				

*varimax rotation: only loadings of 0.4 or greater are shown

Appendix B

Replicating the observational data

A major aspect of the ORACLE research is that it is a longitudinal project, in which the same children are studied as they pass through three years of schooling. The results reported in *Inside the Primary Classroom* were based on the observational data gathered during the first year of the study. The analysis presented in the present volume is mainly concerned to relate these observational data to the tests and other assessments conducted during this first year. However, unlike most process-product studies, where the longitudinal element consists of data gathered at the beginning and end of the school year, the same data-gathering process was repeated with the same children in their subsequent year in school, and most of the children were also studied for a third year. In later volumes, this three-year programme of data collection will be used to analyse behaviour and achievement in a developmental perspective, and to consider such issues as the consistency of pupil and teacher behaviour and the impact on children of transfer to secondary education. But, as well as providing a genuinely longitudinal basis for the study of pupil behaviour and achievement, the subsequent years of data gathering also build an element of replication into the study, as a majority of the data-collection procedures are repeated exactly in the three years. In the present volume, the second year's data is being treated as a replication of the first year's data; specifically, the observational data gathered in the second year will be compared with the analysis of primary classrooms contained in *Inside the Primary Classroom* and summarized in Chapter 2 of this volume.

The principle of replicability is a major element of the scientific method, and the replication of research findings is a common feature of most areas of experimental science. Replication is a much less common feature of social and educational research, but there are a number of reasons why its neglect is unfortunate. Problems of sampling and the generalizability of results are common in this area, and the potential danger that the 'one-off' use of powerful multi-variate techniques, such as factor analysis and cluster analysis, will turn chance fluctuations into apparently meaningful patterns is well known (see *Inside the Primary Classroom*, Appendix 2C). In research using new techniques of data collection on a large scale, and a complex research design involving schools, classrooms, teachers and pupils, as well as a variety of multi-variate statistical methods, it is particularly important to build as many checks on the findings as possible into the research. In the following pages, the findings of the first and second years of observation will be compared, first for the Teacher Record and then for the Pupil Record. These results are presented only for those children who remain in primary or primary/middle schools. Children who transferred to secondary education at the end of the first year are not included. Consequently, while the first year's data were based on 489 pupils in fifty-eight classrooms, the data from the second year presented here are based on 334 pupils in forty classes. The pattern of observing eight children in each class could not be maintained in the second year, as classes did not always stay together.

A number of qualifications have to be made, however, before making this comparison. The children from whom the second year's data were obtained are the same children in the same schools studied in the first year. This has two consequences. Obviously they are a year older, and it is possible that any differences found are a systematic result of increasing age. However, as children of three age groups are included in the study, the data provide a check on this possibility. Secondly, because they are the same children, the replication does not provide a check on biases due to the sampling and selection procedures. This is not the case, however, as regards the data collected on the Teacher Record. The teachers, on the whole, were different from those in the first year. Of the forty teachers involved in the second year of the project, only fourteen had been in the project the previous year.

The Teacher Record

Three codes are made on the Teacher Record at each time signal: one for the interaction the teacher is engaged in, one for the audience for that interaction and one for the curricular area. The relative proportion of observations falling in the various categories of these three variables

Table B.1 Activities on Teacher Record as percentage of observations

	1976–7	1977–8
Questions		
Task fact	3.5	2.7
solution (closed)	2.2	2.4
solution (open)	0.6	0.2
Task Supervision	3.9	3.0
Routine	1.8	1.7
All questions	12.0	10.0
Statements		
Task fact	6.9	7.8
ideas	2.5	2.8
Task supervision telling	12.6	11.8
praising	1.0	0.5
feedback	9.6	11.6
Routine information	6.5	7.4
feedback	2.0	2.1
control	2.3	1.6
small talk	1.3	1.3
All statements	44.7	46.9
Other interaction		
Gesturing	1.9	1.8
Showing	2.6	2.4
Marking	10.1	9.6
Waiting	1.9	1.3
Story	0.9	0.8
Reading	3.4	2.5
Not observed	1.0	0.8
Not coded	0.5	0.2
All other interaction	22.3	19.4
No-interaction		
Adult interaction	1.7	1.7
Visiting pupil	0.4	0.6
No-interaction	17.6	19.9
Out of room	1.3	1.5
All 'no-interaction'	21.0	23.7

in the first and second years of the study are presented in Tables B.1, B.2 and B.3.

Table B.1 shows the relative frequency of use of the twenty-six interaction categories in the two years. The two sets of figures, taken from a mainly different sample of teachers (but teaching the same children in the same schools), show a close similarity. The proportion of teacher questions has gone down by 2.0 per cent in the second year, and the proportion of teacher statements has gone up by 2.2 per cent, leaving the proportion of verbal interactions virtually identical in the two years. Non-verbal interactions are 2.9 per cent lower in the second year, and no-interaction has increased by 2.7 per cent. Small-scale variations also occur in the individual categories, but the over-all pattern is very similar.

Table B.2 Audience of teacher interaction as percentage of observations

Audience	1976-7	1977-8
Individual	55.8	52.8
Group	7.5	11.2
Class	15.1	12.1

Table B.2 gives the proportion of teacher interactions involving individuals, groups and the whole class in the two years. Unlike the interaction categories, the relative proportions of observations in the audience categories do differ to some extent. In the first year, the great majority of teacher interactions were with individual pupils, a much smaller proportion were with the class as a whole and fewer still were with groups. In the second year, as Table B.2 shows, the order of occurrence of the three audience categories remains the same, and the majority of interactions are still with individuals. However, the proportion of observations made of individual interactions is 3 per cent lower, as is the proportion of observations made of class interactions. Group interactions, on the other hand, are up by nearly 4 per cent of observations, half as high again as in the first year. This increase in the amount of teacher interaction with groups is the only substantial difference between the two years of observation with the Teacher Record, and will be discussed in more detail below.

The areas of the curriculum involved in teacher-pupil interaction are shown in Table B.3. Here again the pattern is very similar in the two years. The decrease in practical maths, reading and spoken English is probably the result of the increase in the age of the children. In *Inside*

the Primary Classroom it was shown that the time spent on reading decreased as children got older and, presumably, required less teaching
(p. 79). This is probably also true of the other two activities. Conversely,
the time spent on writing, and on other, more formal, aspects of
mathematics has increased slightly.

Table B.3 Curriculum content

	1976–7	1977–8
Number work	16.0	18.1
Practical mathematics	4.9	2.9
Mathematics	12.4	13.3
Reading	7.9	6.0
Writing	20.6	22.8
Spoken English	3.3	2.0
Creative Writing	6.0	5.9
Art and Craft	10.3	8.7
General	18.7	20.2

In the first volume, considerable attention was given to the analysis
of the relationship between the content of a teacher's interaction and
the audience to which it was addressed. These findings, summarized
here in Chapter 2, showed that interactions with the class as a whole
were very much more likely than other interactions to be directly concerned with the content of the pupils' work (as opposed to task supervision and routine interactions), and particularly were much more
likely to be 'higher cognitive level' interactions. Individual interactions
were the least likely to be task oriented and 'higher cognitive level',
with interactions with a group falling between these. These results were
particularly important both because interactions with individual pupils
dominate the teacher's use of her time, and because individualized
instruction is generally thought to be most appropriate for primary
school children. This finding also challenges the idea of a simple dichotomy between 'formal' and 'progressive' methods, as the enquiry or
discovery approach implicit in higher cognitive level interactions was
found to be most common in class teaching.

It is especially interesting, therefore, to repeat the analysis using the
second-year data. A comparison of the results in the first and second
year is presented in Table B.4. These figures are derived, as before, from
mainly different teachers teaching the same children. The over-all
picture in the two years is very similar. About 28 per cent of verbal

Table B.4 Audience and content of task interactions: Teacher Record

	All verbal interactions	Individual verbal interactions	Group verbal interactions	Class verbal interactions
1976–7				
Higher-level task interactions	9.3	6.9	8.9	16.8
Other task interactions	18.5	15.5	21.3	26.2
All tasks interactions	27.8	22.4	30.2	43.0
1977–8				
Higher-level task interactions	9.8	6.6	14.5	17.8
Other task interactions	18.6	13.7	28.0	28.7
All task interactions	28.4	20.3	42.5	46.5

Figures are given as percentages of verbal interactions (questions and statements).

interactions are directly concerned with the task, and between 9 and 10 per cent of verbal interactions are of the higher-level type, in both years of observation. The contrast between the content of individual and whole-class interactions is also repeated in the second year; the figures for task interactions and for higher-level interactions are approximately the same for individuals over the two years, and for classes over the two years. However, the figures for group interactions change somewhat in the second year. In both sets of figures group interactions lie in between individual and class interactions, in terms of their task content and higher-level content. But in the first year they are closer to the pattern for individual interactions, while in the second year both the task content and higher-level content of group interactions have increased, so that their values are now closer to class than to individual interactions. These comparisons show that the only real difference between the two years in the over-all patterns of interactions is that the proportion of group interactions has increased, and it seems that the content of these interactions has also changed to some extent. These points will be considered in more detail after discussing the replication of the cluster analysis of teachers.

As well as considering the results of the first year's data on teacher interaction for the teachers as a whole, cluster analysis was used to group the original fifty-eight teachers into 'teacher types'. Cluster analysis is a technique for sorting people into groups, whereby the individuals within a particular group are relatively similar to each other, and the groups themselves are relatively distinct from one another. As is explained in Chapter 2, this procedure resulted in the original fifty-eight teachers being divided into four main clusters, which were named *individual monitors, class enquirers, group instructors* and *style changers*. Although the audience to which interactions were addressed is a dominant differentiating feature of the first three styles, as is reflected in their titles, the clusters also differ in important ways with regard to other aspects of teacher-pupil interaction.

The same cluster-analysis procedure was repeated for the forty teachers for whom data were available from the second year of observation. The only difference between the procedures employed in the two years was that, in the first year, the four-cluster solution was chosen as the most satisfactory in accordance with the normal criteria for evaluating cluster analysis. In the second year, a four-cluster solution was decided on in advance, in order to provide a straightforward comparison between the two sets of data.

The cluster profiles for the two sets of four teacher types are shown in Table B.5. The clusters from the two years were initially matched in terms of their similarities in the distribution of audience categories. As can be seen in the bottom three rows of Table B.5, the two sets of teachers fall into very similar groups with regard to the audience for their interactions. In both years there is a group of teachers who are much higher in their use of individual attention than the other teachers, a group who are much higher in their interaction with the whole class and a group who are much higher in their interaction with groups of pupils. As before, there is a group who are more mixed in their use of the various audience categories (these were identified as 'style changers' in the analysis of the first year's data, and were further divided). The relative size of the four clusters differs in the two years, as we would expect with samples of this size. In particular the 'group' cluster is very much larger in the second year, and the 'individual' cluster very much smaller. But despite the relatively small sample sizes,

Table B.5 Replication of teaching styles

		Individual monitors		Class enquirers		Group instructors		Mixed changers	
		76–7	77–8	76–7	77–8	76–7	77–8	76–7	77–8
Questions									
task:	fact	3.9	3.0	4.1	5.7	2.4	2.0	3.4	2.0
	closed solution	1.1	1.8	3.3	2.6	2.0	2.7	2.4	2.0
	open solution	0.3	0.1	1.0	0.2	0.9	0.2	0.6	0.2
task supervision		2.9	3.4	4.1	2.4	3.2	2.4	4.5	3.9
routine		1.3	1.3	2.2	2.0	1.5	0.8	2.0	2.1
Statements									
task:	fact	5.6	7.7	8.0	11.2	11.5	9.3	6.0	5.5
	ideas	2.1	1.3	4.2	3.6	1.0	3.8	2.6	2.1
task supervision:									
	telling	15.8	9.7	11.2	9.8	11.6	11.1	11.8	13.8
	praising	1.0	0.4	1.3	0.6	0.6	0.3	1.1	0.6
	feedback	8.7	8.5	10.9	9.6	15.9	14.5	8.0	9.8
routine:									
	information	5.6	5.9	7.0	7.4	6.7	5.3	6.8	8.9
	feedback	1.8	1.9	2.3	2.4	2.3	1.5	2.0	2.3
	control	2.0	1.8	1.5	2.2	2.4	0.9	2.6	2.4
	small talk	1.3	1.6	1.7	1.4	0.6	1.0	1.4	1.6
Other interaction									
	gesturing	1.8	2.1	0.9	1.4	3.7	2.1	1.8	1.4
	showing	2.4	1.4	3.3	1.4	2.0	2.8	2.6	2.3
	marking	16.4	20.9	5.7	8.4	7.4	9.5	9.4	8.1
	waiting	1.7	1.9	1.6	1.7	2.1	1.1	2.0	1.3
	story	0.6	0.7	1.8	1.9	1.0	1.0	0.7	0.3
	reading	3.0	3.6	3.4	0.9	2.2	3.1	3.8	2.4
Audience									
	individual	66.9	65.1	43.6	42.4	52.5	49.9	55.4	56.1
	group	5.5	2.2	5.9	5.1	17.7	19.0	6.3	7.6
	class	6.9	9.9	31.4	24.1	11.4	4.5	14.6	18.7
	N =	13	4	9	5	7	15	29	16

the identity of the various groups is maintained in the two years.

A comparison of the figures at the foot of Table B.5 with the figures in Table B.2 provides an illustration both of the value of replication, and of the value of using cluster analysis in addition to over-all averages to describe data of this kind. In Table B.2 the main difference between the two years is that the amount of group interaction is half as high again in the second year as in the first year. However, in Table B.5 this substantial increase is not reflected in the figures *within* any one of the clusters. Within each pair of clusters the values for group interaction remain at similar levels. The only pair not conforming to this is the *individual monitors* cluster pair, where there is a decrease in the amount of group interaction. This shows that what has happened is not a general increase in group interaction, resulting either from a shift in teaching patterns across the whole sample or from unreliability in the observation or time sampling, but a sampling fluctuation, by which teachers who make extensive use of group interaction are now more heavily represented in the sample. In the first year *group instructors* made up 12.1 per cent of the sample. In the second year the group cluster makes up 37.5 per cent. However, the amount of group interaction these two clusters of teachers engage in is almost identical. This suggests that the cluster analysis has described stable patterns which can be found within populations of teachers. With these relatively small sample sizes we would expect the relative proportions of different teacher types to differ in two samples. The value of cluster analysis is that it enables us to distinguish differences between two whole sample values caused by this sampling fluctuation from differences caused by a general shift in teaching patterns.

Although the differences in the use of audience categories is a major feature of the clusters, the other interaction categories also differentiate between the clusters in a systematic fashion, and in the analysis of the first year's data it was shown that very similar clusters emerged if the audience categories were omitted from the clustering procedure. Comparing the pairs of clusters which were originally matched in terms of their audience characteristics, it can be shown that, in general, they also match with regard to other interaction categories, especially those categories which were important in describing the original clusters.

In the first year, the *individual monitors* were characterized as being particularly likely to use non-verbal monitoring of pupils' work (marking) as a style of interaction, and as having a low level of questioning and a low level of task interaction. These features are also characteristic of the individual cluster from the second year's data, especially the low level of task interaction and the high level of silent marking.

The *class enquirers* from the first year's analysis were distinguished by having a high level of task questions and a high level of task statements. Both these characteristics are repeated in the 'class' cluster in the second year. The cluster was also conspicuous in the first year for having a much higher level of statements and questions dealing with ideas and problems (higher cognitive level) than the other clusters. The class cluster in the second year is still well above average with regard to this kind of question and statement, but it is not now the highest for them.

The cluster described as *group instructors* in the analysis of the first year's data was dramatically higher than any of the other clusters with regard to interaction with groups. It was also characterized by high levels of factual statements, providing information on task and a high level of verbal feedback. These characteristics are repeated in the 'group' cluster in the second year. However, there is one noticeable difference between the group clusters from the two years. In the first year, the *group instructors* were below average in their use of questions and statements dealing with ideas and problems. Although they were above average on task interactions, these interactions were predominantly concerned with the presentation of facts. In the second year, however, members of the group cluster are the highest with regard to these higher cognitive level interactions. This appears to be a real difference between the group clusters in the two years. The second year's group cluster, which is a much larger proportion of the sample than the first year's, now contains teachers who are using more open-ended methods, with more emphasis on problem solving and ideas.

However, the extent to which these 'new' *group instructors* encourage children to work *co-operatively* in groups is no different from the first year's *group instructors*. In the first year, pupils in these classrooms spent 6.5 per cent of their time working together on tasks, a figure only slightly higher than that for all classrooms (5.2 per cent). In the second year, the equivalent figures are 6.4 per cent for *group instructors'* classes and 5.1 per cent for all classes.

The members of the last pair of clusters were described as *style changers* in the analysis of the first year's data, but the pair is simply described as 'mixed' here, as we do not have data replicating the information used to describe the different kinds of changes. These clusters are the least distinctive, and in most respects appear to be a mixture of the other styles. In the first year more definite 'types' were described by sub-dividing the cluster but, as already stated, this is not possible here. In the first year, two of the distinguishing features of the style were high values for task supervision statements and high values for critical control. Both these results are repeated in the second year. However, a third distinctive feature, a high value for hearing children read, is not repeated.

Fourteen of the teachers in the first year's sample were also included in the second year. All of these remained in the same clusters as before. Unfortunately however, eleven of the fourteen were in the mixed/changers clusters, and so this is a less satisfactory check on the reproduceability of the clusters than if they had been more widely spread between them.

Summary: replicating the Teacher Record data

In general, the comparison of the Teacher Record data for the first and second years has confirmed the analysis and conclusions from the first year alone. The over-all use of interaction, audience and curricular categories remains much the same. The relationship between the audience and content of interactions, in particular the striking difference between class and individual interactions, is confirmed, and the cluster analyses give similar groupings of teachers in the two years.

The cluster analyses also show how the differences between the two years in the amount and characteristics of group interaction is explained by sampling fluctuations, and that within groups of teachers patterns remain very similar. The single exception to this, and the 'new' finding from the second year's analysis, is the discovery of a number of teachers using group interaction in a different, and possibly more interesting and challenging fashion, from those in the first year's sample, although this change is not accompanied by any change in the amount of co-operative group work.

The Pupil Record

Individual pupils were observed in the second year, using the Pupil Record, in exactly the same fashion as in the first. Unlike the second-year teacher data, the pupils were the same as those who had been observed in the previous year. However, pupils transferring to secondary school were not included and so the second year's data are based on 334 pupils.

The Pupil Record codes pupils' behaviour in three areas: the activity they are engaged in, their interaction with the teacher and their interaction with other pupils. One of the major findings from the analysis of the first year's data was the high proportion of lesson time which children spent involved in their work. Including working directly on their task, routine or support activities and waiting for the teacher, 74.3 per cent of the average pupil's time was spent involved in work.

Table B.6 *Pupil activities: Pupil Record (percentage of all observations)*

	1976-7		1977-8	
Working on task	58.1		60.0	
Working on routine	11.9	74.3	10.8	74.1
Waiting for teacher	4.3		3.3	
Distracted	15.9		15.9	
Distracted by observer	0.3		0.2	
Disruptive	0.1	16.5	0.1	16.3
Horseplay	0.2		0.1	
Working/distracted	1.9		2.2	
Interested in teacher	1.7		1.8	
Interested in another pupil	3.4		3.3	
Working on another activity	0.4		0.3	
Daydreaming	0.8		0.9	
Not observed	0.8		1.0	
Not listed	0.1		0	
Total	100		100	

This result is repeated almost exactly in the second year, as is shown in Table B.6. Working directly on the task has increased 1.9 per cent, and routine activities and waiting for the teacher have decreased 1.1 per cent and 1.0 per cent respectively. This leaves the over-all figure virtually identical. Analysis of the first year's data has shown that waiting for the teacher, and involvement in routine, decrease among older children, and that working on task is slightly lower amongst younger children, so that slight changes within the 'involved' category are probably due to the children being a year older. The figures for various forms of distracted and disruptive behaviour are also almost exactly the same over the two years. These categories total at 16.5 per cent in the first year and 16.3 per cent in the second. Similarly, the remaining categories in Table B.6 remain constant between the two years. In Table B.7 the figures for pupil-teacher interaction in the two years are presented. In the first year, 15.8 per cent of a pupil's lesson time is spent interacting with the teacher. This is made up of 2.3 per cent of lesson time as an individual, 1.5 per cent as a member of a group and 12.0 per cent as a member of the class. In the second year, these figures have become 14.5 per cent for total interaction, 2.1 per cent for individual interaction, 2.1 per cent for group interaction and

Table B.7 Pupil-teacher interaction: Pupil Record (percentage of all observations)

	1976-7	1977-8
Individual interaction	2.3	2.1
Group interaction	1.5	2.1
Class interaction	12.0	10.1
Other/unclassified	0.0	0.2
Total	15.8	14.5

10.1 per cent for whole-class interaction. The slight decrease in individual and class interactions, and the increase in group interactions, match the figures from the Teacher Record already discussed. Over-all though, the figures confirm the dramatic asymmetry between the teacher and pupil with regard to interaction. The teacher interacts predominantly with individuals, but the pupil interacts with the teacher mainly as a member of the class.

Table B.8 Pupil-pupil interaction: Pupil Record

	1976-7	1977-8
Interaction as percentage of all observations		
All pupil-pupil interaction	18.6	18.8
Interaction on task	5.2	5.1
Interaction on routine	2.0	1.3
Interaction as percentage of all pupil-pupil interactions		
Interaction on task	28.1	27.1
Interaction on routine	10.8	6.9
Total co-operation	38.9	34.0

The third part of the Pupil Record deals with interactions between pupils. The figures for these interactions in the two years are given in Table B.8. The amount and type of pupil-pupil interactions are virtually identical in the two years. In the first year, 18.6 per cent of observations are of pupils interacting with other pupils, and in the second year the figure is 18.8 per cent. A majority of these interactions involve distractions from work, but a substantial minority are work oriented. In the first year 28.1 per cent, and in the second year 27.1 per cent of pupil-pupil interactions are directly concerned with their task, and a further 10.8 per cent in the first year and 6.9 per cent in the second year are concerned with routine activities connected with the task. This slight drop in the proportion of work-oriented interactions can be predicted from the first year's data, where the analysis showed that such interactions were more common amongst younger children.

Table B.9 Pupils' base: Pupil Record (percentage of all observations)

Pupils' base	1976–7	1977–8
Alone	5.1	4.5
Single-sex pair	15.3	12.6
Mixed-sex pair	2.0	2.3
Single-sex group	30.8	34.2
Mixed-sex group	43.5	44.8
Other/unclear	3.3	1.6
Total	100	100

Table B.9 gives figures for the two years for the base groups in which the target pupils were sitting. These also remain very similar. In both years, about three-quarters of observations were of children sitting in groups, and less than a fifth of observations were of children seated in pairs. (Observations of children seated in pairs do not necessarily mean that the desks were arranged in pairs.)

If the figures for pairs are included in those for groups, in both years there are an equal number of mixed-sex and single-sex groupings.

In addition to providing the over-all figures for pupil activities and interactions, the first year's Pupil Record data were also used to perform a cluster analysis on the target pupils, in the same way that Teacher Record data was used to group teachers into teaching styles. The four 'pupil types' which resulted from this analysis have been described in Chapter 8. These pupil types were differentiated in a number of ways, in particular with regard to the amount of time they spent working, the amount of pupil-pupil interaction they engaged in and the amount and type of their contacts with the teacher.

The same cluster analysis was conducted using the data from the second year's observations on the Pupil Record. As with the replication of the teacher clusters, a four-cluster solution was decided on, in order to match it against the first year's results. The results for the two years with the two sets of clusters arranged into pairs are presented in Table B.10.

Table B.10 Replication of pupil types: Pupil Record (percentage of all observations)

Pupil Activities	Attention seekers 76--7	77–8	Intermittent workers 76–7	77–8	Solitary workers 76–7	77–8	Quiet collaborators 76–7	77–8
Involved								
Co-op task	54.8	59.0	52.4	48.4	65.7	67.5	59.1	61.7
Co-op routine	11.8	10.7	12.0	12.5	11.4	9.7	13.5	10.8
Waiting for teacher	6.4	5.1	3.8	4.7	3.3	2.7	5.5	1.8
Distracted, disruptive, etc.	17.7	15.6	30.1	26.3	11.1	11.3	15.0	14.9
Other	9.3	9.6	1.7	8.1	8.5	8.8	6.9	10.8
Pupil-teacher interaction								
Interaction with								
Individual	5.5	5.7	1.3	1.7	1.4	1.3	2.0	1.4
Group	1.1	1.1	0.7	0.9	0.7	1.2	7.1	4.9
Class	11.3	7.4	6.9	7.1	16.9	13.4	13.5	10.1
Interaction initiated by pupil	2.3	2.2	0.7	0.9	1.1	0.7	1.4	0.5
Pupil-pupil interaction								
Total	19.0	17.7	23.4	27.7	12.4	12.2	19.1	20.3
Directly concerned with task	4.8	4.9	5.7	5.9	3.9	3.6	6.8	6.3
N =	96	54	174	77	156	114	60	89
Percentage of sample	19.5	16.2	35.7	23.1	32.5	34.1	12.3	26.6

As Table B.10 shows, the clusters which emerge from the second year's data can be matched fairly closely to those from the first. In the first year, the first cluster was labelled *attention seekers*. These pupils were second lowest with regard to the amount of time spent on task, and about average with regard to pupil-pupil interaction. Their distinctive feature was that they spent a very high proportion of their time in comparison with other pupils in individual interaction with the teacher, and were much more likely than other pupils to initiate teacher interactions. They also had the highest proportion of time spent in waiting for the teacher. All these characteristics are true of the group labelled *attention seekers* in the second year of observation. The second cluster was labelled *intermittent workers*. This cluster was lowest on the amount of time spent working on task and highest on pupil-pupil interaction. Interaction with the teacher, particularly as a class member, was low. These features are present in a slightly more extreme form in the equivalent group from the second year's data. These pupils are even lower on co-operating on task (even though across the sample as a whole this has increased slightly), and are even higher on pupil-pupil interaction than previously.

The cluster labelled *solitary workers* in the first year's analysis can also be matched very closely to a cluster emerging from the second year's data. In both years, this group was by far the highest in the amount of lesson time spent working, and by far the lowest on interaction with other pupils. In both years they are fairly low on individual and group interaction with the teacher, but are high on interaction as class members. Finally, the group of *quiet collaborators* can also be matched by a second-year cluster. These pupils are second highest in the amount of time spent working, and also second highest on pupil-pupil interaction. Their most distinctive characteristic is that they spend very much more time than other pupils interacting with the teacher as group members, and are also the highest on the amount of time they spend working jointly with other pupils. These results are repeated in the second year. It is clear that this and the other clusters represent distinctive styles of working. The *quiet collaborators* are similar to the *solitary workers* in that they spend above-average amounts of time working, but they also spend nearly twice as much time interacting with other pupils. Similarly, although they resemble the *attention seekers* in the amount of pupil-pupil interaction, the two groups have dramatically different patterns of interaction with the teacher.

In *Inside the Primary Classroom* considerable attention was given to the relationship between teacher and pupil clusters. It is fairly clear that they are not independent, and that some of the variables used in the pupil clustering are likely to be influenced by teacher behaviour. A full analysis of the consistency of pupil behaviour over time and with different teachers will be made in a subsequent volume. It can briefly be noted, however, that the pupils most closely related to a teaching style in *Inside the Primary Classroom* were the *quiet collaborators*, who were mainly found in the *group instructors'* classrooms. The increase in the proportion of teachers falling into the group category is matched by an increase in the proportion of pupils in the equivalent pupil cluster. Similarly, the decrease in the proportion of

intermittent workers could be predicted from the decrease in the proportion of teachers in the *individual monitor*'s cluster.

Summary: replicating the Pupil Record data

This analysis of the second year of data from the Pupil Record confirms
the main findings of the first year. The high level of pupil involvement
in work remains the same in the second year, as do the patterns of
pupil-teacher and pupil-pupil interaction. As before, the largest part of
a pupil's time in class is spent working on his own. About one-seventh
of his time is spent interacting with the teacher, mainly as a class
member. Although the teacher interacts mainly with individuals, any
particular child's share of this attention is necessarily very small. Just
under one-fifth of the pupil's time is spent interacting with other
pupils. A majority of this interaction involvĕs distraction from work,
but over a third is co-operation of some kind.

The four pupil types identified from the cluster analysis of the first
year's Pupil Record data also emerged from a similar analysis of the
second year's observation. These pupil types, characterized principally
by the amount of work and pupil-pupil interaction they engaged in,
and the amount and type of their contacts with the teacher, form
distinctive patterns of classroom behaviour, which were very similar
in the two years of the study.

Analyses of covariance: summary tables

Table C.1 Analyses of covariance: individual scores by teaching style

Covariates	Subjects	Sums of squares						Degrees of freedom			Mean squares		F ratio
		Total	Covariates	Unexplained by covariates	Styles	Residual	Total	Covariates	Styles	Residual	Styles	Residual	
Pre-test	Mathematics	11533	4462	7071	290	6781	408	1	5	402	58.0	16.9	3.43**
	Language skills	11413	3453	7960	442	7518	409	1	5	403	88.4	18.7	4.73**
	Reading	14618	4521	10097	491	9606	411	1	5	405	98.3	23.7	4.15**
Pre-test time on task	Mathematics	11533	4526	7007	251	6756	408	2	5	401	50.2	16.9	3.00*
	Language skills	11413	3481	7932	434	7497	409	2	5	402	86.8	18.7	4.64**
	Reading	14618	4521	10097	496	9601	411	2	5	404	99.2	23.8	4.18**

* significant at the 5 per cent level
** significant at or beyond the 1 per cent level

Table C.2 Mean scores for each teaching style (by initial achievement)

Test	Initial achievement level	Variable	Individual monitors	Class enquirers	Group instructors	Infrequent changers	Rotating changers	Habitual changers	All
Reading	High	Pre-test	18.7	15.0	15.8	16.3	14.7	17.3	16.5
		Post-test	24.5	22.0	21.4	22.2	19.8	21.7	21.9
		Residual change	1.3	0.7	−0.3	0.7	−1.4	−1.0	*
	Medium	Pre-test	15.2	12.3	11.5	12.3	11.5	13.8	12.9
		Post-test	20.7	18.6	17.9	22.3	17.4	18.0	18.9
		Residual change	0.1	0.0	0.0	3.9	−0.6	−1.4	*
	Low	Pre-test	9.4	8.4	5.3	8.1	8.1	8.8	8.2
		Post-test	16.7	13.6	12.4	17.1	14.0	16.0	15.1
		Residual change	0.9	−1.4	−1.4	2.0	−1.3	0.3	
Mathematics	High	Pre-test	19.6	14.4	13.4	14.3	13.3	15.0	15.3
		Post-test	23.1	21.0	17.8	17.8	18.0	20.0	19.9
		Residual change	0.6	1.8	−1.0	−0.5	−0.8	−0.5	
	Medium	Pre-test	15.1	10.4	9.5	12.4	10.9	11.9	11.9
		Post-test	18.6	17.9	16.0	17.5	15.7	16.6	17.0
		Residual change	−0.5	1.6	0.3	0.6	−0.9	−0.6	
	Low	Pre-test	10.9	6.5	4.8	8.4	8.1	7.6	7.9
		Post-test	14.2	13.0	12.4	13.8	13.8	12.0	13.2
		Residual change	−0.2	0.8	−0.3	0.7	0.4	−1.1	
Language	High	Pre-test	15.4	11.2	10.1	12.9	9.9	13.4	12.4
		Post-test	18.3	17.4	16.5	17.0	12.4	17.4	16.5
		Residual change	0.0	1.7	1.4	0.5	−2.8	−0.2	*
	Medium	Pre-test	9.9	7.0	6.6	9.3	7.9	9.7	8.6
		Post-test	13.1	13.7	12.5	13.1	10.7	13.9	12.8
		Residual change	−0.4	1.5	0.5	0.0	−1.9	0.4	
	Low	Pre-test	6.2	4.1	4.3	5.6	6.3	6.4	5.6
		Post-test	10.1	8.5	9.3	11.5	9.3	9.9	9.7
		Residual change	0.1	0.1	0.5	1.9	−0.9	−0.7	

*significant at the 5 per cent level

Table C.3 *Analyses of covariance: class mean scores by teaching styles*

Covariates	Subjects	Sums of squares						Degrees of freedom				Mean squares		F ratio
		Total	Covariates	Unexplained by Covariates	Styles	Residual	Total	Covariates	Styles	Residual	Total	Styles	Residual	
Pre-test	Mathematics	617.43	341.50	275.93	44.92	231.01	57	1	5	51		8.98	4.53	1.98
	Language skills	418.58	121.03	297.55	58.50	239.05	57	1	5	51		11.70	4.69	2.49*
	Reading	411.17	223.99	187.18	37.00	150.17	57	1	5	51		7.40	2.94	2.52*
Pre-test Teacher age	Mathematics	617.43	348.42	269.01	21.81	247.20	57	2	5	50		4.36	4.94	0.88
	Language skills	418.58	140.13	278.45	44.89	233.56	57	2	5	50		8.98	4.67	1.83
	Reading	411.17	229.52	181.65	28.03	153.61	57	2	5	50		5.61	3.07	1.83
Pre-test Time on skill	Mathematics	617.43	350.46	266.97	24.65	242.32	57	2	5	50		4.93	4.84	1.02
	Language skills	418.58	129.97	288.61	56.34	232.27	57	2	5	50		11.27	4.64	2.43*
	Reading	411.17	224.39	186.78	36.98	149.81	57	2	5	50		7.40	3.00	2.46*
Pre-test Proportion of time-on-task class and group work	Mathematics	617.43	361.74	255.69	21.58	234.10	57	3	5	49		4.31	4.77	0.90
	Language skills	418.58	146.74	271.84	33.19	238.65	57	3	5	49		6.64	4.87	1.36
	Reading	411.17	238.30	172.87	28.80	144.07	57	3	5	49		5.76	2.94	1.96

*significant at the 5 per cent level

Table C.4 Analyses of covariance for study skills

Exercise	Skill	Source	Sum of squares	Degrees of freedom	Mean squares	F
Block graph	Concept	Age	0.96	1	0.96	0.84
		Pre-test	11.57	1	11.57	10.10**
		Teaching style	1.6	5	3.2	0.28
		Residual	452.58	395	1.99	
	Layout	Age	0.34	1	0.34	0.27
		Pre-test	1.83	1	1.83	1.45
		Teaching style	24.18	5	4.84	3.89**
		Residual	490.54	395	1.24	
	Accuracy	Age	2.79	1	2.79	1.23
		Pre-test	109.23	1	109.23	48.25**
		Teaching style	12.51	5	2.50	1.11
		Residual	894.34	395	2.26	
	Presentation	Age	37.52	1	37.52	24.26**
		Pre-test	25.04	1	25.04	16.19**
		Teaching style	26.24	5	5.25	3.39**
		Residual	610.82	395	1.55	
Map of classroom	Con-ventions	Age	0.57	1	0.57	0.43
		Pre-test	33.64	1	33.64	25.6 **
		Teaching style	27.25	5	5.45	4.15**
		Residual	518.65	395	1.31	
	Positioning	Age	10.52	1	10.52	1.01
		Pre-test	447.3	1	447.3	42.83**
		Teaching style	148.61	5	29.72	2.85*
		Residual	4125.08	395	10.44	
Clock-face	General	Age	0.02	1	0.02	0.01
		Pre-test	12.67	1	12.67	7.45**
		Teaching style	12.13	5	2.43	1.43
		Residual	668.27	395	1.69	
Sound story	Sequen-cing	Age	1.05	1	1.05	0.15
		Pre-test	163.77	1	163.77	24.13**
		Teaching style	97.69	5	19.54	2.88**
		Residual	2681.37	395	6.79	

243

Exercise	Skill	Source	Sum of squares	Degrees of freedom	Mean squares	F
Instruc-tions	Following instructions	Age	3.39	1	3.39	0.4
		Pre-test	59.23	1	59.23	7.04**
		Teaching style	87.3	5	17.46	2.08
		Residual	3322.44	395	8.41	
Picture story	Compre-hension	Age	29.12	1	29.12	3.73
		Pre-test	168.93	1	168.93	21.64**
		Teaching style	77.04	5	15.41	1.97
		Residual	3083.88	395	7.81	
Questions	Formu-lating questions	Age	12.78	1	12.78	1.82
		Pre-test	133.79	1	133.79	19.09**
		Teaching style	192.06	5	38.41	5.48**
		Residual	2769.01	395	7.01	
Picture completion	Originality	Age	0.02	1	0.02	0.02
		Pre-test	2.09	1	2.09	1.94
		Teaching style	13.01	5	2.6	2.42*
		Residual	396.96	369	1.08	
	Appro-priateness	Age	2.93	1	2.93	1.69
		Pre-test	0.06	1	0.06	0.04
		Teaching style	5.51	5	1.1	0.64
		Residual	639.72	369	1.7	

* significant at the 5 per cent level
** significant at or beyond the 1 per cent level

Table C.5a Analysis of covariance: individual scores by pupil types

Covariates		Sums of squares					Degrees of freedom				Mean squares		F ratio
	Subjects	Total	Covariate	Unexplained by Covariate	Styles	Residual	Total	Covariate	Styles	Residual	Styles	Residual	
Pre-test	Mathematics	12548	5316	7232	61	7170	418	1	3	414	20.4	17.3	1.18
	Language skills	11766	3637	8129	168	7961	419	1	3	415	56.1	19.2	2.92*
	Reading	15408	5041	10367	146	10221	421	1	3	417	48.6	24.5	1.98

* significant at the 5 per cent level

Table C.5b Three-way analysis of covariance: individual scores by pupil types, sex and teaching styles

Sources of variation	Mathematics				Language skills				Reading			
	SS	df	MS	F	SS	df	MS	F	SS	df	MS	F
Total	11523	405			11404	406			14609	408		
Covariate	4519	1			3453	1			4522	1		
Main effects Teaching style	260	5	52.0	3.14**	400	5	80.0	4.26**	473	5	94.7	4.14**
Pupil type	5	3	1.5	0.09	98	3	32.8	1.74	120	3	40.0	1.75
Pupil sex	1	1	1.0	0.04	33	1	33.0	1.74	4	1	4.0	0.17
2-way inter-actions Style × sex	129	5	25.9	1.56	40	5	8.0	0.40	181	5	36.2	1.59
Type × sex	48	3	16.0	0.96	61	3	20.5	1.09	162	3	53.9	2.35
Style × type	308	15	20.5	1.24	363	15	24.2	1.29	544	15	36.2	1.59
3-way interactions	218	12	18.2	1.10	151	12	12.6	0.67	343	12	28.6	1.25
Residual	5967	360	16.6		6774	361	18.8		8292	363	22.8	

** significant at or beyond the 1 per cent level

Bibliography

Anthony, W.S. (1979), 'Progressive Learning Theories: The Evidence', in Bernbaum, G. (ed.), *Schooling in Decline*, Macmillan, London.

Ashton, P., Kneen, P., Davies, F. and Holley, B.J. (1975), *The Aims of Primary Education: A Study of Teachers' Opinions*, Schools Council Research Studies, Macmillan Education, London.

Barker Lunn, J.C. (1970), *Streaming in the Primary School*, NFER, Slough.

Bealing, D. (1972), 'Organization of Junior School Classrooms', *Educational Research*, 14, pp. 231–5.

Bennett, N. (1976), *Teaching Styles and Pupil Progress*, Open Books, London.

Bennett, N. (1978a), 'Educational Research and the Media', *Westminster Studies in Education*, 1, pp. 23–30.

Bennett, N. (1978b), 'Recent Research on Teaching: A Dream, A Belief, and A Model', *British Journal of Educational Psychology*, 48, pp. 127–47.

Bennett, N. and Youngman, M.B. (1973), 'Personality and Behaviour in School', *British Journal of Educational Psychology*, 43, pp. 228–33.

Bernstein, B. and Davies, B. (1969), 'Some Sociological Comments on Plowden', in Peters, R.S. (ed.), *Perspectives on Plowden*, Student's Library of Education, Routledge & Kegan Paul, London.

Bloom, B.S. (ed.) (1956), *Taxonomy of Educational Objectives*, I: Cognitive Domain, Longman, London.

Boydell, D. (1974), 'Teacher-Pupil Contact in Junior Classrooms', *British Journal of Educational Psychology*, 44, pp. 313–18.

Boydell, D. (1975), 'Pupil Behaviour in Junior Classrooms', *British Journal of Educational Psychology*, 45, pp. 122–9.

Brimer, A. (1969), *Bristol Achievement Tests: Interpretive Manual*, Nelson, London.

Brown, G.A. (1975), 'Some Case Studies of Teacher Preparation', *British Journal of Teacher Education*, 1, pp. 71–85.

Bullock Report (1975), *A Language for Life*, HMSO, London.

Burstall, C. (1979), 'Mending the Nets: A Commentary on Class Size Research', *Trends in Education*, DES, London.

246

Burstall, C. and Kay, B. (1978), *Assessment – The American Experience*, Assessment and Performance Unit, Monograph, DES, London.

Cameron-Jones, M. (1979), Pedagogics Project, *Introduction to Teaching: Course Book*, Moray House College of Education, Edinburgh.

Charters, W.W. and Waples, D. (1929), *The Commonwealth Teacher-Training Study*, University of Chicago Press.

Cox, C.B. and Dyson, A.E. (eds) (1969), 'Fight for Education: A Black Paper and Black Paper Two: The Crisis in Education', *Critical Quarterly Society*.

Cronbach, L.J. and Furby, L. (1970), 'How Should We Measure Change – or Should We?', *Psychological Bulletin*, 74, pp. 68–80.

Cronbach, L.J. and Snow, R.E. (1977), *Attitudes and Instructional Methods: A Handbook for Research on Interactions*, Irvington Publisher, New York.

Cropley, A.J. and Maslany, G.W. (1969), 'Reliability and Factorial Validity of the Wallach-Kogan Creativity Tests', *British Journal of Psychology*, 60, no. 3, pp. 395–8.

Department of Education and Science (1978), 'Assessing the Performance of Pupils', *Report on Education, no. 93*.

Dewey, J. (1916), *Democracy and Education*, Macmillan, New York.

Douglas, J.W.B. (1964), *The Home and the School*, MacGibbon & Kee, London.

Downing, J.A. (ed.) (1967), *The i.t.a. Symposium*, NFER, London.

Duckworth, E. (1979), 'Either We're Too Early and They Can't Learn It or We're Too Late and They Know It Already: The Dilemma of "Applying Piaget",' *Harvard Educational Review*, 49, no. 3, pp. 297–312.

Dunkin, M.J. and Biddle, B.J. (1974), *The Study of Teaching*, Holt, Rinehart & Winston, New York.

Eggleston, J.F., Galton, M.J. and Jones, M.E. (1976), *Processes and Products of Science Teaching*, Schools Council Research Studies, Macmillan Education, London.

Elliott, J. (1978), 'Classroom Accountability and the Self-Monitoring Teacher', in Harlen, W. (ed.), *Evaluation and the Teacher's Role*, Schools Council Research Studies, Macmillan Education, London.

Eysenck, A.J. and Eysenck, S. (1975), *Eysenck Personality Questionnaire (Junior and Adult)*, Hodder & Stoughton, London.

Flanders, N.A. (1960), *Teacher Influence on Pupil Attitudes and Achievement*, Final Report, Co-operative Research Programme Project no. 397, University of Minnesota, Minneapolis.

Flanders, N.A. (1976), 'Research on Teaching and Improving Teacher Education', *British Journal of Teacher Education*, 2, pp. 167–74.

Foster, J. (1971), *Creativity and the Teacher*, Macmillan Education, London.

France, N. and Fraser, I. (1975), *Richmond Tests of Basic Skills*, Nelson, London.

Galton, M.J., and Simon, B. and Croll, P. (1980), *Inside the Primary Classroom*, Routledge & Kegan Paul, London.

247

Gardner, D.E.M. (1966), *Experiment and Tradition in Primary Schools*, Methuen, London.

Gray, J. and Satterly, D. (1976), 'A Chapter of Errors: Teaching Styles and Pupil Progress in Retrospect', *Educational Research*, 19, no. 1, pp. 45–56.

Guilford, J.P. (1967), *The Nature of Human Intelligence*, McGraw-Hill, New York.

Haddon, F.A. and Lytton, H. (1968), 'Teaching Approaches and the Development of Divergent Thinking Abilities in Primary Schools', *British Journal of Educational Psychology*, 38, pp. 171–80.

Hargreaves, D. (1966), *Social Relations in a Secondary School*, Routledge & Kegan Paul, London.

Harnischfeger, A. and Wiley, D. (1975), 'Teaching/Learning Processes in Elementary Schools: A Synoptic View', *Studies of Education Processes*, no. 9, University of Chicago.

Harris, C.W. (ed.) (1963), *Problems in Measuring Change*, University of Wisconsin.

Hilsum, S. and Cane, B.S. (1971), *The Teacher's Day*, NFER, Slough.

HMI survey (1978), Department of Education and Science, *Primary Education in England: A Survey by HM Inspectors of Schools*, HMSO, London.

HMI survey (1979), Department of Education and Science, *Aspects of Secondary Education in England: A Survey by HM Inspectors of Schools*, HMSO, London.

Jackson, B. (1964), *Streaming: An Education System in Miniature*, Routledge & Kegan Paul, London.

Kemp, L.C. (1955), 'Environmental and Other Characteristics Determining Attainment in Primary Education', *British Journal of Educational Psychology*, 25, pp. 67–77.

Kogan, N. (1971), 'A Clarification of Cropley and Maslany's Analysis of the Wallach-Kogan Creativity Tests', *British Journal of Psychology*, 62, no. 1, pp. 113–17.

Lacey, C. (1970), *Hightown Grammar: The School as a Social System*, Manchester University Press.

McIntyre, D., Griffiths, R. and MacLeod, G. (1977), *Investigations in Microteaching*, Croom Helm, London.

McIntyre, D. and MacLeod, G. (1978), 'The Characteristics and Uses of Systematic Classroom Observation', in McAleese, R. and Hamilton, D. (eds), *Understanding Classroom Life*, NFER, Slough.

Nash, R. (1976), *Teacher Expectation of Pupil Learning*, Routledge & Kegan Paul, London.

Newson, J. and Newson, E. (1976), *Seven Years Old in the Home Environment*, George Allen & Unwin, London.

Nie, N.H., Hull, C.H., Jenkins, J.G., Steinbrenner, K. and Bent, D.H. (1975), *Statistical Package for the Social Sciences*, 2nd Edition, McGraw-Hill, Berks.

Nisbet, J.D. and Entwistle, N.J. (1969), *The Transition to Secondary Education*, Hodder & Stoughton, London.

O'Connor, E. (1972), 'Extending Classical Test Theory to the Measurement of Change', *Review of Educational Research,* 42, no. 1, pp. 73–97.

Page, G.T. and Thomas, J.B. (1977), *International Dictionary of Education,* Kogan Page, London.

Parlett, M. and Hamilton, D. (1976), 'Evaluation as Illumination' in Tawney, D. (ed.), *Curriculum Evaluation Today: Trends and Implications,* Schools Council Research Series, Macmillan, London.

Plowden Report, (1967), *Children and their Primary Schools* (2 vols), Report of the Central Advisory Council for Education in England, HMSO, London.

Rutter, M., Mangha, B. and Ouston, J. with Smith, A. (1979), *Fifteen Thousand Hours: Secondary Schools and their Effects on Children,* Open Books, London.

Salomon, G. and McDonald, F.J. (1970), 'Pre-test and Post-test Reactions to Self-Viewing One's Teaching Performance on Video Tape', *Journal of Educational Psychology,* 61, no. 4, pp. 280–6.

Simon, A. and Boyer, E.G. (eds) (1970), *Mirrors for Behaviour: An Anthology of Classroom Observation Instruments,* Research for Better Schools, Philadelphia.

Solomon, D. and Kendall, A.J. (1979), *Children in Classrooms – An Investigation of Person Environment Interaction,* Praeger Publishers, New York.

Stake, R.E. (1967), 'The Countenance of Educational Evaluation', *Teachers College Record,* 68, pp. 523–40.

Stenhouse, L. (1975), *An Introduction to Curriculum Research and Development,* Heinemann Educational Books, London.

Strasser, B. (1967), 'A Conceptual Model of Instruction', *Journal of Teacher Education,* 18, no. 1, pp. 63–74.

Taba, H. (1966), *Teaching Strategies and Cognitive Functioning in Elementary School Children*; United States Office of Education (USOE), Co-operative Research Project No. 1574, San Francisco State College.

Tann, C.S. (1980), 'A Study of Groupwork in Primary and Lower Secondary Schools', unpublished PhD thesis, University of Leicester.

Thurstone, L.L. (1938), 'Primary Mental Abilities', *Psychometric Monographs,* no. 1.

Tisher, R.P. (1970), 'The Nature of Verbal Discourse in Classrooms', in Campbell, W.J. (ed.), *Scholars in Context: The Effects of Environment on Learning,* John Wiley, Australasia.

Trown, E.A. and Leith, G.O.M. (1975), 'Decision Rules for Teaching Strategies in Primary Schools: Personality-treatment Interactions', *British Journal of Educational Psychology,* 45, pp. 130–40.

Warburton, F.W. (1964), 'Attainment and the School Environment', in Wiseman, S. (ed.), *Education and Environment,* Manchester University Press.

Ward, M. (1979), *Mathematics and the Ten Year Old,* Schools Council, Methuen, Educational, London.

Wilkinson, M. (1977), *Lessons from Europe: A Comparison of British and Western European Schooling,* Centre for Policy Studies.

Willis, P.E. (1977), *Learning to Labour: How Working Class Kids Get Working Class Jobs,* Saxon House, Westmead.

Winer, B.J. (1970), *Statistical Principles in Experimental Design,* International Student Edition, McGraw-Hill, New York.

Worthington, F. (1974), 'A Theoretical and Empirical Study of Small-Group Work in Schools', unpublished PhD thesis, University of Leicester.

Wragg, E.C. (1978), 'A Suitable Case for Imitation', *The Times Educational Supplement,* 15 September, p. 18.

Youngman, M.B. (1979), *Analysing Social and Educational Research Data,* McGraw-Hill, Berks.

Index